'A decades-long expansion has unmoored community-based alternatives to state justice from their early theoretical and critical promise. Adopting the mantel of 'restorative justice', these alternatives tend to fix their operation within a technical ethos that secures success as naturalised solutions to state-defined problems. Maglione's thoughtful analysis clarifies and highlights the importance of retrieving contemporary political, social and cultural theorising to provide fluid ways to engage restorative initiatives. Drawing on key theories, this book successfully grinds novel critical lenses that bring into focus complex political arenas by which to engage democratic, unsettled, nomadic, subaltern and constantly emerging practices of restorative justice'.

—**George Pavlich**, *University of Alberta, Canada*

'In a work of cutting-edge criticism and sparkling originality, Maglione explores the most prominent political implications for restorative justice in our time. His penetrating encounter with contemporary political thought examines the problems of diversity and democracy, community and identity, sovereignty and oppression. This will become an essential handbook for both the theory and creative practice of restorative justice'.

—**Phil Carney**, *University of Kent, U.K.*

'For at least a generation, restorative justice has seemed to be a unique answer to the crises of criminal justice. So, there has been huge growth in interest in the study, practice, law and policy development of restorative justice. Yet, does the reality of this growth live up to the various claims and hopes of restorative justice? What do we know about the relationship between restorative justice and political theory? In his superbly creative book, Maglione shepherds us to think, and rethink, the relationships between restorative justice and fundamental political and social concepts like sovereignty, community, identity, difference, equality and subalternity. In doing so, we are better equipped to read the past, present and future or restorative justice; and to reimagine its wider potential contribution to addressing social, political and cultural injustices'.

—**Cyrus Tata**, *University of Strathclyde, U.K.*

'Even though this is a book I would have loved reading when I started discovering restorative justice, reading it today feels equally important and certainly like a gift. Embedded within both a critical and imaginative strand in restorative justice literature, the book aims at deconstructing and reconstructing restorative justice's main tenets from different and rich political-philosophical angles and threads, by creating a sustained dialogue with the work of important political philosophers. In line with his previous work, the author remains committed to open up paths within the restorative justice movement by stimulating the development of a critical and radical political imagination around restorative justice.

This book is timely and important, because as older generations of scholars leave the restorative justice field, younger generations are searching for innovative, daring and engaging analyses that can widen our intellectual horizons and deepen our political and ethical commitments towards justice'.

—**Brunilda Pali**, *University of Amsterdam, The Netherlands*

'*Restorative Justice and Contemporary Political Theory* is a provocative book in the best sense of the word. In it, Maglione provokes us to reconsider our assumptions about harm and justice through our encounter with six important theorists. His skilled conceptual excavation allows us to ask more of restorative justice, so that we might push it toward becoming more than an ossified and institutionalised justice mechanism'.

—**Andrew Woolford**, *University of Manitoba, Canada*

'Restorative justice came out of the shadows to inspire a worldwide movement of social justice. While we are still learning to do restorative justice practice well, the theory and norms underpinning this practice have been neglected. Like any other justice intervention that claims to offer a better experience for victims, offenders and communities, restorative justice must proceed with responsibility and a careful justification of its practices and proposals. Maglione's contribution could not be more timely as it adds to the scant theoretical restorative justice literature, helping us to navigate our critical thinking. The book provides a descriptive account of contemporary theories, while offering a critical analysis that allows us to connect theoretical norms with practice. It is not often that a book dedicated to restorative justice theory is offered'.

—**Theo Gavrielides**, *Restorative Justice for All (RJ4All)*

Restorative Justice and Contemporary Political Theory

Outlining an original analysis of the political dimension of restorative justice, this book seeks both to enhance the critical comprehension of this phenomenon and to forge new tools for acting politically through restorative justice, inviting restorative justice scholars, practitioners and advocates to become a radical political movement.

Restorative justice is widely studied, nationally and internationally legislated, and increasingly practised; however, the growth of relevant policy, practice and research has been only marginally accompanied by the development of updated, theoretically informed and critical reflections on the relationships between politics and restorative justice. This is a significant problem since neglecting the political dimension may limit the capacity of the restorative justice movement to critically appreciate its possible role in confronting oppressive social and political arrangements. This book addresses this gap by providing reflections on restorative justice in relation to six complex political concepts – difference, sovereignty, community, identity, equality and subalternity. Engaging with the thoughts of Gilles Deleuze, Giorgio Agamben, Jean-Luc Nancy, Judith Butler, Jacques Rancière and Gayatri Chakravorty Spivak, each chapter works as a prism to unravel and reconstruct creatively restorative justice unearthing its political conditions and effects.

Providing an innovative contribution to our thinking about the political nature and significance of restorative justice from the specific perspective of political theory, *Restorative Justice and Contemporary Political Theory* will appeal to both students and scholars of restorative justice specifically and of criminal justice and criminology more broadly.

Giuseppe Maglione is Lecturer in Criminology and Director of the Restorative Justice Clinic in the School of Social Policy, Sociology and Social Research at the University of Kent, UK.

Routledge Critical Studies in Crime, Diversity and Criminal Justice

Edited by
Patricia Faraldo Cabana
University of A Coruña, Spain
and
Nancy A Wonders
Northern Arizona University, USA

The works in this series strive to generate new conceptual and theoretical frameworks to address the legal, organisational and normative responses to the challenges that diversity and intersectionality present to criminal justice systems. This series aims to present cutting edge empirically informed theoretical works from both new and established scholars around the world.

Drawing upon a range of disciplines including sociology, law, history, economics, and social work, the series encourages different approaches to questions of mobility and exclusion with a cross-section of theorists, empiricists, and critical policy researchers. It will be key reading for scholars who are working in criminal justice, criminology, criminal law and human rights, as well as those in the fields of gender and LGBTI studies, migration studies, anthropology, refugee studies and post-colonial studies.

Race, Recognition and Retribution in Contemporary Youth Justice
The Intractability Malleability Thesis
Esmorie Miller

Legal Professionals Negotiating the Borders of Identity
Operation Streamline and Competing Identity Management
Jessie K. Finch

Campus Sexual Violence
A State of Institutionalized Sexual Terrorism
Sarah Prior and Brooke A. de Heer

Sexuality in the Swedish Police
From Gay Jokes to Pride Parades
Jens Rennstam

Restorative Justice and Contemporary Political Theory
Critical Encounters
Giuseppe Maglione

For more information about this series, please visit: https://www.routledge.com/criminology/series/CDCJ

Restorative Justice and Contemporary Political Theory

Critical Encounters

Giuseppe Maglione

Routledge
Taylor & Francis Group
LONDON AND NEW YORK

First published 2025
by Routledge
4 Park Square, Milton Park, Abingdon, Oxon OX14 4RN

and by Routledge
605 Third Avenue, New York, NY 10158

Routledge is an imprint of the Taylor & Francis Group, an informa business

British Library Cataloguing-in-Publication Data
A catalogue record for this book is available from the British Library

Library of Congress Cataloging-in-Publication Data
Names: Maglione, Giuseppe, author.
Title: Restorative justice and contemporary political theory : critical encounters / Giuseppe Maglione.
Description: Abingdon, Oxon ; New York, NY : Routledge, 2025. | Series: Routledge critical studies in crime, diversity and criminal justice | Includes bibliographical references and index.
Identifiers: LCCN 2024035897 (print) | LCCN 2024035898 (ebook) | ISBN 9781032287454 (hardback) | ISBN 9781032287461 (paperback) | ISBN 9781003298359 (ebook)
Subjects: LCSH: Restorative justice. | Reparation (Criminal justice)
Classification: LCC HV8688 .M338 2025 (print) | LCC HV8688 (ebook) | DDC 364.6/8—dc23/eng/20240903
LC record available at https://lccn.loc.gov/2024035897
LC ebook record available at https://lccn.loc.gov/2024035898

ISBN: 978-1-032-28745-4 (hbk)
ISBN: 978-1-032-28746-1 (pbk)
ISBN: 978-1-003-29835-9 (ebk)

DOI: 10.4324/9781003298359

Typeset in Times New Roman
by Apex CoVantage, LLC

To Eve – ***no distance amounts to absence, I encounter you every day.***

Contents

Acknowledgements

Discussions in Florence with Emilio Santoro and the AdirMediazione team, in Oslo with the late Nils Christie and Krisztina Luraas, in Edinburgh with Jamie Buchan and Siobhan Butler and in Canterbury with Phil Carney have encouraged me to expand my understanding of justice. Jamie and Phil read parts of the manuscript and provided valuable suggestions. Routledge reviewers and the Critical Studies in Crime, Diversity and Criminal Justice book series editors made helpful and encouraging recommendations. More recently, students on my restorative justice courses at the University of Kent gave me crucial feedback. The Kent Criminology Group offered the perfect balance of intellectual stimulation and camaraderie, creating an environment conducive to finalising this work. Thanks to the support of the School of Social Policy, Sociology and Social Research, within the Law, Society, and Social Justice Division at the University of Kent, I had the opportunity to benefit from Tim Lundy's exceptional editing skills.

1 Encountering Restorative Justice

This book consists of six critical encounters between restorative justice and contemporary political theory. Its purpose is to contribute to creating a space for political thinking about, and political action through, restorative justice. From this angle, the following pages provide a rich, original and innovative critical toolbox to address the lack of theoretical-political engagement with restorative justice.

The word *encounter* derives from Latin – *in* (meaning 'in') and *contra* (meaning 'against') – denoting both a moving towards someone or something and an opposition, a moving away from them. This etymology seems to reflect the fact that encounters combine the striving towards others, our exposure to them, and the resistance that the world inevitably opposes to us. The term *critical*, meanwhile, derives from the Greek word *kritikē*, meaning 'the faculty of judging'. Critique is not a mere fault-finding exercise, a purely negative and destructive operation, but a positive and constructive endeavour to discern value and to express a stance towards the world we encounter.

A *critical encounter* is, therefore, a moment and space for moving towards someone or something, learning from being exposed to those encountered, experiencing the challenges of being open to others and then engaging with a process of discernment. It involves considering the value of whom or what has been encountered and considering their impact on us.

Facilitating a critical encounter between restorative justice and contemporary political theory, making the former learn, be challenged and be assessed from the latter, is both significant and timely.

Restorative justice remains a largely undertheorised field, and this deficiency has detrimental consequences for its development. Namely, in a time when restorative justice is experiencing momentous growth, the dearth of sustained political-philosophical meditation around the direction of such an expansion may cause its form, substance and direction to be accepted as natural and taken for granted. This could then lead to the stifling of those creative energies which have animated restorative justice as a collective enterprise and hinder their radical social impact. Specifically, neglecting the links between politics and justice may limit the capacity of the restorative justice movement to appreciate the connections between individual harms and socio-political contexts, between relational repair and social justice, thus thwarting its potential to address oppressive social, cultural and political arrangements.

DOI: 10.4324/9781003298359-1

The relationships between politics and restorative justice are notably neglected, with very few exceptions (Pavlich, 2005; Gavrielides and Artinopoulou, 2013; Aertsen and Pali, 2017; Woolford and Nelund, 2019). George Pavlich's (2005) work is a precious critical analysis, largely inspired by Michel Foucault's writings, of the governmental rationales that have legitimised restorative practices in the Western context. Gavrielides and Artinopoulou's (2013) collection is an ambitious endeavour to re-elaborate the philosophical foundations of restorative justice, from a variety of normative perspectives, ranging from Aristotelian thought to Ubuntu philosophy. Similarly, Aertsen and Pali's collection (2017) deconstructs and reconstructs restorative justice, often highlighting its political justifications and effects. More recently, Woolford and Nelund's (2019) monograph on the politics of restorative justice probes into how intersecting socio-political contexts impact on restorative justice's political significance, role and effects.

In addition to these book-length analyses, over the last 20 years a few specific critical studies have contextualised the rise in popularity of restorative justice within a wider understanding of policy and the political process in the UK (Gray, 2005; Walklate, 2005; Maglione, 2019a, 2019b), Australia (Richards, 2011) and the United States (Cohen, 2019). Others have reflected on the articulations between restorative justice politics and oppressive (gendered and racialised) arrangements (e.g. Daly and Stubbs, 2013; González and Schiff, 2024), including within postcolonial contexts (Moyle and Tauri, 2016). Some have argued for a political reorientation of restorative justice focused on promoting equality and human relationality (González, 2014) or democratic civic engagement (Dzur, 2011), whilst others have scrutinised the interaction between politics and language in restorative justice (González and Buth, 2019).

These studies have made remarkable contributions to the critical understanding of the politics of restorative justice, often from a socio-legal standpoint. The following pages adopt a different (political-philosophical) perspective, drawing on an unexplored set of theories and theorists. This book is driven by the conviction that this type of scrutiny may elucidate the generative connections between how we conceive and organise the polity and how we think of and respond to conflicts and harms, and then in turn how specific ways of understanding and practising justice generate specific political effects. This operation, however, does not amount to formulating a single, unified political theory of restorative justice. Instead, this book forays into different contemporary political-philosophical theories, experimenting with how they could both enhance the current understanding of, and inspire political action through, restorative justice. The final result is a polemical rhapsody, featuring a diverse range of thought-provoking perspectives, methods and concepts aiming to stimulate the reader's imagination.

Along these lines, this book provides reflections on restorative justice in relation to six complex political concepts – *difference, sovereignty, community, identity, equality and subalternity* – by engaging with political thinkers who have developed a sustained examination of these categories. Each chapter, respectively, offers an analysis of how the thought of Gilles Deleuze, Giorgio Agamben, Jean-Luc Nancy, Judith Butler, Jacques Rancière and Gayatri Chakravorty Spivak could be used as a prism to unravel and reconstruct restorative justice, creatively. Before diving into such analyses, each chapter provides a brief background of those authors' thoughts, their methods and main concepts. The reader is encouraged to actively engage with those reflections and strategically select and employ the tools laid down. In this way, it is possible to generate fresh insights into the vexed questions of the definition, history, cultural significance, relationships with social identities and institutionalisation of restorative justice, as well as its links with criminal justice.

This book then aims to engage politically with, not only read politically, restorative justice. This means that it seeks both to intensify our understanding of the emergence and possible trajectories of restorative justice and to forge new tools for political action through restorative justice. Each chapter, thus, is both an analytical exploration and an attempt to sketch out potential pathways for the restorative justice movement towards a radical and critical restorative praxis.

Regarding this work's disciplinary and conceptual boundaries, political theory, here, is broadly conceived as the theoretical reflection on the nature and organisation of political life and its limits. It is the space of an encounter between theory, understood as the process of critical understanding, and politics, seen as the process of imagining and conducting the polity. The authors discussed, rather than conforming to rigid disciplinary positionings, have all worked across disciplinary boundaries. Much of the generativity of their thought depends on this defiance of preset intellectual identities. Yet the question of politics, and the theoretical engagement with it, remains central to their intellectual journeys. Their theories offer radical analytical and normative frameworks to problematise restorative justice against the backdrop of the relationships between justice and politics. Framing the debate in this way aims to fill the gap concerning a thorough, philosophically informed analysis of restorative justice as a political phenomenon – that is, as integral to the organisation of the polity. This approach may possibly lead to envisioning new and different futures for the restorative justice movement, thereby presenting important praxeological implications.

Similarly, the expression 'restorative justice' is used in the following pages as a broad signpost for the social movement which has organically emerged around a range of informal justice practices since the 1970s, in the Western world, advocating for dialogic and reparative responses to harms. Each chapter will engage with this idea and then unpack it, break it down, expand it and thoroughly reformulate it. This minimal working definition presents the advantage of being relatively comprehensive and open-ended, enabling a generative engagement with restorative justice's rather fluid (and often contested) operational, conceptual and normative dimensions.

The absence of a neat, systematic narrative across the following chapters reflects both this disposition to cross disciplinary boundaries and the choice to use a comprehensive working definition of restorative justice. In fact, instead of presenting a single argument, the book unfolds through six distinct stories. The aim is not merely to replicate the chosen authors' thought but to attempt 'to use it, to deform it, to make it groan and protest' (Foucault, 1975/1980: 54), without subsuming it to a greater whole. In this way, it is possible to express and harness the diversity of the theories and theorists encountered.

Diversity, here, refers both to theoretical pluralism, that is, the availability of multiple, sometimes conflicting, theoretical frameworks, and to each theory's conceptual richness. Honouring such diversity holds a dual significance. Heuristically, it enables the generation of knowledge that lends itself to multiple applications, fostering new interpretations of the world. Normatively, if we adhere to the principles of democratic science, theoretical pluralism possesses intrinsic value, empowering the reader to select among different ontological, epistemological and methodological options, ultimately promoting new possibilities not only for knowledge but also for life.

Clearly, this approach relies on the reader's willingness to both challenge their common sense and actively participate in reassessing some of their certainties. The refusal to formulate a ready-to-use, grand political theory of restorative justice is driven by the desire to treat the reader as an active companion (rather than a silent passenger) in this journey.

Each theory and the respective authors have been selected for two interlinked orders of reasons. On a general note, these theories and theorists have yet to be monographically considered by the restorative justice literature, whilst they are all renowned for their conceptual creativity and transdisciplinarity. From a substantive perspective, they offer a repertoire of critical instruments capable of both rethinking the historical development of restorative justice (with a specific focus on its political conditions) and proposing ideas for its future political roles. The selected theorists can all be described as 'continental' philosophers writing about fundamental political questions. Their approaches are historically informed and sensitive to the entanglement of power and knowledge and the material and cultural realms. Their descriptions are normative, their proposals are radical, and they tackle the roots of the problem whilst suggesting fundamental options for a future to come. These authors contest prevailing interpretations while reinventing them critically, confronting established authorities and envisioning new paths for change. From this angle, they help in problematising accepted narratives of the history of restorative justice whilst providing instruments to scrutinise the growth and formalisation of restorative justice by connecting it to broader political questions.

Notwithstanding these commonalities, there are also conspicuous conceptual and methodological differences between Deleuze's Spinozian–Nietzschean orientation, Agamben's and Nancy's broadly Heideggerian approaches and the Hegelian–Marxist theories advocated by Butler, Rancière and Spivak. The problem is not the existence of tensions, though, but the lack thereof. This book's open-ended texture attempts to honour theoretical plurality and methodological diversity, deemed as conditions for critical understanding, by experimenting, playing with existing theories to raise new, daring questions about the basic tenets of restorative justice.

The book starts off by encountering a thinker who dedicated his intellectual life to transcending conventional cultural boundaries, advancing a thought built around *difference* – Gilles Deleuze. Through Deleuze, this chapter reflects on how we can draw a dynamic portrait of the multiple processes which constitute restorative justice without falling into anachronism and reductionism, whilst multiplying restorative justice's potential for forging new forms of solidarity.

Deleuze, in particular through the concept of assemblage (developed with his intellectual companion Félix Guattari), enables us to analyse restorative justice by combining different spheres: natural and cultural, semiotic and material, individual and social, psychic and political. Adopting this perspective, this chapter generates a multidimensional and intensive understanding of restorative justice. It then outlines the idea of a *nomadic restorative justice*, a political strategy of nurturing the creative, unbounded libidinal energies that inform restorative encounters by creating new spaces for enhancing people's capacities.

The following chapter reflects further on the relations between politics and restorative justice by connecting them to ontological issues. In doing so, it encounters a key figure in contemporary political theory – Giorgio Agamben. His work is used as a prism through which to address the relationships between *sovereignty* and restorative justice and the implications of an embodied form of justice whilst investigating the model of human life integral to restorative encounters. Agamben's philosophical archaeology traces the fundamental categories of restorative justice back to their origin, unearthing their ontological-political stakes. Here, 'origin' does not denote the specific point in time when something begins but rather the fluid array of cultural forces that over time have shaped that subject. These forces demand critical scrutiny, which can then support the development of a radical *restorative justice to come*. This view suggests abandoning the juridical-sovereign models which are implied by the current process of institutionalising restorative justice and instead seeking politically engaged, means-oriented models of restorative praxis.

Similarly to Agamben's analysis, the chapter on Jean-Luc Nancy explores the themes of relationality and *community* in restorative justice from a political-ontological angle. Nancy offers material to rethink restorative justice as a hospitable space delivered from criminal justice, aiding us in reimagining community as a condition for exposing human beings' sociality without collapsing their singularities into identities.

Restorative justice, in fact, is often described as a form of relational justice, an endeavour to cure broken social bonds. The involvement of communities in restorative processes is integral to this representation. Yet relationality and community are not self-evident concepts, and the frequent claim that restorative justice's 'communitarian' nature is cast against criminal justice's 'individualism' requires political-philosophical analysis.

Nancy's work constitutes one of the most thorough contemporary critiques of both individualism and communitarianism. From his vantage point, both approaches revolve around a reified entity – either 'the individual' or 'the community' – endowed with an objective identity around which politics should be shaped. Both disregard the fact that the human condition is always necessarily shared, that being is always being-in-common. Human beings are not defined by a common natural quality determining their identity but rather by their necessary exposure to each other. This chapter equips us with a sensibility to rethink the very core of restorative justice, whilst pointing to a *restorative justice singular plural* as an effort to counter the denial of difference exerted by capitalist forces on humans' quest for justice.

The issues of relationality and identity are also at the centre of the chapter on Judith Butler, a contemporary American philosopher deeply interested in how the imbrication of political power and cultural frameworks contributes to creating spaces of oppression or emancipation.

Butler provides instruments to reflect on how restorative encounters can be spaces wherein participants perform their 'selves' and enrich their personhood, whilst unearthing the political implications of a form of justice which recognises interdependence, vulnerability and social precarity. By creatively appropriating Butler's theories, it is possible to rethink how restorative encounters influence *identity-making* processes and then to formulate a space for developing emancipatory strands of action and thought.

Encountering Butler's wide-ranging, transdisciplinary critique prompts a radical reflection on key claims surrounding restorative justice – the focus on interdependence, the critique of state justice, non-violence – whilst helping to imagine a *restorative justice otherwise*. This is a critical understanding of restorative justice as a political praxis informed by the awareness of the mutually constitutive links between social vulnerability and resistance, individuality and interdependence, subjectivation and subjection.

The chapter on French philosopher Jacques Rancière argues that the dynamics taking place during restorative encounters should be considered as distinctively political processes. People caught in those interactions, in fact, find themselves provided with or lacking the rights and duties to perform particular kinds of meaningful action, such as negotiating or rejecting assigned identities. This approach poses the problem of whether and how restorative encounters ensure *equality* between participants or instead enforce an unequal distribution of those rights and duties.

Rancière helps us rethink stakeholders' positions within restorative encounters by reflecting on how to enable people to articulate their own *logos* whilst raising the question of how restorative facilitators can promote social equality. Hence, this chapter provides fresh insights to widen and deepen the discussion on the politics of restorative justice, connecting broad issues of institutionalisation and de-institutionalisation with the specific functioning of restorative practices. It also outlines a *democratic restorative justice*, the process of infusing equality into restorative encounters whilst uncovering the limitations of existing forms of justice, questioning their foundations and effects, establishing new relations, allowing new voices to emerge and politicising what is at stake.

The final chapter expands on the theme of equality in restorative justice, encountering Gayatri Chakravorty Spivak, a literary critic whose work is informed by feminist concerns, Marxist analysis and deconstruction. Spivak has dedicated her career to engaging with *subalternity*, the condition of being at once politically disempowered, economically deprived and culturally silenced. Searching for, obtaining or being denied the experience of justice always take place in specific contexts wherein human beings encounter each other. These contexts are often marked by struggles between those who are left at the margins, disenfranchised and suffering, and those who have the power to oppress both materially and culturally. Restorative justice is not immune to such dynamics. Through Spivak, it is possible to reflect on how restorative justice can perpetuate political and cultural exploitation whilst imagining a decolonised, ethical restorative justice.

Encountering Spivak means not only enriching the critical vocabulary of restorative justice but also reflecting on the positionality of such vocabulary, adding a further crucial layer to our analysis. Ultimately, Spivak may serve as a catalyst for restorative justice to become an active force towards the establishment of a justice that is more than Western justice. From this perspective, this chapter points to a *subaltern restorative justice*, a reflection on how subalternity could inform justice practices understood as intersectional interventions aiming to redress unbalanced power dynamics. This would lead to dialogues which incorporate different concepts of the world and address power differentials related to gender, class and culture in a bid to address interlocking experiences of oppression.

The book also includes some concluding reflections on recurrent themes across the different chapters, looking particularly at the ontological and ethical-political dimensions of a justice that aims to generate and nurture just relations. The goal is to identify some crucial issues that need to be further addressed in order to develop a critical and political restorative praxis.

As Aristotle argued in the *Nicomachean Ethics* (350 BCE/1999), theory does not simply refer to abstract thought divorced from mundane concerns but to the contemplation of the most important things in the pursuit of a good life – that is, theory is always normative. From this angle, each chapter sketches out different paths for restorative justice to play a significant political role in addressing social, cultural and political oppression.

These analytical-normative reflections ultimately seek to keep restorative justice as dynamic and open as possible, with the awareness that closing off this field will ossify its radical potential and that the separation of intellectual critique and political action from imagining justice will lead to injustice.

References

Aertsen, I. and Pali, B. (eds.) (2017) *Critical Restorative Justice*. Oxford: Hart.

Aristotle (350 BCE/1999) *Nicomachean Ethics*. Indianapolis, IN: Hackett.

Cohen, A. J. (2019) 'Moral Restorative Justice: A Political Genealogy of Activism and Neoliberalism in the United States'. *Minnesota Law Review*, 104: 889–953.

Daly, K. and Stubbs, J. (2013) 'Feminist Theory, Feminist and Anti-racist Politics, and Restorative Justice'. In Johnston, G. and Van Ness, D. (eds.) *Handbook of Restorative Justice*, 149–70. Cullompton, UK: Willan.

Dzur, A. W. (2011) 'Restorative Justice and Democracy: Fostering Public Accountability for Criminal Justice'. *Contemporary Justice Review*, 14(4): 367–81.

Foucault, M. (1975/1980) 'Prison Talk'. In Gordon, C. (ed.) *Power/Knowledge: Selected Interviews and Other Writings, 1972–1977*, 37–54. New York: Pantheon.

Gavrielides, T. and Artinopoulou, V. (eds.) (2013) *Reconstructing Restorative Justice Philosophy*. Farnham, UK: Ashgate.

González, T. (2014) 'Reorienting Restorative Justice: Initiating a New Dialogue of Rights Consciousness, Community Empowerment and Politicization'. *Cardozo Journal of Conflict Resolution*, 16: 457–77.

González, T. and Buth, A. J. (2019) 'Restorative Justice at the Crossroads: Politics, Power, and Language'. *Contemporary Justice Review*, 22(3): 242–56.
González, T. and Schiff, M. (2024) 'The Uncertain Future of Restorative Justice: Anti-Woke Legislation, Retrenchment and Politics of the Right'. *William & Mary Journal of Race, Gender, and Social Justice*, 30(1): 1–52.
Gray, P. (2005) 'The Politics of Risk and Young Offenders' Experiences of Social Exclusion and Restorative Justice'. *British Journal of Criminology*, 45(6): 938–57.
Maglione, G. (2019a) 'The Political Rationality of Restorative Justice'. *Theoretical Criminology*, 23(4): 54–62.
Maglione, G. (2019b) 'The Restorative Justice Apparatus: A Critical Analysis of the Historical Emergence of Restorative Justice'. *Social & Legal Studies*, 28(5): 650–74.
Moyle, P. and Tauri, J. M. (2016) 'Māori, Family Group Conferencing and the Mystifications of Restorative Justice'. *Victims & Offenders*, 11(1): 87–106.
Pavlich, G. (2005) *Governing Paradoxes of Restorative Justice*. London: Routledge-Cavendish.
Richards, K. (2011) 'Restorative Justice and "Empowerment": Producing and Governing Active Subjects through "Empowering" Practices'. *Critical Criminology*, 19: 91–105.
Walklate, S. (2005) 'Researching Restorative Justice: Politics, Policy and Process'. *Critical Criminology*, 13(2): 165–79.
Woolford, A. and Nelund, A. (2019) *The Politics of Restorative Justice: A Critical Introduction*, 2nd ed. Black Point, NS: Fernwood.

2 Encountering Desire

Becoming, Desire and Justice

How can we rethink the history of restorative justice without falling into anachronisms? How can we draw a dynamic portrait of the politics of restorative justice avoiding simplifying reductionisms? How can we conceptualise critically the institutionalisation of restorative justice? How can we multiply restorative justice's potential for forging new forms of solidarity?

This chapter argues that addressing these questions requires a sustained engagement with different domains and their interconnections: natural and cultural spheres, semiotic and material elements, individual and social bodies, psychic and political processes. The main figure encountered in these pages is Gilles Deleuze, a thinker who dedicated his intellectual life to transcending well-established ontological, epistemological and conceptual boundaries.

A prominent figure in contemporary French philosophy, Deleuze advances a materialist, vitalist and empiricist theory which foregrounds *desire* and *becoming* as, respectively, the fundamental force and dynamic structure of reality. Much of his work is an endeavour to analyse how desire and becoming are socially captured and individually experienced. He challenges foundational Western philosophical notions, such as being, identity, representation and, more broadly, the negative – that is, thought articulated around basic dialectical dichotomies (being/non-being, matter/form, interiority/exteriority). Deleuze focuses on how things *become* rather than how they *are*, thinking of reality as a dynamic field wherein an array of forces combine, clash and coalesce, producing individual and social bodies. His philosophical work is shaped as a creative practice, an artistic intervention to generate new concepts and, in this way, new forms of thinking, seeing, speaking – in short, new possibilities for life. With Félix Guattari, in *Capitalism and Schizophrenia* (Deleuze and Guattari, 1972/2013, 1980/2013), his most ambitious work, Deleuze describes how desire is consolidated and dispersed, whilst arguing that the aim of thinking should be unearthing and questioning our desire to be subjugated, thereby propelling us towards revolutionary behaviour at both micro and macro levels.

The following pages 'play with' Deleuze to generate a multidimensional and dynamic understanding of restorative justice. They creatively appropriate one Deleuzian–Guattarian instrument in particular – the concept of 'assemblage'

DOI: 10.4324/9781003298359-2

(*agencement* in French) (Deleuze and Guattari, 1980/2013: 2) – experimenting with how it may contribute to unpacking and reconstructing critically and politically restorative justice.

Deleuze is like a *machine* capable of folding and unfolding restorative justice in unexpected and thought-provoking ways, widening our intellectual horizons and pushing us towards the very limits of our common understanding of what restorative justice is, could be and ought to be. Here, there is no prophetic solution but the struggle to forge new methodological, conceptual and normative tools that others will have to take up. This chapter endeavours to reproduce this puzzling experience, conjuring up the multiple vibrations that traverse the Deleuzian machine.

Encountering Gilles Deleuze

Deleuze's intellectual journey can be broken down into four main phases, characterised by the emergence of specific themes or approaches. Despite such variations, these stages are all underpinned by the conviction that philosophy is the expression of thought's active and positive function, explicated in the creation of concepts. Deleuze's overarching aim is confronting chaos whilst defying *microfascisms*, that is, human tendencies towards self-oppression. Perhaps, rather than discrete phases, it might be more apt to consider Deleuze's career in terms of intellectual layers, each relying upon the previous and connected to the next, producing the stratified character of his philosophical itinerary.

In his early works, Deleuze acts as an interpreter of other philosophers and writers: David Hume (1953/2001), Friedrich Nietzsche (1962/1983), Immanuel Kant (1963/2008), Marcel Proust (1964/2008) and Henri Bergson (1966/1991). Writing as a highly original historian of philosophy, Deleuze produces thought-provoking and counter-intuitive readings of these authors, who will deeply influence his entire intellectual journey. A few years later, Deleuze finds his own philosophical voice through his groundbreaking works *Difference and Repetition* (1968/2014) and *The Logic of Sense* (1969/2015). Both books bring forward some of Deleuze's main pre-existing themes – sense, sensation, difference and repetition – by weaving them together whilst further expanding them in unique ways. By contrasting sensation with meaning and difference with identity, Deleuze lays the groundwork for his epistemology and ontology during this period.

In the late 1960s, whilst writing two books on Baruch Spinoza (1968/1992, 1970/2001), Deleuze first encounters Guattari, and their collaboration marks the emergence of a new intellectual stratum, epitomised by the two volumes of *Capitalism and Schizophrenia*, a work on Franz Kafka (1975/1986) and the late *What Is Philosophy?* (1991/1994). *Capitalism and Schizophrenia* is, in many respects, Deleuze's most overtly political work, though it draws from various elements produced during his earlier philosophical explorations, highlighting the genuinely political nature of his entire journey. Volume 1, *Anti-Oedipus* (Deleuze and Guattari, 1972/2013), offers a scathing critique of the Freudian–Marxist narrative of innocent libidinal energies repressed by social institutions. Deleuze and Guattari maintain that social reproduction and economic production are intrinsically linked:

the nuclear family privatises social reproduction as capital privatises economic production. From this angle, they challenge the capitalist nature of psychoanalysis and its Oedipal model of sexual relationships which reduces desire to fixed identities. On the contrary, Deleuze and Guattari advance the concept of diffuse and subjectless desire and unearth the microfascist tendencies which traverse the social and individual body. Volume 2, *A Thousand Plateaus* (Deleuze and Guattari, 1980/2013), is an effort to formulate a historical social ontology animated by a specific normative commitment. This effort results in the elaboration of what Deleuze and Guattari call *nomadic thought*, a perspective operationalised through an array of innovative concepts, among which the idea of *assemblage* with its emphasises multiplicity and difference, crossing ontological, epistemological and normative boundaries, is probably one of the most well-known.

The final stage of Deleuze's work, lasting until his death in 1995, includes works on art – for example cinema (1983/2013, 1985/2013) – and artists – particularly Francis Bacon (1981/2017) – as well as his book on his friend the late Michel Foucault (1986/2006). This phase primarily involves the application of concepts developed earlier to specific subjects, renewing his thought in the process, and addressing subjects as different (yet entangled) as power, artistic-visual practice and sensation.

Overall, this intricate intellectual itinerary bears the marks of at least four philosophers who significantly influenced Deleuze throughout his career: Spinoza, Hume, Nietzsche and Bergson. Deleuze interprets Spinoza as the philosopher of the body, immanence and ethics, Hume as the champion of empiricism and radical subjectivism, Nietzsche as the philosopher of power and genealogy and Bergson as the scholar of the relationships between life, virtuality and time. These thinkers collectively share an interest in the concept of becoming, viewing reality as a field of active forces whilst unearthing the connections between ethics and politics. To this list, we should add Kant, Freud and Marx, with whom, before and after the encounter with Guattari, Deleuze continued to engage in dialogue, challenging their claims around the nature of reason, the psyche and production.

The ultimate result of Deleuze's multiple intellectual engagements is a composite philosophical approach. His ontology contests the privilege given to things and substances, and therefore to extension, foregrounding intensive forces – *desire* – as the basic components of reality. His epistemology disputes the very idea of reason as an a priori way of relating to (and knowing) the external world. Deleuze posits that there is nothing external to our thought; rather, everything is part of a world in which human thought and life are integral. Knowledge is the result of our interaction with the world we are inherently part of. He advocates for 'machinic' production, a subjectless and self-sustaining process of generating reality, encompassing more-than-human and other-than-human entities (Deleuze and Guattari, 1972/2013: 102, 1980/2013: 506). His goal is not to rediscover the eternal or the universal but to find the conditions under which something new is produced and then determine it, by creating new concepts (Buchanan, 2021: 52). Ontology and epistemology, however, in Deleuze's framework, are preceded by politics. Reality and our knowledge of it are an expression of forces which constitute us. From this normative angle, Deleuze interrogates our desire for subjugation, proposing to disentangle us first from our own internal forms of self-oppression, hierarchy and fixity, which converge in our identity, and then from oppressive social institutions, as a path to micro- and macro-revolutionary action.

Deleuze's Approach

Thinking about restorative justice through the concept of assemblage presents numerous advantages. Namely, it provides both analytical creativity and normative coherence, generating new ways of critiquing and then reimagining restorative justice. Additionally, it allows for a journey across the entire Deleuzian itinerary, connecting multiple aspects of his work and promoting wider engagement with this thought-provoking author.

The concept of assemblage is one of the results of Deleuze and Guattari's endeavour to describe the heterogeneous aspects of the reality human beings are enmeshed within (Deleuze and Guattari, 1980/2013: 2). Assemblage is thus a social-ontological instrument; not a static entity or a thing, but a dynamic way of looking at reality by connecting creatively different material elements (things, bodies, actions, passions) and signs (words, discourses), according to a specific diagram. Contrary to what the name might imply, in fact, assembling does not mean lumping together disparate elements of reality. Instead, it requires examining reality by highlighting specific connections among different types of elements, making them resonate with each other.

By adopting this perspective, it is possible to generate an understanding of reality as an open-ended network (and not a seamless and organic whole) of human, non-human and other-than-human elements, of different scales and orders, sustained by an underlying force – *desire* (Buchanan, 2021: 47; DeLanda, 2006: 4). This understanding of reality is consistent, dynamic and oriented. Consistency arises from the fact that the assemblage reconstructs a certain phenomenon by focusing on how desire, the de-individualised flow of intensities which produce reality, informs such phenomenon. Desire is inherently productive; it is not an impulse towards something but a primal energy cast against the unformed matter which constitutes the background of life (Buchanan, 2021: 66).

Thinking in these terms involves making visible the active forces which constitute reality, as well as their clashes, combinations and intersections, which can lead to stability or conflict, at different speeds and with varying effects. Dynamism is related to the fact that these elements are not simply put together but change in quality and quantity, extension and intensity, whilst interacting with each other. The properties of the assemblage emerge from this interaction between components. This inherent dynamism is organised by a diagram, or 'abstract machine' (Deleuze and Guattari, 1980/2013: 81), a set of relations which develop across these elements and signs, endowing the process with a meaningful orientation. These relations exist independently of those components and follow a direction given by the forces underlying the entire assemblage. In terms of effects, the assemblage both makes and unmakes reality, as expressed vividly by Deleuze and Guattari, who describe it as 'stratifying' reality (Deleuze and Guattari, 1980/2013: 46). This means that the assemblage produces strata or layers of reality (material and discursive) in the face of unformed social matter – what Deleuze and Guattari emphatically call the 'body without organs' (1980/2013: 173) – whilst also harnessing the desire of unbecoming. The reality produced is not a unified whole, but a multiplicity characterised by relations enacted by the assemblage. There is no predetermined purpose or end-point to this process; the effects are produced serendipitously through the dynamic and creative connections that constitute the assemblage.

In short, the assemblage aids in dynamically reconstructing a certain phenomenon – in our case, restorative justice – crossing both ontological and epistemological boundaries. It does so by charting how the heterogeneous components of restorative justice become and unbecome, fluidify and solidify, looking at them as part of a constellation of interconnected material and discursive elements, in movement, at different speeds and in different directions. As this chapter will reveal, the assemblage's functioning is inherently normative: by reconstructing restorative justice in this way, it also points to new and different possibilities for thinking of and doing justice.

Assembling Restorative Justice

The process of 'assembling' restorative justice begins with the arrangement of different material and semiotic elements. Material components constitute the content of the restorative justice assemblage, its machinic dimension, whilst semiotic elements pertain to its expressive side (Deleuze and Guattari, 1975/1986: 81). Material and discursive elements are dynamically connected and inscribed onto each other (Buchanan, 2021: 33; DeLanda, 2006: 12). Such components can be envisioned as lines: *molar* lines (rigid lines, such as those in the hierarchical and bureaucratic institutions regulating restorative justice), *molecular* lines (fluid and primal lines, such as the feelings and sensorial experiences that take place during restorative encounters) and *lines of flight* (like the development of a critical restorative justice), which work as the paths along which change is actualised and can transform assemblages creatively. The terms molar and molecular, here, have nothing to do with size; instead, they refer to qualitative states. Molarity involves the translation of desire into transcendental, fixed signifiers, whereas molecularity implies unstructured, high-speed flows. They are not in opposition but rather linked as each other's potential – a molar line can become molecular, and vice versa. Then, depending on how these lines combine, a supple or a rigid reality will be generated. The restorative justice assemblage includes those two dimensions (material and semiotic) along these three different lines (molar, molecular, flight), which intersect, overlap and clash, generating different types of effects over time.

Semiotic Elements

Molecular semiotic elements provide the restorative justice assemblage with an open discursive texture. These components encompass a range of signifiers that can be articulated in different ways, remaining open to contestation and interpretation. Conversely, molar denotes codified signifiers which provide the assemblage with a semiotic rigidity. In the first group, we should include the key concepts of *harm, stakeholders, encounter, facilitator, reparation* and *transformation*. In the latter group, we should include *policy* (legal, regulatory and administrative) on restorative justice enacted by institutional apparatuses. Clearly, there is a fundamental connection between these two groups: molar semiotic components are a development of the molecular semiotic elements, as much as the molecular is nothing but the molar's potential. These components, taken individually, pre-exist the restorative justice assemblage, but it is within the assemblage that by interacting according to distinctive relationships, they engender the reality we call 'restorative justice'.

Harm denotes the negative consequences of a behaviour deemed by a range of stakeholders as morally wrong. *Stakeholders* are the participants in restorative justice processes, 'victims' (or the 'person who has been harmed'), 'offenders' (or the 'person who has harmed') and 'communities', who have a direct stake in the harm and its consequences (Christie, 1977; Johnstone, 2011). Harms, in fact, 'belong' to relevant victims, offenders and communities, since they experience them directly, making the involvement of these direct actors necessary. The *encounter* is the time and space wherein the active participation of relevant stakeholders is enacted (Zehr, 2005). Here, responsibility is assumed, parties are heard, emotions are harnessed and personal accountability is activated (Dignan, 2002). The presence of a *facilitator* is a key condition for the encounter to be restorative, on the assumption that parties will not be able to find restoration by themselves (an idea somewhat conflicting with the concept of stakeholding mentioned above). *Restoration* indicates a critique of retribution (understood as the deliberate infliction of pain as a form of just desert), which emphasises the re-establishment of agency by correcting the material, psychological and symbolic dimensions of harm. It also seeks to heal the supposed social bond between stakeholders corroded by harm. *Transformation* refers to the stakeholders' journey of personal self-improvement, seen as a condition or consequence of repairing harm.

These key molecular semiotic components, which form a minimal 'restorative vocabulary', are informed by scientific, religious and moral-philosophical perspectives which endow the assemblage with its epistemic foundations (cf. Maglione, 2019: 654). Victimology provides restorative justice with the idea of a victim's marginalisation and the rise of victimhood as an academic subject (and political resource) (Garland, 2001: 11). Thus, it promotes the direct involvement of crime victims in criminal justice and the necessity of satisfying the victim's needs to 'be heard' and 'speak out'. The emergence of the 'third way criminologies' (Hughes, 2007: 23), which focus on crime as an effect of the progressive erosion of the moral fabric of local communities (Braitwhaite, 1989; Duff, 1992, 2000; Dzur, 2003) to be addressed with (moralising) community-based interventions, underpins much of the semiotic repertoire of restorative justice, particularly the concepts of harm and stakeholding. Within this context, a central topic has been the emergence of 'everyday' youth offenders. Restorative justice has historically been conceptualised as a third way response to the youth 'problem', centring on responsibilisation by holding youth offenders accountable for the harm caused, as well as by requiring reparation for the consequences of crime.

This cultural background also includes sociological propositions around the 'eclipsing' of moral communities (cf. Etzioni, 1993; Giddens, 1998), as an effect of the combined action of conservative individualism and post-war social democracy, against which restorative justice aims to revitalise communities by involving them in response to harm. Penal minimalism is also relevant here, as the position advocating for the civilisation of punishment and the problematisation of legal language and its stigmatising effects (Christie, 1977). Religious and moral-philosophical perspectives contribute to the epistemic foundations of the assemblage as well. The 'therapeutic' and 'self-help' (Richards, 2005) movements have supported the development of restorative justice as a self-described healing and empowering form of justice which focuses on closure, forgiveness and reconciliation. Mennonites' and Quakers' ethical doctrines, with their focus on non-violent response to wrongdoing, spiritual rehabilitation and community-based and inclusive justice processes, also have been a source of semiotic material for restorative justice (Liebmann, 2007). Lastly, Westernised versions of Indigenous cultures and practices have played a similar role. This is the case for Navajo peacemaking, Māori conferencing and South African Ubuntu, which have provided a culturally specific platform used by Western scholars and policymakers as both a historical explanation of and a justification for the emergence of restorative justice (Zehr, 2005).

This complex, yet not exhaustive, molecular semiotic material is integrated into molar semiotic components such as regulatory decisions, laws and administrative measures – policy. Taken together, molecular and molar semiotic components constitute the discursive dimension of the restorative justice assemblage.

Over the last 30 years, a wide number of public policy measures have been enacted by local, national and international bodies regulating restorative justice. They weave together molecular semiotic aspects whilst infusing legal authority into (some of) them, on the basis of policymakers' preferences. This implies a molarisation of those semiotic elements – that is, their qualitative transformation from organic and supple discourses to legally sanctioned 'order-words' (Deleuze and Guattari, 1980/2013: 88). At the international level, examples of this process are the passing of the United Nations 'Declaration of Basic Principles of Justice for Victims of Crime and Abuse of Power' (1985); the Council of Europe Committee of Ministers Recommendations No. R(99)19 and CM/Rec(2018)8 concerning respectively mediation in penal matters and restorative justice; the United Nations 'Basic Principles on the Use of Restorative Justice Programmes in Criminal Matters' (2002); and the European Union Directive 2012/29/EU establishing minimum standards on the rights, support and protection of victims of crime (The Victims' Directive). Worldwide, an increasing number of national policies and laws on restorative justice are passed every year. There seem to be two general models of policy regulation of restorative justice: centralised (i.e. policy documents dedicated entirely to restorative justice) and diffuse (single norms introducing specific interventions with a limited reach). In the United States, 32 states now have either specific legislation on restorative justice or single normative dispositions on this subject within regulatory frameworks which discipline other matters (González, 2020). In Europe, Belgium and Norway have developed a centralised approach whilst the United Kingdom has developed decentralised regulation. Aotearoa New Zealand is another example of centralised regulation. A further recurrent distinction is between restorative justice regulations for youth and adults. In the case of youth offenders, the youth's interest has to be balanced against the victim's interest, whilst for adults such balance is struck in a different way since there are no specific concerns regarding the offender's welfare. Non-statutory documents also represent an important macro-regulatory area. These span from regulatory bodies' initiatives to governmental recommendations. They continue to play a critical role in creating institutional space for restorative justice, increasing public recognition and, to some extent, legitimacy and provision.

Material Elements

Material molecular elements encompass the affective states experienced by individuals involved in restorative encounters. From a molar perspective, instead, material elements consist in the organisations (councils, charities, NGOs, etc.), which structure the social field and enable restorative justice encounters.

During restorative justice encounters, multiple sensory modalities unfold (cf. McClanahan and South, 2020). This is the embodied dimension of such encounters, wherein flesh-and-bones individuals physically meet. Waiting for the other stakeholders, sitting on an office chair in a waiting room or in the facilitator's office. Entering a more or less anonymous office, the pale-coloured walls, the absence or the presence of a table. The smell of a place unfamiliar and perhaps perceived as hostile or as a place of hope. And then seeing the other, victim or offender, person who has been harmed or person who has harmed, taking a seat in a pre-arranged space. Looking away, staring. A sense of fear or awe. The silence and the small talk before the encounter starts, the surprise, shame and fright given by the sudden appearance of the other. Listening, perhaps being interrupted, modulating the voice, trying to be concise, sometimes sticking with the restorative script. The silence which more or less frequently takes over the encounter. Smiling or crying. Touching a pen or a piece of paper, taking notes whilst the other is speaking. Fiddling, scratching one's head, caressing one's face. Shaking hands or physically withdrawing. Restorative encounters are constituted by embodied sensorial experiences (sight, sound, taste, smell and touch) like these, expressive of affective states, which interact often subtly yet significantly.

These sensory modalities are assembled in distinctive ways – that is, their functioning is generated through their interaction with other components of the assemblage. These modalities' strength (i.e. their frequency, or how often they occur), reciprocity (the symmetry or asymmetry of the interpersonal relations – for example who plays a more dominant or recessive role during encounters), density (the intensity of the connection across bodies partaking in a restorative encounter), stability (the presence or absence of disturbances from a condition of equilibrium) and solidarity (the interdependence of emotional and cognitive performance across participants) are all increased or decreased, affected and affecting, depending on how the other molecular and molar semiotic and material elements are playing with each other (cf. Colman, 2008).

The design of the built environment 'materialises' the semiotic elements of the assemblage whilst providing a stage for those sensorial experiences. Courthouses' layouts express rigid positions within the justice process, as well as principles of hierarchy, accountability and responsibility. Correctional facilities' architectural diagrams express the pains of solitude and the deprivation of freedom. Restorative justice practitioners have characteristically advanced the need to redesign the spaces in which justice occurs as restorative spaces (Hobson, Payne, Bangura and Hester, 2022). These are spaces wherein listening and cooperation from all sides can be facilitated by the organisation of the proximate environment. From this perspective, the circle plays a critical role. This is a 'personal' space wherein no physical hierarchy can be established or recognised, insofar as everyone occupies the same position as everyone else. The circle is often presented as re-enacting Indigenous traditions of conflict resolution (Greenwood, 2005). A second structured form is the triangle (Brigg, 2003), wherein parties sit next to each other facing the facilitator. This is a 'sharper' organisation of the space, in which parties occupy positions which symbolise different roles with respect to the facilitator. Historically, this is an early form of contemporary restorative justice encounters, characterising victim – offender reconciliation programs (VORPs) developed in Canada and the United States in the late 1970s. Today, however, there seems to be a tendency to invest more in the circle than the triangle, especially in the case of youth justice. These two different models of designing the encounter embody different values. Circles, in fact, embrace a transformative discourse, whilst the triangle is more consonant with reparative intent. Both designs are said to create horizontal relationships, underplaying the role of the facilitator as an expert in the process, external to its content. A recent innovation in this context is the idea of the 'restorative city' (e.g. Straker, 2019). This represents an attempt to create a new, expansive restorative space, supposedly beyond the triangle and circle as enclosed and artificial spaces. Restorative cities diffuse and systematise those semiotic components by injecting them into existing organisations, aiming to create a restorative space which surrounds human life and through which human life is cultivated.

A final molar material element consists of institutional bodies: conventional criminal justice agencies, communitarian institutions and distinctive restorative justice organisations which operationally enable the 'delivery' of restorative justice. Police have been one of the first agencies to endorse restorative justice, by training officers in restorative approaches and actually running restorative justice services (Davis, 1992; Clamp and Paterson, 2016). One of the reasons for this appeal has been that restorative justice, as a policing option, resonates with community policing and community resolution techniques as instruments for responsibilising, for example, youth offenders. Probation services have administered restorative justice programmes since the 1970s, whilst prisons are a more recent space in which restorative justice has found some applications. In this context, restorative justice is either a penal option in addition to conventional punishment or independent from it, such as a condition for probation, an element of the sentence or an option given outside the sentencing framework (Daly, 2016). Restorative justice can also count on the support of a wide range of communitarian institutions, such as third sector agencies, non-governmental organisations and voluntary groups involved in doing restorative justice within and outside criminal justice settings, such as victim support organisations and specific institutional bodies created to lead the implementation of restorative justice (e.g. the 'restorative justice councils' which oversee the development of training and service delivery in, for example, the United Kingdom, the United States and Norway).

Abstract Machine and Body Without Organs

This multiplicity of semiotic and material elements is connected and orientated by an *abstract machine*, a diagram which cuts across the elementary components charted earlier, giving them consistency (Deleuze and Guattari, 1980/2013: 81; cf. DeLanda, 2006: 30). These connections are of different types; some consist of conflicts, others of combinations, overlaps or intersections. This emerging diagram is a field of relational forces – a 'rhizome' – neither a permanent structure nor a pre-existing form, but rather a dynamic field with a basic orientation (Deleuze and Guattari, 1980/2013: 2). This diagram is the product of two different machinic processes: *structural individuation* and *functional sequencing* of semiotic and material elements.

The semiotic and material elements constituting restorative justice are individuated – that is, synthesised from that state of radical potentiality, a magma of virtual relations – through a contingent process which responds to local and partial conditions. The abstract machine is the connection across those forces, the condition of their individuation as a singular meaningful object: in our case, restorative justice. This connection is not an outcome achieved once and for all, but a continuous process which makes molar and molecular elements interact. Restorative justice emerges as a configuration of individual bodies in search of responses to discrete actions qualified empirically as harms and normatively as wrongs. It involves the interaction between legal and non-legal, institutional and non-institutional actors, working in specific spatial environments. This configuration is only one possible form which could be given to dialogic-reparative practices, yet it is historically the most stable, the one which has more deeply colonised practitioners, reformers and scholars' imagination.

The second dimension of the abstract machine is functional sequencing. This means that once individuated, restorative justice is explained and justified sequentially. This happens by posing the abstract signifier 'conventional criminal justice in crisis' as the backdrop against which restorative justice is cast. Conventional criminal justice is a constellation of generalisations about the justice system, described as affected by a crisis of legitimation produced by criminal justice's incapacity to fulfil victims' needs and address reoffending. Restorative justice is therefore explained and justified as a functional response to such a crisis. The basic semiotic diagram 'harm – stakeholding – encounter – reparation' constitutes this response.

Both structural individuation and functional sequencing are libidinal processes. They express a productive tendency towards the codification of social reality. This machinic tendency, though functional, engenders tensions as well. There are tensions between semiotic components informed by standard criminal justice notions (such as victim and offender) and specific restorative concepts (the person who has harmed and the person who has been harmed). The former concepts express a distinctive criminal justice language, molarising identities and stigmatising, whilst the latter denote a more 'humane' understanding of the stakeholders involved in restorative encounters. Similarly, there are tensions between victimological research findings, which put forth the idea of restoration as victim satisfaction, and the penal minimalist idea of restoration as offender reintegration. There are complex relationships between material and semiotic elements as well. Material elements do not simply provide 'a platform' for the latter to be put in action. Instead, they produce or reproduce semiotic elements themselves impacting on the semiotic structure of the restorative justice assemblage. The spatial form of restorative encounters as a triangle or a circle affects the content of the encounter which will then take place, and the participation of certain stakeholders (professionals such as police officers or social workers, as often happens in the case of youth restorative justice conferences) materially alters the encounter as well, rendering it more or less inclusive or formal.

The restorative assemblage, orientated by the abstract machine, is cast against a non-organised background constituted by affective relations and populated by multiplicities, a 'body without organs' (Deleuze and Guattari, 1980/2013: 173). This background adds a further dimension to our analysis, a dimension which will then be crucial when trying to unearth the assemblage's normative level. The body without organs is the limit of the assemblage, 'what remains when everything is stripped away' (Deleuze and Guattari, 1980/2013: 174). It is the virtual of restorative justice, the pre-individuated *justice-desiring flows* which pre-exist the organised versions of restorative justice. Such flows are a tangle of affective multiplicities in their constant becoming which are then individuated and connected by the abstract machine. Affect, here, refers to the product of an encounter of bodies, their intensive molecular variation, lived and ethical, active or reactive, in time and space, in transformation. In our case, these affective relations are the entanglement between different justice-desiring flows, the libidinal energies expressed by the tension towards active and reactive affections traversing bodies whose powers are limited, coerced and decreased (that is, harmed) by destructive engagements with others' powers. More fundamentally, here, 'justice is desire' (Deleuze and Guattari, 1975/1986: 49), which means that what bodies strive to do when limited by other powers is to produce a new reality, generating new multiplicities. Multiplicities are the intensive mutations and gradations constituting bodies, unfolding over time and without spatial boundaries. The challenge, at this point, is deciphering what happens to this justice-as-desire, this emission of multiplicities, when the assemblage is set in motion, when this complex machine starts capturing and organising those magmatic flows.

Setting in Motion the Assemblage

Once the elements constituting the restorative assemblage are drawn, it becomes possible to look at this composite 'subject' dynamically, that is, to explore the historical processes which animate the restorative assemblage and then to describe how this actually functions and its effects.

From this angle, the restorative assemblage is the product of the 'coding', 'territorialisation', 'deterritorialisation' and 'reterritorialisation' of justice-desiring flows (Deleuze and Guattari, 1980/2013: 102). *Coding* involves ordering flows by creating bodies (i.e. the identification of discrete individuals in search of justice); *territorialisation* is the ordering of bodies by turning them into consistent entities (e.g. as victims, offenders or communities); *deterritorialisation* is the flight from such ordering (the rejection of legal labels proposed by critical restorative justice theories); and *reterritorialisation* is the return to fixed ordering (Buchanan, 2021: 42). Coding is an operation of fixing molecular relations in static legal entities (Smith, 2012: 169–70). What is coded is the exchange of energy constituting the justice-desiring flows which pre-exist legal structures and identities. Territorialisation involves the production of connective forces which ensure stable reality, deterritorialisation involves the unmaking of that reality, allowing the chaos (the intensive differences which make up reality) in, and reterritorialisation entails the reproduction of connections and organisation.

The restorative justice assemblage appears, from a historical perspective, as a collection of heterogeneous components extracted from justice-desiring flows, which, once coded (i.e. referred back to discrete human bodies rather than more-than-human or non-human entities), are territorialised (i.e. traced onto sets of self-organising social processes). At the same time, these flows undergo concomitant processes of deterritorialisation and reterritorialisation. Here is where the dynamism characterising the assemblage becomes visible. Thinking in terms of molecular and molar lines only means focusing on the static aspects of the assemblage. Lines of flight, instead, activate the assemblage, rendering it unstable and unpredictable in its effects (cf. Buchanan, 2021: 89). The critique of the culturally colonising effects of restorative justice or of its problematic impact on youths when administered as a moralising intervention can be interpreted as lines of (partial) flight from well-established cultural and operational frameworks within restorative justice.

The assemblage, then, 'stratifies' material and semiotic components, preventing the emergence of lines of flight (Deleuze and Guattari, 1980/2013: 46–63). *Stratification* is the capture of free-floating intensive forces, which constitute human and non-human bodies by layering them upon each other, giving them consistency (Buchanan, 2021: 36–8). Stratification equates with imprisoning intensities, locking singularities and organising molecules. The product of this process is the actualisation and stabilisation of power relations, resulting ultimately in regular social meanings, organisms, subjects. These strata constrain human bodies, and this process of capture is a form of 'machinic enslavement' (Deleuze and Guattari, 1980/2013: 498).

Organic reparation-orientated justice practices, blossoming at the very margins of criminal justice systems in the 1970s in the Global North, are one of the strata of the restorative justice assemblage. They stratify justice-desiring flows, turning them into machines (semiotic-material connections of bodies and discourses in the form of early victim–offender reconciliation programs or conferences) plugged into other machines (e.g. probation or court proceedings). What is usually defined as the institutionalisation of restorative justice is nothing but another layer of the process of assembling restorative justice, of turning justice-desiring flows into discrete social machines.

Institutionalisation as State Capture

The scholarly literature describes the institutionalisation of restorative justice as the gradual shift of this constellation of ideas and associated practices, during the 1990s, from the margins of social control systems to the mainstream (cf. Maglione, Marder and Pali, 2024). One of the manifestations of this phenomenon is the increasing incorporation of restorative justice practices into state policy frameworks, a trend supported by large sections of the restorative justice movement (e.g. Walgrave, 2000). The primary rationale behind this support is operational: policy is believed to ensure the wide and deep development of restorative justice, in terms of implementation, funding and capacity (Poama, 2015). When viewed through the lens of the assemblage, the institutionalisation of restorative justice can be conceptualised as a process of coding and territorialisation of justice-desiring flows, driven by the state. The result of this process is then stratified as legal practices, devoid of the multiplicity characterising justice-desiring flows.

Deleuze and Guattari draw their concept of *the state* from Pierre Clastres's idea (1980/2010) of the existence of a unifying regulative principle that precedes social and economic formations. This principle facilitates the emergence of, for example, the nuclear family or the Fordist factory by neutralising social antagonisms and producing a unified, collective subjectivity. Along these lines, Deleuze and Guattari view the state as a centripetal wave that captures flows and variations by introducing a transcendent foundational subject to enable the systematisation of life. The state rationalises spaces, establishes rights over a territory and structures the social world (Deleuze and Guattari, 1980/2013: 449), presenting its violence as always necessary, creating the right of appropriation by appropriation (ibid., 1980/2013: 520). The state subjugates justice-desiring flows in two interrelated ways: by relating them to a central legal structure (i.e. legalisation) and by manipulating their underpinning desire (i.e. microfascism). In both cases, the aim is for the state to expand its sovereignty and to fulfil its libidinal tendency to accumulate and stabilise further power over the social world.

Justice-desiring flows, as seen earlier, are social relations which bind bodies together in their generation of mutually power-enhancing events, operating in a smooth, unorganised space (Holland, 2008: 80), exterior to representation, diffused and polymorphous. The state submits these flows to its totalising, unifying and signifying force by identifying and then representing them as fixed and universal entities, in the form of specific legal categories, such as individual responsibility, obligation to redress, repair and punishment. Identification is the condition of representation: something must be identified before it can be represented. However, social reality – in our case, justice-desiring flows – is a stream of pure differences, and identifying them entails their obliteration. Identities, in fact, are fixed predicates which extrapolate defined objects from reality, in this way denying multiplicity and engendering a form of social repression which will then constitute inherently deficient subjects (i.e. stakeholders with the crystallised identities of victims or offenders).

Legalisation is a complex process, whose final output is 'the law', a pure form, absolutely empty, objectless, whose only message is that we are guilty (Deleuze, 1970/2001: 4) and that the distribution and hierarchisation of bodies are necessary. This is fundamentally a dialectic process, animated by *ressentiment*, since the legal totalisation of justice-desiring flows entails a superior unity generated out of a negative conflict between lower elements: unorganised flows are dangerous and must be organised by means of legalisation. This process destroys connections, linearises and oversimplifies; it imposes negative and extrinsic rules, as well as a transcendent ideal which derives everything from an original principle (truth) and relates everything to an ideal (justice), coalescing in a single entity (the state).

The other aspect of the state capture of justice-desiring flows involves the manipulation of the very libidinal energy constituting those flows. This manipulation results in *microfascism* – the love for being subjugated, an internal death drive which can be manipulated by external actors. Fascist (and microfascist) desire is the desire for codes to replace free flows, creating rigid boundaries and immobilising flows. Obliterating desire involves causing death – that is, the decomposition of the body's relations, its immobility and degree zero of intensity. This is achieved by turning justice-desiring flows into codified lists of harms and responses to them, a classificatory attempt which disguises the very formative context within which certain harms occur. This obliteration is then complemented by the generation of new self-destructive libidinal energy.

In fact, turning those flows into discrete restorative practices, a sequence of codified steps which lead from microdisorders to social order, may appeal to restorative justice practitioners or advocates since it promises to render predictable what is regulated, becoming the condition for translating chaotic organic processes into discrete sets of mechanical operations. This may be appealing since it reduces the emotional and cognitive labour required to handle organic flows, making things apparently smoother. And this is also the mark of legalisation's strength: it produces a form of grey joy that subtly colonises one's freedom, until freedom is paralysed. The very demand, widely shared by the restorative justice movement, to endlessly scale up restorative justice by regulating it, increasing capacity, exemplifies this libidinal tension towards legal self-oppression. Legal abstraction and generalisations penetrate restorative justice, deadening its relational multiplicities. Referral routes kept by criminal justice agencies, the possibility of resuming the standard track if the restorative process is unsatisfactory and the quality certification of restorative providers are examples of this process. The institutionalisation of desire curtails the vital energy which constitutes justice-desiring flows (Deleuze, 1962/1983: 137).

Nomadic Restorative Justice

Assembling restorative justice is both a heuristic and a normative operation. Unearthing the multiplicity of semiotic-material lines, reconstructing their underlying diagram and background, charting how their becoming is immobilised by state capture – all of this means creating new spaces for thinking differently about and thus transforming restorative justice. Further developing these lines, it is possible to point to a *nomadic* development of restorative justice (cf. Woolford and Ratner, 2003). This entails reactivating the becoming of the justice-desiring flows which underpin restorative justice. This reactivation is a process of experimentation, an open-ended, reflexive dismantling of legal operations, creating new spaces for encountering bodies and enhancing their capacities, not without its share of challenges.

The key element of this normative approach is the notion of 'becoming-other' – the cultivation of the affective power of justice against any form of representation, universalisation and totalisation through identity (Deleuze, 1968/2014: 41). Becoming-other is not an end in itself but an active response to a problem unveiled by historical analysis: the current molarisation and stratification of restorative justice. Becoming-other means nurturing the non-linear, transversal, non-hierarchical relations of forces constituting justice. Justice, here, is the moving, open-ended configuration of desiring bodies in search of mutual enhancement, the synthesis of those forces into events which are always specific instead of their representation into fixed and universal legal orderings.

The problem is determining which relations of forces are relevant and which ones are to be cultivated. This evaluative operation is as much ethical as political, and it has implications for the creation of an enhanced social (nomadic) subjectivity. Whilst legal morality consists of constraining rules against which one is judged in relation to the transcendent values of good and evil, producing 'lacking' subjects, ethics is a normative commitment to maximise connections that expand possibilities of life, whose 'good' cannot be determined universally or outside of a concrete situation. Law judges individuals based on how they are and should be, condemning them to infinite debt to a superimposed society, whilst ethics is the consideration of who we are becoming and may become: it is an immanent, evaluative and affirmative analysis of our capacity to live.

A nomadic restorative justice proposes 'ethical tests' and not legal judgements (Deleuze, 1970/2001: 41). These tests involve analysing the affective compositions of relations between bodies taking place in encounters, wherein good relations are those ones which mutually enhance bodies' powers. For these encounters to be affectively active means for them to be configured as *events*. An event is a vibratory block of space-time, constituted by forces, which communicates with other blocks. A *just* rhythm is created within such events when those forces are balanced against each other, enabling the possibility of both affecting and being affected by others' bodies. These encounter-events force us to think (Deleuze, 1968/2014: 183) about the forces that constitute bodies, forces we are never conscious of (Deleuze, 1968/1992: 226), whilst becoming-other, regenerating ourselves as something new, in the very process of encountering other bodies. This is neither the rational process of self-assertion nor that of recognition. At stake is not reconfirming our knowledge, beliefs and emotions but the emptying of oneself, opening up to the other, enabling a rupture of our own habits, whilst affirming a new way of seeing the world and our place within it (cf. O'Sullivan, 2006: 1).

Harm, Art and Dangers

From this perspective, harm is an investment of energy that leads to the ethical decomposition of the other's power. This should be addressed by local, expansive, flexible and contingent connections that mutually enhance bodies' capacities. This, in turn, would forge new, *minor* lines of flight instead of the microfascist legalisation of social relations. The 'minor' is a tendency towards the continuous variation of everybody (Deleuze and Guattari, 1980/2013: 124): defiance of canonical models, investment in collective action, politicisation of personal matters, experimentation with language and opening possibilities for the people to come (Bogue, 2011: 135). Whilst the 'major' adheres to a fixed standard and external grounding – an identity – the minor is standardless, focusing not on who we are but on who we may become (Deleuze and Guattari, 1980/2013: 123). Major is the standard which hierarchises statements by making them resonate with one central point, imposing binary structures and axioms and devitalising the organic through detached signification. It uses order-words which compel obedience. Becoming-other/minor works from inside and against majoritarian language, undoing it. It deterritorialises language – in our case, the individualising legal language enfolding institutional restorative justice – rendering everything political (Deleuze and Guattari, 1975/1986: 17). It produces intensive qualities, the proliferation of series and polyvalent connections.

A practice that embodies this minoritarian political element is *affective art*. Art is affective when, like in Kafka and Bacon, it creates the conditions for new connections and lines of flight from the law (including from the internal law – i.e. identity) to arise. Art, here, neither expresses meaning nor represents things nor imitate nature; instead, it undoes legal guilt, interiority and emptiness by suspending law and its representational, unifying and totalising machine (Deleuze, 1981/2017: 2), by hindering the subject that this violence enacts. Deleuze sees the subject as a relatively stable connection of lines, a pattern of syntheses which fold in on themselves, creating self-awareness. The legalisation of justice-desiring flows is nothing but the creation of an outside which enfolds bodies' affective multiplicity, resulting in legal subjects with fixed traits, hierarchically organised, a 'facialisation' of the body (Deleuze and Guattari, 1980/2013: 199). Dismantling this rigid legal subjectivity becomes art's main political aim, to be achieved not simply by fighting repressive institutions but by de-individualising bodies. This means disentangling them from their own microfascist desire for legal repression and forging the conditions for creating new collective solidarities. Affective art decouples justice (a mutually power-enhancing event) from law (a totalising structure), moves back and forth from the molar to the molecular and produces differences in order to enhance our collective 'potency' (Deleuze, 1970/2001: 3). The horizon of this intervention is 'irresponsibility', the radically innocent life of play (Deleuze, 1962/1983: 21), of pure immanence, of possibilities of becoming, folding and unfolding potential. This life is always a potential life (Deleuze, 1993/1998: xiv).

However, becoming-other and minoritising our life artistically present dangers as well. Lines of flight can be negative; differences are inhabited by identities that produce, certify or perpetuate subjugated subjectivities. A nomadic approach must, then, not only reactivate lines of flight but also be aware of the processes of recodification and reterritorialisation implicit in any power dynamic – that is, not only in the institutionalisation of restorative justice but also in its de-institutionalisation. This ambivalence is constitutive of the very concept of desire. Desiring power means also desiring the repression of the multiplicity embodied by justice-desiring flows.

So far, we have focused on the destructive effects of the microfascist, state-led capture of flows; however, the opposite process, of molecular decoding and deterritorialising, can also be seized upon by violent machines, turning into a pathological condition. This is what happens with capitalism, which deterritorialises and decodes but then blocks the development of revolutionary energies. Capitalism produces its own unfreedom by freeing desiring-production from capture and repression by other codes and representations whilst it recaptures it (e.g. in state nationalism and the nuclear family). This is why advocating for becoming-other is, in itself, not a 'solution' but always a dangerous political strategy. When promoting disentanglement from the legal machine, the goal is not to create an uncontaminated state of becoming but to cultivate the potential of such becoming, producing a permanent state of disentanglement from ourselves. This is always an incomplete and hazardous process, a continuous straining towards de-individualisation, descending to the edge of our abyss to nourish our becoming.

Beyond Deleuze

Assembling restorative justice means breaking down this subject, shattering it into multiple lines of different matter, letting them morph into each other, recombining them together and producing unexpected combinations, overlaps, tensions and clashes. The assemblage is not only a heuristic device but also a normative orientation, a struggle for becoming and for nurturing our potential, with the awareness of its dangers.

Deleuze helps us see justice-desiring flows as the unformed background of restorative justice. 'Restorative justice' is one possible way of assembling those flows, that unformed affective matter, one way of recombining them in semiotic and material elements, according to a certain diagram. This formed matter – restorative justice – is a historical phenomenon, always in motion. The institutionalisation of restorative justice, here, appears as one way of coding and territorialising those flows into machines and then of stratifying them into legal frameworks. The law fixes those flows through representation and identification. This process is libidinal – it entails desiring oppression, a condition which affects many of those propounding the legalisation of restorative justice today. Desiring oppression becomes normal when machines like the law appropriate organic flows by insinuating order into them and exploiting their libidinal creative energies.

This awareness should not lead towards nostalgic longing for a pure version of restorative justice, a regression to an original state. Those justice-desiring flows are an always-present virtual stream within the legalised version of restorative justice. What is at stake here is cultivating their potential for becoming-other, turning encounters into artistic, mutually body-enhancing practices. There is no dialectic between the legal organism and art. Art is the suspension of the legal machine, with an awareness of the dangers of deterritorialisation and lines of flight. There is no reconciliation between these two terms.

Deleuze leaves us, then, with a Francis Bacon-like portrait of the disquieting forces which constitute us, the primal matter which leads to emancipation as much as oppression. This painting is constitutively in the process of being drawn. Deleuze pushes us towards rediscovering the potency animating the yet-to-be-achieved production of reality without indicating a prophetic direction about how to use our potency. Could these lines be turned against themselves? Could freeing the justice-desiring flows integral to restorative justice destroy the assemblage itself? Is that freeing from the law a step towards a capitalistic justice? Deleuze reminds us that these are inevitable dangers and that confronting them is a lifelong task when justice, and an ethically and politically just life, is at stake.

References

Bogue, R. (2011) 'The Minor'. In Stivale, C. (ed.) *Gilles Deleuze: Key Concepts*, 131–41. Montreal, Quebec, and Kingston, Ontario: McGill-Queen's University Press.

Braithwaite, J. (1989) *Crime, Shame and Reintegration*. Cambridge, UK: Cambridge University Press.

Brigg, M. (2003) 'Mediation, Power, and Cultural Difference'. *Conflict Resolution Quarterly*, 20(3): 287–306.

Buchanan, I. (2021) *Assemblage Theory and Method*. London: Bloomsbury.

Christie, N. (1977) 'Conflicts as Property'. *British Journal of Criminology*, 17(1): 1–15.

Clamp, K. and Paterson, C. (2016) *Restorative Policing: Concepts, Theory and Practice*. London: Routledge.

Clastres, P. (1980/2010) *Archaeology of Violence*. Los Angeles: Semiotext(e).

Colman, A. (2008) 'Sensory Modality'. In *A Dictionary of Psychology*. Oxford: Oxford University Press, https://www.oxfordreference.com/view/10.1093/acref/9780199534067.001.0001/acref-9780199534067-e-7508. Accessed 2 January 2024.

Daly, D. (2016) 'What Is Restorative Justice? Fresh Answers to a Vexed Question'. *Victims & Offenders*, 11(1): 9–29.

Davis, G. (1992) *Making Amends: Mediation and Reparation in Criminal Justice*. London and New York: Routledge.

DeLanda, M. (2006) *A New Philosophy of Society*. London: Continuum.

Deleuze, G. (1962/1983) *Nietzsche & Philosophy*. New York: Columbia University Press.

Deleuze, G. (1966/1991) *Bergsonism*. New York: Zone Books.

Deleuze, G. (1968/1992) *Expressionism in Philosophy: Spinoza*. New York: Zone Books.

Deleuze, G. (1993/1998) *Essays Critical and Clinical*. London: Verso.

Deleuze, G. (1953/2001) *Empiricism and Subjectivity: An Essay on Hume's Theory of Human Nature*. New York: Columbia University Press.
Deleuze, G. (1970/2001) *Spinoza: Practical Philosophy*. San Francisco, CA: City Light Books.
Deleuze, G. (1986/2006) *Foucault*. London: Bloomsbury.
Deleuze, G. (1963/2008) *Kant's Critical Philosophy*. London: Continuum.
Deleuze, G. (1964/2008) *Proust and Signs*. London: Continuum.
Deleuze, G. (1983/2013) *Cinema I: The Movement-Image*. London: Bloomsbury.
Deleuze, G. (1985/2013) *Cinema II: The Time-Image*. London: Bloomsbury.
Deleuze, G. (1968/2014) *Difference and Repetition*. London: Bloomsbury.
Deleuze, G. (1969/2015) *The Logic of Sense*. London: Bloomsbury.
Deleuze, G. (1981/2017) *Francis Bacon: The Logic of Sensation*. London: Bloomsbury.
Deleuze, G. and Guattari, F. (1975/1986) *Kafka: Toward a Minor Literature*. Minneapolis: University of Minnesota Press.
Deleuze, G. and Guattari, F. (1991/1994) *What Is Philosophy?* London: Verso.
Deleuze, G. and Guattari, F. (1972/2013) *Anti-Oedipus*. London: Bloomsbury.
Deleuze, G. and Guattari, F. (1980/2013) *A Thousand Plateaus*. London: Bloomsbury.
Dignan, J. (2002) 'Restorative Justice and the Law: The Case for an Integrated, Systemic Approach'. In Walgrave, L. (ed.) *Restorative Justice and the Law*, 168–90. Cullompton, UK: Willan.
Duff, A. (1992) 'Alternatives to Punishment – Or Alternative Punishments?' In Cragg, W. (ed.) *Retributivism and Its Critics*, 44–68. Stuttgart, Germany: Steiner.
Duff, A. (2000) *Punishment, Communication and Community*. New York: Oxford University Press.
Dzur, A. (2003) 'Civic Implications of Restorative Justice Theory: Citizen Participation and Criminal Justice Policy'. *Policy Sciences*, 36(3): 279–306.
Etzioni, A. (1993) *The Spirit of Community*. New York: Crown Books.
Garland, D. (2001) *The Culture of Control: Crime and Social Order in Contemporary Society*. Oxford: Oxford University Press.
Giddens, A. (1998) *The Third Way: The Renewal of Social Democracy*. Cambridge, UK: Cambridge University Press.
González, T. (2020) 'The Legalization of Restorative Justice: A Fifty-State Empirical Analysis'. *Utah Law Review*, 5(3): 1057–98.
Greenwood, J. (2005) *The Circle Process: A Path for Restorative Dialogue*. Center for Restorative Justice & Peacemaking, School of Social Work, University of Minnesota, https://rjp.d.umn.edu/resources/victim-offender-mediation/circles. Accessed 13 November 2023.
Hobson, J., Payne, B., Bangura, K. and Hester, R. (2022) '"Spaces" for Restorative Development: International Case Studies on Restorative Services'. *Contemporary Justice Review*, 25(2): 143–62.
Holland, E. W. (2008) 'Schizoanalysis, Nomadology, Fascism'. In Buchanan, I. (ed.) *Deleuze and Politics*, 74–97. Edinburgh: Edinburgh University Press.
Hughes, G. (2007) *The Politics of Crime and Community*. Basingstoke, UK: Palgrave.
Johnstone, G. (2011) *Restorative Justice: Ideas, Values, Debates*, 2nd ed. London: Routledge.
Liebmann, M. (2007) *Restorative Justice: How It Works*. London: Jessica Kingsley.
Maglione, G. (2019) 'The Restorative Justice Apparatus: A Critical Analysis of the Historical Emergence of Restorative Justice'. *Social & Legal Studies*, 28(5): 650–74.
Maglione, G., Marder, I. and Pali, B. (2024) *Restorative Justice at a Crossroads: Dilemmas of Institutionalisation*. Abingdon: Routledge.
McClanahan, B. and South, N. (2020) '"All Knowledge Begins with the Senses": Towards a Sensory Criminology'. *The British Journal of Criminology*, 60(1): 3–23.
O'Sullivan, S. (2006) *Art Encounters Deleuze and Guattari: Thought beyond Representation*. Basingstoke, UK: Palgrave.
Poama, A. (2015) 'Restorative Justice: The Institutional Turn'. *Raisons Politiques*, 59(3): 7–16.
Richards, K. (2005) 'Unlikely Friends? Oprah Winfrey and Restorative Justice'. *Australian and New Zealand Journal of Criminology*, 38(3): 381–99.
Smith, D. (2012) *Essays on Deleuze*. Edinburgh: Edinburgh University Press.

Straker, C. (2019) 'Conclusion: The Restorative City – A Challenge about Means and Ends'. *The International Journal of Restorative Justice*, 2(2): 325–31.
Walgrave, L. (2000) 'How Pure Can a Maximalist Approach to Restorative Justice Remain? Or Can a Purist Model of Restorative Justice Become Maximalist?' *Contemporary Justice Review*, 1(4): 415–32.
Woolford, A. and Ratner, R. S. (2003) 'Nomadic Justice? Restorative Justice on the Margins of Law'. *Social Justice*, 30.1(91): 177–94.
Zehr, H. (2005) *Changing Lenses: A New Focus for Crime and Justice*, 3rd ed. Scottsdale, PA: Herald Press.

Legislation

Council of Europe Committee of Ministers, Recommendation CM/Rec(2018)8 of the Committee of Ministers to Member States Concerning Restorative Justice in Criminal Matters (Adopted by the Committee of Ministers on 3 October 2018 at the 1326th Meeting of the Ministers' Deputies).
Council of Europe Committee of Ministers, Recommendation No. R(99)19 of the Committee of Ministers to Member States Concerning Mediation in Penal Matters (Adopted by the Committee of Ministers on 15 September 1999 at the 679th Meeting of the Ministers' Deputies).
Directive 2012/29/EU of the European Parliament and the Council of 25 October 2012 Establishing Minimum Standards on the Rights, Support and Protection of Victims of Crime, and Replacing Council Framework Decision 2001/220/JHA [The Victims' Directive], OJ L315/57.
United Nations Economic and Social Council (ECOSOC) Resolution 2002/12, 'Basic Principles on the Use of Restorative Justice Programmes in Criminal Matters', UN Economic and Social Council, 37th Plenary Meeting, 24 July 2002, New York, Annex, ESCOR, 2002, suppl. no. 1, E/RES/2002/12 (24 July 2002).
United Nations General Assembly Resolution 40/34, 'Declaration of Basic Principles of Justice for Victims of Crime and Abuse of Power', UN General Assembly, 40th session, 29 November 1985, A/RES/40/34.

3 Encountering Sovereignty

Being, Politics and Justice

From Giles Deleuze, we learned to think of restorative justice not merely as a penal mechanism or as a social movement, but as a heterogeneous and dynamic network of forces captured by state apparatuses. In a similar way, this chapter furthers the analysis of the multiple dimensions of restorative justice, reflecting specifically on the relationships between sovereignty and restorative justice from a political-ontological perspective. In doing so, the following pages encounter a key figure in contemporary political theory, Giorgio Agamben.

Agamben's work revolves around the study of the political stakes of ontology and the ontological stakes of politics. He maintains that to understand our current political landscape we must historicise our political categories (e.g. sovereignty, democracy, human rights) to the point of tracing them back to their origin (or *archē*). This concept does not denote the specific point in time when something begins but rather the fluid array of cultural forces that over time have shaped our contemporary political ideas. Agamben's central argument is that such forces are all rooted in how the Western world has grappled with or disengaged from the fundamental ontological question of *what it means to be human*.

The following sections delve deeper into this set of issues in order to excavate the conditions that make restorative justice possible and then to sketch out a restorative justice to come. This exploration engages both with Agamben's early writings on language (1982/1991) and with his more recent, nine-volume *Homo Sacer* project on the foundations of Western politics (2017).

At the core of Agamben's journey lies a conviction of the inseparable relationship between language, being and politics. Language is both what characterises human beings and what marks that specific human activity known as politics. Exactly as human language presupposes and yet excludes the existence of an animal voice that preceded meaningful speech, so the political community presupposes animal life and yet keeps it at the margins of the polis. This inclusive-exclusive model permeates Western culture and politics: from human rights to totalitarianism, from social democracy to the capitalist commodification of culture. Agamben's main claim, in fact, is that totalitarianism and capitalism are not historical aberrations but rather expressions of the ontological foundation of Western civilisation. The

DOI: 10.4324/9781003298359-3

task of a progressive politics and culture is to unveil and address this problematic continuity, interrupting the political-ontological paradigm which keeps haunting the Western world (Agamben, 1990/1993, 1996/2000).

Encountering Agamben's philosophical thought compels us to question well-known claims around restorative justice: How can restorative justice truly differ from criminal justice? What are the political implications of an embodied form of justice? What model of human life is integral to restorative encounters? Agamben also furnishes tools for radically reimagining restorative justice. He maintains that the means for deposing the contradictions of Western political and cultural traditions lie in a politics completely divorced from sovereignty. This coming politics proposes the development of an emancipatory ethical and political way of living. As the final sections of this chapter argue, this perspective suggests abandoning legal models of restorative justice which are implied by the current process of institutionalisation, and instead seeking radical, politically engaged, means-oriented forms of restorative praxis.

Encountering Giorgio Agamben

Agamben occupies an influential position within contemporary political theory, eliciting both admiration and criticism. His work represents a distinctive effort to unravel the intricate relationship between violence and law, aiming to provide tools for responding to the commodification of life inherent in Western modernity (Murray, 2010). His approach is radical and strategic, focusing on the conditions of possibility of our present whilst opening up avenues for new forms of political thought and action. His critical analyses involve a painstaking dissection of the structure of Western modernity, highlighting the fundamental dichotomies which characterise our culture: man and animal, language and discourse, potential and act, political life and biological life. Agamben then describes the multifarious apparatuses devised by Western civilisation to make sense of those dichotomies. He focuses particularly on the unintended and destructive consequences of hiding the tensions that traverse those fundamental concepts or of prioritising one concept over the other, leading to cultural, ethical and political impasses. Denying the 'animal' origin of 'man', for example, leads to neglecting a crucial dimension of human life – its descent and natural environment. This critical operation is preliminary to the deactivation of such dichotomies and the envisioning of an alternative future. Agamben does not attempt to prophesy a definitive escape from the dilemmas of modernity; instead, he invites the reader to engage with his fragmentary sketches, allusive paths and incomplete maps of a world yet to come.

Agamben draws from a wide array of philosophical influences, including Martin Heidegger, Aristotle, Walter Benjamin, Hannah Arendt and Michel Foucault. From Heidegger, Agamben inherits a critical interest in the foundational question of what it means to be human. Like the German philosopher, Agamben contends that the defining feature of humanity is language. However, he diverges from Heidegger by asserting that Western philosophy's treatment of the relationship between 'being human' and language has always been highly problematic (cf. Mills, 2014). His diagnosis is that philosophical thought has presupposed and posited a foundation for being and language in *negativity* (Agamben, 1982/1991). Language does not belong to humans, yet they are thrown into it and constantly use it. This creates a form of negativity, a void, since humans are defined by something they do not own (Murray, 2010: 13). To some extent, language 'owns' humans, since without language humans would lose their defining feature. Agamben describes this negative ground of language as *voice*, which is included by exclusion into language in order for this to make sense. This negativity is repressed by Western civilisation and yet continues to exert influence on culture and politics.

In *Infancy and History* (1978/1993), Agamben suggests that a way of overcoming this negative foundation is the notion of *infancy*. Infancy represents the experience of language as such, not a prelinguistic state to which humans should return but an integral aspect of the experience of language. Infancy refers to the split between language and voice, the active origin of civilisation which keeps influencing humans' present condition, which should thus be recognised and reconstructed, historically and philologically. Along these lines, during this early stage of his intellectual journey, Agamben advocates for a rediscovery of *criticism*, as outlined in *Stanzas* (1977/1993) and *The Idea of Prose* (1985/1995). Criticism, for Agamben, signifies an effort to recompose the fractures which characterise a language founded in negativity. Agamben argues against presupposing an ineffable (negative) origin of both the human being and the community. We should instead recognise the 'ungroundedness of human praxis, neither presupposed incomprehensible foundation nor nihilist senselessness, but foundation of man in man, of language in its communicability' (Whyte, 2008: 77–8). Western civilisation, in contrast, has tended to conceal its own ungroundedness by separating and excluding what defines humans and by grounding the very idea of polity on this ontological separation.

Language and Politics

Agamben's understanding of the connection between language and politics becomes apparent when considering his (Aristotelian) assertion that language not only constitutes the foundation of human existence but also serves as the basis for the political community: *logos* defines both humans as political animals and the very idea of the polis as their community. Therefore, both the negativity inherent in language and the ways in which Western civilisation has sought to fill this void project themselves into politics. This link between language and politics is explored in *The Coming Community* (Agamben, 1990/1993) and even more so in the multivolume *Homo Sacer* project (Agamben, 2017). Here, Agamben provides a historical analysis of specific empirical examples of the negative foundation of Western politics. His starting point is Foucault's (2008) thesis that a crucial political transformation occurred in the Western world from the seventeenth century onwards – the shift from sovereign power to biopower, from the sovereign's right to take a subject's life (or let them live) to political institutions which treat human life, at the level of the population, as a political subject to be fostered. Agamben, however, contends that rather than being specific to the modern era, biopower and sovereignty are fundamentally intertwined: sovereign power has a necessary biopolitical dimension, aiming to manage the population as a living organism to be controlled and exploited.

Agamben invokes some of his key sources – Schmitt, Benjamin, Aristotle and Arendt – to conceptualise this intertwinement. Schmitt, a political theorist with connections to the Third Reich, notoriously affirmed that the defining characteristic of the sovereign is their power to decide when to suspend the law and establish a *state of exception*, positioning themselves as the subject who institutes the law whilst being outside its constraints (Schmitt, 2005). Benjamin, one of the most eclectic cultural critics of the twentieth century, responded to Schmitt by claiming that the 'real' exception is external to the law and cannot be subsumed within it (Benjamin, 2021). Agamben combines elements of both perspectives: he accepts Schmitt's position that in the state of exception the law is in force but loses its signification, whilst incorporating Benjamin's idea that in the real state of exception there is always a non-legal *potential* able to overcome sovereign power (Agamben, 2003/2017). What remains to be ascertained is the actual content of the exception, the object of the decision and the source of the overcoming of sovereign capture. Aristotle provides an answer here: it is *life* that is the object of the exceptional decision (Aristotle, 350 BCE/1981).

The result of this conceptual patchwork is a conception of political sovereignty as the self-grounding decision of violently separating political life (*bios*) from biological life (*zoē*), which ultimately reflects the exclusion by inclusion of animal sound to generate meaningful human language. Yet just as linguistic exclusion produces a negative residue (the voice) (Agamben, 1982/1991) and a split between humans and language, so the political exclusion of natural life generates a problematic secondary result, which Agamben, following Benjamin, terms *bare life* (Agamben, 1995/2017). Bare life is the by-product of including natural life in politics by exclusion, creating a life infinitely *abandoned* (cf. Nancy, 1993; see next chapter) to sovereign violence – that is, without any political or legal protection. Drawing on Arendt – a political philosopher and Holocaust survivor – Agamben argues that this sovereign process of capturing life is epitomised by the concentration camp. The camp is the clearest form of inclusion of life by exclusion, the stripping of any relational and linguistic faculty from the human being, who is reduced to bare life.

To overcome these ontological-political predicament, Agamben posits the need for a non-sovereign ethics, one that does not rely on concepts like legal responsibility, culpability or punishment (Agamben, 1998/2017, 2017/2018), which conceal and enable the sovereign exception. In *Remnants of Auschwitz* (1998/2017), Agamben outlines an ethos of bearing witness to that which cannot be witnessed – a new ethical perspective that counters the ethical premises of exceptional politics.

In the last volumes of the *Homo Sacer* project, Agamben further develops his critical analysis with innovative conceptual tools. In *The Kingdom and the Glory* (Agamben, 2009/2017), sovereignty is complemented by economic government, the administration of humans and things, which includes both juridico-political and managerial elements. A comprehensive analysis of Western politics requires an appreciation of this managerial paradigm, bringing to the fore how the governmental management of people's life complements the sovereign exclusion. In *The Highest Poverty* (2011/2017) and *The Use of Bodies* (2014/2017), Agamben lays the groundwork for a new model of politics. He argues for deactivating the ontological apparatus that sustains the biopolitical violence informing sovereignty, proposing a politics articulated around the concepts of *use, gesture, profanation, destitution* and *form-of-life*. Agamben advocates for a notion of life in the continuous process of freeing itself from sovereign apparatuses and their destructive effects. The aim is not the abolition but the deposition of these oppressive yet foundational structures of Western culture, politics and society. The fractures between biological and political life, with bare life as its by-product, between animal and man, potential and act, poetry and philosophy, are to be profaned (Agamben, 2005/2007). This involves being restored to a state where the possibilities of life can be freely used and enjoyed instead of exclusively appropriated and owned by a sovereign. This is a messianic life – a life of pure potentiality – to counter the destructive effects of the Western political and cultural machine, rediscovering the capacity of our ungrounded being to generate a political community which includes without exclusion.

Agamben's Approach

In *The Signature of All Things* (2008/2009), Agamben, looking backward at his intellectual journey, outlines his method, defined as *philosophical archaeology*. This approach seeks to expose what remains unarticulated in how a certain tradition generates and transmits knowledge on a particular subject, in this way controlling its intelligibility (Primera, 2019). Agamben's focus is on the capacity for development of the past – that is, on the fact that the past is replete with missed opportunities and unexplored paths that could have led to different outcomes. These unexplored paths can still be unearthed, in this way restoring their potential to change our present. By doing so, philosophical archaeology enables us to reimagine our current condition and open up new possibilities for the present.

Hence, philosophical archaeology involves reconstructing the past to uncover the dynamic conditions of possibility of the present, rather than its static origin. From this angle, Agamben scrutinises the structure of those apparatuses of power which canonise the past by turning it into authoritative traditions, passing on to the present self-evident knowledge and natural ways of being and doing (Murray and Whyte, 2011). From religious institutions to political organisations, from administrative agencies to cultural authorities, philosophical archaeology directly engages with the historical unfolding of the traditions that such apparatuses generate and solidify. To achieve this, Agamben undertakes complex philological analyses, tracing the etymology of terms, uncovering the historical formation of meanings and highlighting opportunities which are not stabilised by traditions. These analyses emphasise the context-bounded nature of the ways in which institutions 'word' our understanding of ourselves and the world (Kotsko and Salzani, 2017).

The language-mediated connection between being and politics constitutes the political-ontological condition of Agamben's archaeological method. In fact, by excavating the paradigms of tradition, it is possible to bring to light the bonds between ontology and politics, as well as their problematic by-product: a life without historical ground, separated from its linguistic nature and exposed to violence.

This approach is ultimately an attempt at revealing the ways Western culture has dealt with the 'being – language – politics' connection bringing to the fore, in different contexts (e.g. from the emergence of sovereignty to the commodification of language), the covering over of those foundational, yet not natural, fractures. This method demonstrates that sovereignty is a groundless, self-affirming authority that demands subjection to its content-free rules, serving as a fragile cover over the Western political void. Sovereignty entails the systematic production of what Agamben (1995/2017) calls *homines sacri*, bare life at the margin of the polity which contributes to maintaining the polity's boundaries. The deadly effect of this dynamic becomes visible within twentieth-century totalitarian states, which perform the mass-killing of human groups deemed noxious to the rest of the population. Similarly, Agamben's analysis of the commodification of language shows how language is transformed into a self-referential spectacle that results in the loss and destruction of meaningful presence in the world.

Yet philosophical archaeology is not merely a description of our present condition and its historical archē. This very historical-critical excavation opens the possibility of radical change fuelled by the *potential* which characterises human beings. Drawing from Aristotle, Agamben argues that our possibilities of becoming never entirely exhaust themselves into acts: there is always an ineliminable potential, a pre-individual resistance to actualisation which defines our being and which can be used to make another life possible (Agamben, 1995/2017: 42). This residue, displaced in history as missed opportunities, can be recovered and revitalised. Agamben's critique implies the retrieval of this potential by creating new spaces for thought and action. This constructive dimension is developed though specific concepts (e.g. destitution, use and form-of-life) rooted in that idea of an active force defining the human being – an energy which can never be fully realised but serves as an ontological reservoir of power to radically transform cultural and political life (cf. Deleuze's idea of desire in the previous chapter). Philosophical archaeology thus becomes a method not only for understanding the past but also for engaging with the present and actively shaping the future.

A Political Ontology of Restorative Justice

Writing a political ontology of restorative justice involves questioning how this form of justice addresses (and could address) the fundamental relationship between being and politics. This operation entails delving into how different understandings of what it means to be human (among other humans) inform different understandings of justice.

Restorative Justice and Human Presence

What is the archē of restorative justice? Restorative justice can be conceptualised as the historical re-emergence of something that (liberal) criminal justice both denies and presupposes, something excluded by inclusion – *human presence*. Human presence is the lived experience that serves as a condition for legal judgements. Human presence is akin to an infinitely potential yet meaningless sound (cf. Agamben, 1982/1991) whose translation into legal discourse requires that presence be excluded. This transformation allows humans to acquire significance within the legal context, separating insignificant human behaviour from meaningful legal action and harm from wrongdoing, rendering humans suitable to be judged and punished.

This dynamic implies that criminal justice is essentially a penal machine: the mere entry into the criminal justice realm, such as by being accused of a crime, results in the capture (i.e. the legalisation) of human presence as criminal justice's negative foundation. Criminal justice, from this angle, is primarily geared towards punishment by diminishing one's potential for being and becoming. This suggests that the ultimate goal of the criminal justice process is not the judgement but rather the punishment achieved by removing human presence upon entry into that context. In this way, in fact, criminal justice fulfils a greater aim than merely enforcing criminal law and controlling crime – it ensures the perpetuation of the Western sovereign machine by restraining human potential and enforcing obedience to a self-referential authority.

This negative foundation is justified by criminal justice's 'katechonic' function (Agamben, 2000/2005: 109). The term *katechon* originates from theology, initially being used by Saint Paul to describe the mysterious entity that restrains the Antichrist from unleashing the Apocalypse. In political theory, this figure has been often interpreted as a theological transposition of the state, acting as the entity that prevents social anomie and violence. Criminal justice's separation and removal of human presence similarly fulfils a katechonic function – the prevention of the supposed anarchy that human presence might generate if not excluded. Nevertheless, human presence remains as a silent condition of criminal justice, included by exclusion. To claim that criminal justice serves to prevent or respond to anarchy is a way of concealing the inherent groundlessness of the idea of sovereign justice, which is designed to submit humans to content-free rules of self-referential power.

Just as Western metaphysics constructs a model of a self-sufficient human being (Heidegger, 2001), so criminal justice, by isolating culpable acts from human interactions, harm from wrongdoing, meaningful legal persona from meaningless human presence, contributes to the persistence of sovereignty in the political, social and cultural landscape. Similar to how ontological negativity was obliterated in the history of being, so human presence is denied in modern, katechonic criminal justice. However, this negativity resurfaces as a problem in the postmodern era. In fact, the katechonic function revealed its limitations historically when various embodied subjectivities broke free from their state of marginalisation, articulating demands for the acknowledgement of their human presence. Starting in the 1970s, crime victims' demand to occupy a more central position on the criminal justice stage, stating their need for recognition of the personal experience of victimisation, lacerated the katechonic veil, letting criminal justice's negative foundation violently erupt and leading to a legitimacy crisis within the realm of criminal justice.

The rise of restorative justice can be interpreted as a response to this historical impasse – the re-emergence of the suppressed foundation of criminal justice, the attempt at disconcealing (mainly victims') human presence through embodied encounters. Restorative justice, in fact, is built around the belief that flesh-and-bones human beings who have been harmed need a safe physical and emotional space wherein to 'heal' and find 'closure' (Johnstone, 2011). This notion of safety refers to a state of immunisation, which is at the same time both backward-looking (from the emotional, physical and financial consequences of victimisation) and forward-looking (from the risks and dangers of future victimisation). Likewise, those who have caused harm are provided with an opportunity to directly confront the human consequences of their actions.

Restorative justice revolves around meeting demands for participation, inclusion and the direct expression of one's experiences. Participants are enabled to communicate their emotions and seek answers to some decisive questions – such as why the crime happened to them, why they responded as they did, what to do in case of re-occurrence and how to make meaning out of this tragic happening (Zehr, 2005). 'Speaking out' and 'being heard' are the main forms this active participation takes in the restorative justice process (Van Ness and Strong, 2022).

The disconcealment of human presence in restorative justice is finally expressed through the obligation to 'take care' of the harmed person and their well-being by making amends, providing material and emotional reparation or restitution. Making amends includes elements such as apology, changed behaviour and restitution from offenders to victims, as well as the offender's promise of behavioural change. Restorative justice often emphasises the need for a symbolic statement that acknowledges the legitimacy of victims' status and recognises the emotional harm they have experienced (Strang, 2003; Strang and Sherman, 2003). Restorative encounters, then, seek to provide a concrete and viable alternative to the possibility, already enshrined in law, of mere material or financial reparation by offering opportunities for emotional, psychological and symbolic restoration (Johnstone, 2011). The exploration of the offender's shame (Braithwaite, 1989) is a further expression of the new demands of care towards the victim, as well as the manifestation of the offender's fundamental sentiment of being an embodied subject (Agamben, 1998/2017) vis-à-vis the victim.

Restorative Exception

The main difference between restorative and criminal justice is that the former responds to the exclusion of human presence enacted by the latter. However, a significant commonality between these two models of justice should now be considered: both include by exclusion something which precedes human presence – the 'mere fact of life' (Agamben, 1995/2017: 10). From a political-ontological perspective, restorative and criminal justice share this foundational continuity that demands critical scrutiny.

Both restorative and criminal justice, in fact, are built on the exclusion of what Aristotle referred to as zoē, biological or natural life as distinguished from political life (bios). Aristotle's account of the origins of the polis revolves around the relegation of natural life to the domestic sphere and, thus, its exclusion from the political realm. Natural life is stripped of any political significance and deprived of any protection; it is thus abandoned to the unconditional power of sovereignty.

From this angle, restorative justice appears to be characterised by an entanglement between bodily life and legal power. Participants in restorative encounters enter a distinctively 'grey' space, wherein life is suspended between law and non-law, external rules and interpersonal agreements, bureaucracy and bodily encounters, facilitators and criminal justice gatekeepers. Participants hold legal rights and responsibilities, much like in criminal justice. However, the encounter does not serve to ascertain, solidify or challenge those legal positions. Instead, it functions as a space wherein human restoration will take place, a space for healing, closure and reparation. Yet both criminal and restorative justice perform the same crucial political operation: depoliticising human interactions (i.e. harms) and turning them into culpable acts. In doing so, the mere fact of life expressed by those human interactions, processes and ways of living is placed outside the political sphere. The actions of 'victims' and 'offenders' are individualised, abstracted from their social and political context and thus excluded from the protection of the political order. Victims and offenders become personally responsible either to the state (criminal justice) or to some other embodied subjects (restorative justice) for their (depoliticised) acts of transgression. This juridical process of depoliticisation, and the consequent individualising treatment of culpable actions, is what connects criminal justice to restorative justice, their common foundational matrix.

Throughout the restorative and criminal justice process, in fact, the lives of victims and offenders become politically irrelevant yet politically indispensable ('sacred', as Agamben [1995/2017: 10] would claim). They serve as the condition of the functioning of sovereign apparatuses, which enable both forms of justice (e.g. through policing and prosecution). This 'exceptional' capture generates lawfulness by producing deviance. Lawfulness is an empty ideal constructed through the isolation and exclusion of certain (deviant) actions from the political sphere, the establishment of an arbitrary differential residue which will be abandoned to the very sovereign justice that created it.

Although this dynamic occurs in both restorative and criminal justice processes, in the former the law does not conceal the exceptional capture of life, as it does in the latter. In restorative justice, in fact, the law (not only politics) is suspended while still in force, bringing the nexus between sovereignty (expressed by the decision to depoliticise the harm, its premises and consequences) and the body to light, in a singular way. This means that in restorative justice a double exclusion takes place: from both the political and legal domains. Participants in restorative encounters are simultaneously 'handed over' to politics and law while being 'banned' from them. Politics and the law linger on the threshold of those encounters, neither completely outside nor inside. This threshold represents a zone of indistinction in which human presence may be disconcealed but not freed from the sovereign logic. This constitutes the political-ontological limit of restorative justice: its potential for emancipation is curtailed by the sovereign power. The restorative disconcealment of being does not completely transcend the logic of the state.

The by-product of this dual ban is the creation of a distinctive *embodied life*. This concept neither equates to biological life nor to human presence. Instead, it is life exposed to the sovereign power that informs restorative encounters. This power depoliticises and delegalises human presence, whilst establishing a fluid threshold between life, law and politics (Agamben, 1995/2017: 141). Embodied life is also the standard of inclusion in restorative justice – only those who adhere to this ideal are considered suitable for participation in restorative encounters; others are excluded from them.

Anthropological Machine

How is this embodied life shaped within restorative encounters? Specific subjectivating processes take place in those exceptional spaces. Humans involved in those encounters, in fact, are subtly encouraged to conform to a specific model of a subject (cf. Agamben, 2002/2004). This model combines qualities that overlap with the those characterising the liberal criminal justice subject – *culpability, free will* and *purposefulness* – with other features which are specific to the restorative justice realm – *embodiment, disempowerment* and *resilience* (cf. Maglione, 2017).

The restorative subject is inherently culpable. Here, culpability denotes that once human beings enter the realm of justice, their actions acquire new meanings sanctioned by the legal order. This entails that they are subjected to a particular form of violence – the violence that removes the mere fact of life. This violence sanctions human beings and makes them *entirely* culpable. Restorative justice requires a preliminary admission of responsibility – that is, the offender's acknowledgement of having committed culpable, willed and instrumental actions against a victim. Similarly, the victim must detach themselves from the social and political context within which harmful behaviours occurred. This results in a double separation – both the offender and the victim are removed from their social and political life whilst subjected to restorative justice.

This culpability is then interiorised. Agamben contends that Christian theology originally developed the idea of introjected culpability based on Aristotle's ethics. In the *Nicomachean Ethics* (350 BCE/1999), Aristotle, in fact, argues that actions can be attributed to agents because they choose them. The concept of choice makes it possible to claim that people are responsible for what they do (Agamben, 2017/2018: 37) and thus can be punished. This idea of choosing makes people own their actions, and this serves as a prerequisite for individualising justice (as well as ethics and politics). Once choice is qualified as either 'good' or 'bad', it will produce the notion of culpable harm and, therefore, of punishable action. Actions and actors become indissolubly linked, making it possible to hold individuals accountable. The interiorisation of culpability as a shadow of freely willed actions is the precursor of the concept of individual responsibility that deeply informs both criminal justice and restorative justice.

The final common quality between restorative and criminal justice is the presumption that the ideal subject always acts instrumentally (Agamben, 2017/2018). The belief that the ultimate goal of every action is the good pursued by the actor leads to a separation and opposition between ends and means. Human actions are seen as mere means and never ends in themselves, mere actualisations of an external end-good. Whether this external good driving action is rationally chosen or biopsychologically or socially determined is irrelevant. What matters is that there is no alternative to instrumental action (except 'madness', which requires specific legal arrangements). As a consequence, an ontological gap between human beings and their good emerges. The good does not lie within humans but rather in the external world. The existence of such an external good retrospectively justifies the existence of punishable actions.

Among the features unique to restorative justice, embodiment demands specific attention (Maglione, 2017). It refers to the material condition of causing harm or being harmed by a clearly identifiable individual, not a social structure or organisation. The emphasis on the need to speak up, listen and be listened to, as well as the need for physical safety and material repair, entails a connection between the body, as a natural entity, and thoughts, feelings and behaviours. The encounter between victim and offender, happening in a shared physical space where flesh-and-blood human beings encounter each other's suffering, exemplifies this embodied characteristic. Embodiment is also closely linked to the emotional nature of restorative subjects. Concepts such as healing, closure, forgiveness and reconciliation all align with an understanding that the restorative subject's needs revolve around emotions, moods and feelings. Being disempowered, mainly in terms of psychological or individual dis-empowerment (instead of social or political disempowerment), is also linked to this idea of embodiment. Although disempowered, this subject retains the capacity to act or react positively, demonstrating a unique quality of resilience. This is expressed through the choice to partake in the restorative processes, meet the other party, express needs and advance requests, mediate over them and decide the process' outcome (e.g. by refusing or accepting apologies or compensation). This embodied subject ultimately appears as a combination of a passive capacity ('can be judged') with an active capacity ('can repair the wrong/harm'), engaged in earning their redemption (Bazemore, 1998) through symbolic and material actions, within a shared 'community'.

In summary, these subjectivating processes function as a mechanism which shapes life, complementing the inclusive-exclusive process of restorative exception (Agamben, 2009/2017). The end result, the restorative subject, is an internally split entity. On the one hand, this subject's culpable, freely willed and instrumental actions project the human good outside of itself. This means that the good is not a dimension inherent in human beings but rather an external reward to be achieved by actions for which one is responsible. This operation dooms the restorative subject to the unfulfillable pursuit of preset external goods (e.g. reintegration in the community, forgiveness of the victim, acts of reparation), diminishing people's ethical and political potential to reimagine and enact non-violent forms of community. On the other hand, its embodied, disempowered and fusional features produce an entity made of a bundle of sensations and feelings exposed to the sovereign restrictions of restorative encounters as spaces that capture the mere fact of life. This subject is the opposite of the 'Muselmann' described by Agamben (1998/2017: 807) as a paradigmatic dweller of the concentration camp – a complete witness who nevertheless cannot bear witness precisely because he has been stripped of every relational and linguistic capacity. In contrast, participants in restorative encounters are loaded with relational and embodied capacities. They appear as *hyper-witnesses* (of the sovereign power to capture life through justice) who require external direction to achieve their good, and thus as governable entities with diminished potential.

Institutionalisation as Loss of Experience

The sovereign capture of life is further developed by the institutionalisation of restorative justice. To some extent, this process erases what initially appeared as the 'original' element of restorative justice – the disconcealment of human presence. In fact, the formalisation through policy and the canonisation through tradition of organic restorative practices (and of the movement who advocated for them) is a flagrant example of the destruction of the experiential nature (i.e. the anarchic and autonomous potential) of informal methods of responding to harm. Through this process, restorative justice becomes commodified, bureaucratised and technicised.

Policy – that is, the top-down, formal regulation of practice – construes restorative justice as a discrete object – a practice with codified steps, aims and goals – presented as a means for realising restorative principles. Despite its seemingly benign nature, this sovereign appropriation commodifies restorative justice, transforming various historical processes into ahistorical entities, human interactions into objects, depleting their potential (cf. Agamben, 1977/1993). Policy translations of restorative justice seem to hold an intrinsic value, representing the materialisation of Leviathan's will and the seal of its authority, cancelling the context-bound historical experiences that constitute restorative practices and the social movement behind them. This policy fetishism stands in stark contrast to the recognition of the disconcealment of human presence that the restorative justice movement originally advocated. Penal policy literally *defines* this experiential process of recognition (*definire* in Latin means confining, enclosing within bounds), ordering its fluid nature from outside and reducing its complexity to a transparent thing: a katechonic sequence of commanded steps leading from microdisorders to social order (cf. Pali and Maglione, 2023). This operation renders restorative justice regulable within the realm of law. Restorative justice, in fact, becomes integral to the juridical apparatus, a legal means to achieve victims' satisfaction and reducing reoffending. These are essentially criminal justice ends, with the proviso that the victim here is only the person categorised by criminal justice as the material or direct victim, not the broad society represented by the state/crown.

In this manner, restorative justice loses much of its potential 'otherness', its pluralistic nature as a bottom-up approach that seeks to address human presence's ambivalence and, at times, destructiveness (Maglione, 2018).

Tradition – that is, the emergence of authoritative approaches to restorative justice – produces bureaucracy. This is a subtly invasive form of legal violence, epitomised by Arendt (2006: 252) as the 'word-and-thought-defying banality of evil'. Bureaucracy blurs the boundaries between law-making and law-preserving violence (cf. Benjamin, 2021), generating what it claims merely to enforce. This violence is akin to a self-augmenting organism which creates its own demand, making itself necessary even when it does not deliver on its promises of predictability and efficiency (cf. Arendt, 1970: 38). It generates more regulations, relentlessly, as a Moloch which grounds itself whilst expanding its deadening reach. Then, even when regulations remain largely unapplied, they nevertheless create the very condition for appealing to the 'rule book', when, for instance, conflicts arise on what to do and how. A layer of material sovereign violence is added when such rules are backed up by the possibility of resorting to violence to enforce them. This violence is expressed by sanctioning those who do not comply with the rules canonised by authoritative traditions – for example, by excluding them from the restorative community or impeding their services.

Both policy and tradition systematically transform justice practices into technical apparatuses. These apparatuses deny the sociality of the world, reproducing it as an entity lacking presence (Agamben, 1977/1993). They relentlessly extract representations from the social domain and store them, revealing the world as a stock of phantasms (Heidegger, 1954/2013). Over time, these apparatuses evolve into ends in themselves. This is because they are automatic (they seek the instrumentally rational best solution), self-augmenting (they increase without decisive human intervention), unitary (they produce a whole which is taken for granted), universal (they apply everywhere) and, finally, autonomous (the means becomes the end) (cf. Ellul, 1964: xi). Consequently, they gradually become sovereign machines that continuously increase their power.

In summary, institutionalisation limits the potential of human presence, ultimately leading to the expropriation of the very substance justice practices are made of – *language* as expression of human potential. The authoritative regulation of restorative encounters involves contrasting participants' experiences with phantasmatic participation. This entails bringing lived experiences into alignment with abstract, hollow and self-sustaining commands that dictate what can be done and known. Policy is rooted in a katechonic mistrust of experience, which must therefore be expropriated, translated into Leviathan's language and thereby transformed into nullified property that is no longer under the control of those actually living it. Restorative encounters are no longer experiences but commodified objects, deprived of their historical practical significance, formalised and canonised. Here, destruction means fracturing the anarchic structures of knowledge that nourish horizontal justice practices, transforming them into tradition. The establishment of restorative 'quality marks', compulsory national training standards and government-led restorative 'hubs' and the subsequent exclusion of practices that do not conform to such standards are concrete examples of this destruction. Through the incremental commodification, bureaucratisation and technicisation of lived experiences, restorative justice slowly becomes *spectacle*, in Guy Debord's sense, an entity alien to itself (Debord, 1994).

Restorative Justice to Come

Agamben's political ontology provides critical tools for addressing the contradictions within restorative justice whilst liberating its potential, gesturing towards a justice without violence, an inappropriable praxis able 'to make the world into the highest good' (Benjamin, 2003: 170; cf. Agamben, 2014/2017).

The first step is to overcome the presuppositional ban-structure of restorative justice, exposing its inherent contradictions. This involves undoing the sovereign bond between law and violence which characterises institutionalised restorative justice. The elimination of any reference to sovereignty becomes possible only if the mere fact of life is never separated and removed, never included by exclusion to found restorative encounters. This requires imagining forms of deposition (Benjamin, 2021) of legal violence that pave the way for a new *form-of-life*. This concept refers to the impossibility of isolating life to establish politics or justice. A form-of-life is a life that emerges once the Western political-ethical separation between natural life and political life is deactivated. This justice to come will offer an 'escape from utilitarian subject – object relations and juridical instrumentalism, and from substantivist conceptions' (Whyte, 2011: 156) of justice rooted in punishment and premised on stable identities. It will be a justice of means without ends, integral to a form-of-life populated by beings with no nature, no purpose, no biological destiny or vocation – a justice and life of potential beings.

This idea is developed by Agamben in *The Coming Community* (1990/1993) (a work influenced by Jean-Luc Nancy, see next chapter), wherein he formulates a concept of community that does not presuppose commonality or identity as a condition for belonging. What Agamben terms 'whatever singularities' (1990/1993: 1) is a mode of being that appropriates itself, allowing for the formation of a community based on the co-belonging of singularities, immune to exclusion. Such singularities are the perpetual taking place of humanity. They constitute the stake in the struggle between the state and a humanity that seeks no recognition from the law or institutionalised tradition but manifests itself as the process of commoning. It will not be possible to enact this life, politics and justice if we do not free ourselves from those legal traditions which immobilise our potential. A coming restorative justice should thus embrace a new and different idea of ethical responsibility (Agamben, 1998/2017). Contrary to juridical interpretations of responsibility, which frame it in terms of debt and culpability, responsibility must be thought as unassumable, as something which the subject is consigned to but which it can never fully appropriate as its own. Non-legal responsibility precedes the designations of good and evil, and it is rooted in an understanding of ethics as the 'doctrine of happy life' (Agamben, 1998/2017: 777). This idea is based on the recognition that human nature is devoid of preset essence, vocation or destiny and that evil arises from the decision to repress potentiality.

Practising a Justice to Come

How can one liberate restorative justice from sovereign violence and realise a justice integral to a form-of-life that restores the potential of human beings? Agamben provides a range of interconnected instruments.

Profanation is the act of freeing things from the 'sacred' names that set them apart for the benefit of a few and returning them to their free or common use (Agamben, 2005/2007: 73). It involves redeeming life from the sovereign ban, transforming the state of exception into a situation wherein the anomic power is appropriated by everyone. In this way, the life produced and captured by the biopolitical function of sovereignty is redeemed as a 'happy life' – a life stripped of any essential identity. Profaning restorative justice means rejecting the admission of legal responsibility as a condition to enter restorative encounters, as well as the sacred categories of victim and offender. Open collective spaces should be created to address individual choices enmeshed within total social processes which contribute to destructive behaviours, imagining new forms of social-individual responsibility.

Agamben's notion of *use* denotes a new relationship with things that transcends both the utilitarian conception of use and the logic of exchange. This new relationship involves seeking spaces where people could enjoy things beyond the law rather than in open conflict with it (Agamben, 2014/2017). The notion of use in question rejects the idea of legitimate ownership. Use is contrasted here with property and (policy) appropriation, as it does not simply represent a different way of owning but a theory of relationship with the world that is independent from the paradigm of appropriation. In restorative encounters, use involves the creation of new forms of sociality. Legal categories could be appropriated and infused with new meanings towards non-violent forms of conflict resolution (a theme which will feature again in this book, in the chapters on Jacque Rancière, Judith Butler and Gayatri Chakravorty Spivak).

Gesture constitutes another instrument to counteract the disintegrative tendencies inherent in legalising justice. It involves bringing about a new world as a non-statist, non-teleological, non-identitarian community-to-come (Agamben, 1978/1993, 2017/2018). Gesture is a pure praxis that is free from any pre-existing end, a pure means. Restorative justice should embrace the absolute gesturality of human beings by incorporating artistic forms of reparation that embody the pure mediality of gestures. Art can create spaces for engagement among individuals involved in harms, fostering communal praxis that suspends guilt and responsibility in favour of co-belonging to a form-of-life.

Destitution means deactivating rather than abolishing the law. It represents a mode of potentiality that is not exhausted in its transition to act. Whereas in liberal criminal justice the individual is compelled to act through external commands, destitution exposes the possibility of a human life 'in which the single ways, acts, and processes of living are never simply *facts* but always and above all *possibilities* of life, always and above all power' (Agamben, 1996/2000: 4.5). This form-of-life is entirely outside the grasp of the law and entails using the world without appropriating it. Destitution brings about a state of infancy (Agamben, 1978/1993), a pre-individuated space in which to experience the fullness of language connected to its voice and the world as a space of possibilities. This justice to come halts and deactivates the sovereign machine. By simply overthrowing it, in fact, sovereignty will reconstitute itself but in different forms or shapes. Destitution, instead, is about creating new, playful relationships and spaces for political engagements.

The image of restorative justice emerging from the combination of these instruments is crucially different from what restorative justice is becoming and, to some extent, has always been (Maglione, 2018). This restorative justice to come critiques both criminal justice and the legal mentality within restorative justice, exposing the contradictions within these sovereign structures. It reveals criminal justice's focus on acts more than interactions, personality more than systems, breach of social order more than broken human relationships. It contests the katechonic mentality, the idea of punishment as an antidote to the violated social order, as based on metaphysical illusions of sovereign control. It promotes the development of an ethical-political justice movement advocating for anarchist forms of sociality, for direct forms of discussing transgressions of people's freedoms as symptoms of 'communal inadequacies' (McKinney, 2012: 16). These non-sovereign restorative processes are not mere alternatives to (and apparently less punitive than) penal mechanisms but are ethical-political practices meant to neutralise sovereign relationships – that is, domination, hierarchy, violence. A self-critical stance towards the development of institutional models of restorative justice is also integral to this approach. Institutionalisation, on the one hand, appears to scale up restorative justice; on the other, it ends up transforming it into a mechanism which reproduces sovereign violence. Ultimately, this critique has the potential to hinder the sovereign machine that informs restorative justice by contesting its depoliticising function. In this way, restorative justice would open up spaces for reinventing social relationships beyond juridical institutions, practices and mentalities.

Beyond Agamben

Agamben's political ontology generates radical insights into the logic, aims and functions of restorative justice and its relations with criminal justice. Appreciating the metaphysical logic of justice and linking this to the very foundations of the Western conception of politics empowers us to consider some unexplored dimensions of restorative justice and to connect these to wider and deeper issues concerning Western history, politics and society.

The first finding relates to the archē of restorative justice, its origin and aim – disconcealing human presence, which is neutralised and hidden by criminal justice. This involves rethinking crime as harm, that is, as a material and/or psychological disruption of one's life to be addressed through embodied encounters between human beings directly involved in experiencing such harms.

Despite this significant difference, restorative justice presents a fundamental similarity with criminal justice – its presuppositional ban-structure. This means that both models share a deeper foundational dynamic: the removal of their common conditions of possibility – the mere fact of life – pushed outside the edifice of justice. However, such exclusion does not entail elimination but just an exceptional relation with what is excluded. The mere fact of life will play a vital threshold-position, enabling, as a negative foundation, both criminal and restorative justice.

Political ontology also sheds light on the anthropological machine enacted by restorative encounters and how such events contribute to turning humans into certain types of subjects. The subject shaped within restorative justice presents some qualities which overlap with the features typical of the criminal justice subject – culpability, free will and purposefulness – and others which are specific to restorative justice – embodiment, disempowerment and resilience.

The contentious issue of the institutionalisation of restorative justice finds a critical reformulation within this theoretical framework. The policy incorporation of restorative justice, originally a fluid range of crafty practices at the very margins of institutional apparatuses of social control, advocated by an organic social movement, represents a paradigmatic form of sovereign appropriation of an informal model of justice. Bottom-up justice practices are separated and removed from their environment in order for the law-as-discourse to take place. The commodification, bureaucratisation and technicisation induced by policy appropriation cause a loss of experience. This entails the neutralisation of the striving towards freeing life from oppressive apparatuses, which the historical emergence of restorative justice has embodied.

Political ontology is not only a set of radical diagnostic instruments. It also provides tools to reflect on what a coming restorative justice could be. Revealing the inconsistencies of the presuppositional ban-structure of restorative justice, profaning the artificial separation and removal of life at its heart, imagining gestures to open restorative encounters to new use, amounts to destitute the legal violence which informs restorative justice as a device which accepts a legal, and thus violent, notion of ethical responsibility.

How to use these instruments is only sketched by Agamben; his elusive writing is consistent with the content of his work – an ever-coming thought which requires the reader's active engagement with those tools in order to make them work. This thought is not only a set of instruments, though; it is instead an intensive 'space' for generating a different way of thinking, whose unique feature is connecting language, being and politics in order to cultivate human potential – the very substance of justice.

References

Agamben, G. (1982/1991) *Language and Death: The Place of Negativity*. Minneapolis: University of Minnesota Press.

Agamben, G. (1977/1993) *Stanzas: Word and Phantasm in Western Culture*. Minneapolis: University of Minnesota Press.

Agamben, G. (1978/1993) *Infancy and History: On the Destruction of Experience*. London: Verso.

Agamben, G. (1990/1993) *The Coming Community*. Minneapolis: University of Minnesota Press.

Agamben, G. (1985/1995) *The Idea of Prose*. Albany: SUNY Press.
Agamben, G. (1996/2000) *Means without End: Notes on Politics*. Minneapolis: University of Minnesota Press.
Agamben, G. (2002/2004) *The Open: Man and Animal*. Stanford, CA: Stanford University Press.
Agamben, G. (2000/2005) *The Time That Remains: A Commentary on the Letter to the Romans*. Stanford, CA: Stanford University Press.
Agamben, G. (2005/2007) *Profanations*. New York: Zone Books.
Agamben, G. (2008/2009) *The Signature of All Things: On Method*. New York: Zone Books.
Agamben, G. (1995/2017) 'Homo Sacer: Sovereign Power and Bare Life'. In *The Omnibus Homo Sacer*, vol. 1. Stanford, CA: Stanford University Press.
Agamben, G. (1998/2017) 'Remnants of Auschwitz: The Witness and the Archive'. In *The Omnibus Homo Sacer*, vol. 3. Stanford, CA: Stanford University Press.
Agamben, G. (2003/2017) 'State of Exception'. In *The Omnibus Homo Sacer*, vol. 2.1. Stanford, CA: Stanford University Press.
Agamben, G. (2009/2017) 'The Kingdom and the Glory: For a Theological Genealogy of Economy and Government'. In *The Omnibus Homo Sacer*, vol. 2.4. Stanford, CA: Stanford University Press.
Agamben, G. (2011/2017) 'The Highest Poverty: Monastic Rules and Form-of-Life'. In *The Omnibus Homo Sacer*, vol. 4.1. Stanford, CA: Stanford University Press.
Agamben, G. (2014/2017) 'The Use of Bodies'. In *The Omnibus Homo Sacer*, vol. 4.2. Stanford, CA: Stanford University Press.
Agamben, G. (2017) *The Omnibus Homo Sacer*. Stanford, CA: Stanford University Press.
Agamben, G. (2017/2018) *Karman: A Brief Treatise on Action, Guilt, and Gesture*. Stanford, CA: Stanford University Press.
Arendt, H. (1970) *On Violence*. London: Harvest Books.
Arendt, H. (2006) *Eichmann in Jerusalem: A Report on the Banality of Evil*. London: Penguin.
Aristotle (350 BCE/1981) *The Politics*. London: Penguin.
Aristotle (350 BCE/1999) *Nicomachean Ethics*. Indianapolis, IN: Hackett.
Bazemore, G. (1998) 'Restorative Justice and Earned Redemption: Communities, Victims and Offender Reintegration'. *American Behavioral Scientist*, 41(6): 768–813.
Benjamin, W. (2003) 'Notes to a Study on the Category of Justice'. In Jacobson, E. (ed.) *Metaphysics of the Profane: The Political Theology of Walter Benjamin and Gershom Scholem*, 166–7. New York: Columbia University Press.
Benjamin, W. (2021) *Toward the Critique of Violence*. Stanford, CA: Stanford University Press.
Braithwaite, J. (1989) *Crime, Shame and Reintegration*. Cambridge, UK: Cambridge University Press.
Debord, G. (1994) *The Society of the Spectacle*. New York: Zone Books.
Ellul, J. (1964) *The Technological Society*. New York: Vintage Books.
Foucault, M. (2008) *The Birth of Biopolitics: Lectures at the Collège de France, 1978–1979*. Basingstoke, UK: Palgrave Macmillan.
Heidegger, M. (2001) *Being and Time*. Oxford: Blackwell.
Heidegger, M. (1954/2013) *The Question Concerning Technology and Other Essays*. New York: Harper.
Johnstone, G. (2011) *Restorative Justice: Ideas, Values, Debates*. London: Routledge.
Kotsko, A. and Salzani, C. (2017) *Agamben's Philosophical Lineage*. Edinburgh: Edinburgh University Press.
Maglione, G. (2017) 'Embodied Victims: An Archaeology of the "Ideal Victim" of Restorative Justice'. *Criminology & Criminal Justice*, 17(4): 401–17.
Maglione, G. (2018) 'Pushing the Theoretical Boundaries of Restorative Justice: Non-Sovereign Justice in Radical Political and Social Theories'. In Gavrielides, T. (ed.) *Routledge International Handbook of Restorative Justice*, 21–31. London: Routledge.

McKinney, C. (2012) *An Anarchist Theory of Criminal Justice*. The Anarchist Library, https://theanarchistlibrary.org/library/coy-mckinney-an-anarchist-theory-of-criminal-justice. Accessed 10 June 2022.

Mills, C. (2014) *The Philosophy of Agamben*. London: Routledge.

Murray, A. (2010) *Giorgio Agamben*. London: Routledge.

Murray, A. and Whyte, J. (eds.) (2011) *The Agamben Dictionary*. Edinburgh: Edinburgh University Press.

Nancy, J.-L. (1993) *The Birth to Presence*. Stanford, CA: Stanford University Press.

Pali, B. and Maglione, G. (2023) 'Discursive Representations of Restorative Justice in International Policies'. *European Journal of Criminology*, 20(2): 507–27.

Primera, G. (2019) *The Political Ontology of Giorgio Agamben: Signatures of Life and Power*. London: Bloomsbury.

Schmitt, C. (2005) *Political Theology: Four Chapters on the Concept of Sovereignty*. Chicago: University of Chicago Press.

Strang, H. (2003) 'Justice for Victims of Young Offenders: The Centrality of Emotional Harm and Restoration'. In Johnstone, G. (ed.) *A Restorative Justice Reader: Texts, Sources and Context*, 286–93. Cullompton, UK: Willan.

Strang, H. and Sherman, L. (2003) 'Repairing the Harm: Victims and Restorative Justice'. *Utah Law Review*, 1: 15–42.

Van Ness, D. and Strong, H. (2022) *Restoring Justice*, 6th ed. Cincinnati, OH: Anderson.

Whyte, J. (2008) 'Its Silent Working Was a Delusion'. In Clemens, J., Heron, N. and Murray, A. (eds.) *The Work of Giorgio Agamben: Law, Literature, Life*, 66–81. Edinburgh: Edinburgh University Press.

Whyte, J. (2011) 'Politics'. In Murray, A. and Whyte, J. (eds.) *The Agamben Dictionary*, 156–7. Edinburgh: Edinburgh University Press.

Zehr, H. (2005) *Changing Lenses: A New Focus for Crime and Justice*, 3rd ed. Scottsdale, PA: Herald Press.

4 Encountering Community

Community, Exposure and Justice

In the previous chapter, Giorgio Agamben's political ontology brought to the fore some of the fundamental questions characterising restorative justice, such as the problematic links between justice, community and sovereignty, the issues of institutionalisation as a loss of experience, and the problems related to the idea of an embodied and relational justice. This chapter further explores the themes of *relationality* and *community*, adopting a theoretical stance drawn from the work of French philosopher Jean-Luc Nancy.

Restorative justice is often presented as a form of relational justice, an endeavour to heal broken social bonds (Zehr, 2005). The participation of communities in restorative processes is integral to this representation. Yet relationality and community are far from self-explanatory concepts, and the recurrent claim that restorative justice's 'communitarian' nature is cast against criminal justice's 'individualism' requires philosophical scrutiny (cf. Braithwaite, 1989).

Nancy's work constitutes one of the most profound and wide-ranging contemporary critiques of both individualism and communitarianism. From his perspective, both approaches revolve around a reified and impoverished entity – either 'the individual' or 'the community' – endowed with an objective identity around which politics should be shaped. Both neglect the fact that the human condition is always necessarily shared, that *being* is always *being-in-common*. This means that human beings are not defined by a common essential quality determining their identity but rather by their necessary exposure to each other.

Nancy's philosophical scope is broad, being influenced by philosophers like Georg Wilhelm Friedrich Hegel, Martin Heidegger and Jacques Derrida. *The Inoperative Community* (Nancy, 1986/1991), a work on the question of community, and *Being Singular Plural* (Nancy, 1996/2000), a manifesto for a relational ontology, are probably his most famous works, even though his philosophical production was relentless until his death in 2021.

Throughout his intellectual journey, Nancy shows that community is not a project of fusion but a process of resistance against power; not a place, state or condition with preset boundaries and exclusionary effects but an endless process of *commoning* intrinsic to human existence. Justice, within this context, is the

DOI: 10.4324/9781003298359-4

ever-coming, always-incomplete endeavour to enable the sense of the world – that is, human beings' constitutive relationality – a task which is at once ontological, political and ethical.

This chapter adopts this conceptuality as a lens to scrutinise restorative justice's theoretical tenets. From this angle, what is at stake in the restorative encounter is a confrontation with the world, the tying and untying of relational bonds. The acknowledgement of humans' own worldly and singular-plural origin shapes restoration as an active response to humans' mutual exposure and to the possible breaking or stifling of social bonds. Restoration, here, is a form of ontological repair, the endeavour to generate sense out of human beings' groundlessness, resisting any attempt at covering over or denying this existential void, whilst engaging with the very process of becoming human 'out of it'.

How can we rethink restorative justice as a hospitable space delivered from criminal justice? How can we restore just relations shaken by a loss of coexistence? How can we reimagine community in restorative justice as a condition for exposing human beings' sociality without collapsing their singularities into identities? Nancy's delicate exploration of our existence as being-with equips us with a sensibility to rethink the very core of restorative justice.

Encountering Jean-Luc Nancy

Nancy's oeuvre consists of dozens of volumes and essays on an extensive range of subjects from Christianity to globalisation, from cinematographic practice to the early German Romantics. His thought unfolds through broad chronological phases, wherein themes and approaches evolve incrementally, through a recursive engagement with a few main thinkers and theories.

Nancy's first intellectual phase, spanning the 1970s, is characterised by a sustained dialogue with classical and contemporary philosophical figures and expressed by creative commentaries on their thoughts. In this period, often with his long-time friend and colleague Philippe Lacoue-Labarthe, Nancy deals critically with Jacques Lacan's concept of subjectivity (Nancy and Lacoue-Labarthe, 1973/1992), Hegel's ideas of mediation and speculation (Nancy, 1973/2001), Kant's philosophical language (Nancy, 1976/2007) and the early German Romantics' theory of literature (Nancy and Lacoue-Labarthe, 1978/1988).

During the 1980s, Nancy produces some of his most original works. In 1980, Nancy and Lacoue-Labarthe organise a conference on Derrida and politics to stress Derrida's central role in contemporary philosophy, whilst providing a platform for a conversation between philosophy and politics. This incipient interest is then solidified by the creation in the same year of the Centre for Philosophical Research on the Political, dedicated to pursuing philosophical rather than empirical approaches to political questions (Nancy and Lacoue-Labarthe, 1983/1997).

In this period, Nancy writes probably his most acclaimed book – *The Inoperative Community* (1986/1991). Here, he deconstructs Western political thought as characterised by a nostalgic longing for an 'original' community. This is a morally higher entity produced by the merging of individual subjects, who will then draw their sense from such a fusional and intimate 'super-subject'. This work is marked by Nancy's interest in Heidegger's question of being-with as well as in literary critics Georges Bataille and Maurice Blanchot's idea of community as 'neither a work to be produced, nor a lost communion, but rather as a space itself' (Nancy, 1986/1991: 19).

The 1990s represent a critical stage of Nancy's work, characterised by the codification of his distinctive ontological approach. In this period, he further develops a commitment to a relational ontology, as explicitly outlined in *Being Singular Plural* (Nancy, 1996/2000). Nancy formulates an idea of the social bond as independent of any substantial and exclusive identity. The book's fundamental argument is that existence *is* coexistence. Being is always already *being-with*: what is common to each single human being is their being inevitably exposed to one another. The notion of *singular-plural beings* underscores the idea that whilst we are unique individuals (singular) we receive our meaning from our being together with other beings (plural). Along these lines, Nancy reframes fundamental Western political and cultural concepts, such as sovereignty, war, the body, technology and identity, deconstructing their underlying theoretical foundations.

During the 2000s, Nancy applies more consistently this conceptual apparatus to a variety of specific subjects while formulating some 'constructive' political proposals. *The Creation of the World or Globalization* (Nancy, 2002/2007a) reflects on globalisation and its impact on our being-in-the-world, undertaking a rethinking of the world-destroying and world-forming dimensions of globalisation. On the one hand, with globalisation, there is the uniformity produced by a global economic and technological logic leading to devastation. On the other hand, there is the possibility of an authentic world-forming activity – that is, the creation of *sense*. Nancy describes sense in terms of an incomplete struggle for justice, understood as a task and responsibility for each human being. This perspective is then integrated with an understanding of democracy, summed up in *The Truth of Democracy* (Nancy, 2008/2010), not as a given form of government but as a process of political contestation, a force of resistance to capitalist power and the only way to restore a relational world.

Nancy's Approach

Nancy's main philosophical influences, stretching across his entire intellectual journey, are Hegel, Heidegger and Derrida. Nancy's encounter with Hegel dates back to his postgraduate work in the mid-1960s at the Sorbonne, under Paul Ricoeur's supervision. Nancy approaches this great German philosopher unconventionally, rejecting Hegel's foundational idea of the dialectical structure of reality whilst retrieving his phenomenological critique of individualism (Norris, 2015). The dialectical opposition of forces which informs reality is not exhausted in what Hegel calls 'sublation' (in German *Aufhebung*), a synthesis which dissolves these conflictual forces but, Nancy argues, remains open as a dynamic field, never exhausted and never completed. In *The Speculative Remark* (1973/2001) and then in the more recent *Hegel: The Restlessness of the Negative* (1997/2002), Nancy advances this creative appropriation of Hegel, proposing a notion of being and reality as constitutively relational and dynamic.

A similar creative relationship ties Nancy's thought to Heidegger. Nancy re-elaborates well-known Heideggerian themes – the end of metaphysics, the question of being, death, spatiality and relationship with the world – focusing particularly on the concept of being-with, developed by Heidegger in *Being and Time* (1927/1962), as both prior to and constitutive of being. Nancy contests the idea of a solid metaphysical ground of being, arguing, with Heidegger, that this ground is *withdrawing*, leaving human beings in a world of emptied-out entities – such as sovereignty, God, nature – which need to be reckoned with and addressed. This task is, today, *the* human task par excellence. Against Heidegger, however, Nancy rejects the understanding of community as the historical completion of human sociality, a destiny to be realised (as in the Nazi *Volk*), proposing instead an interpretation of community as an essentially incomplete process of commoning, as sketched out in Bataille and Blanchot.

Derrida's deconstruction, finally, provides Nancy with a philosophical approach that questions the binary and hierarchical oppositions which characterise Western foundational cultural and political constructs. Deconstruction does not simply uncover and deactivate oppositions but also creates in this way a space for new concepts to arise, on the threshold between the old and new regimes, between violent hierarchies and their suspension (see also in this book the chapter on Gayatri Chakravorty Spivak). Adopting this perspective, Nancy deconstructs the ontology of topics such as existence, embodiment, freedom, community and communism, reconstructing their conceptual contradictions and ontological limitations.

The result of these creative readings is a unique philosophical style that, to some extent similarly to Agamben's method, unhinges the ontology of some foundational Western ideas whilst showing their intrinsic political implications. Nancy opposes to such concepts a distinctively materialist, bodily ontology which emphasises the fact that being is necessarily relational as bodies are necessarily exposed to each other and, therefore, that ontology is necessarily a political ontology of bodies. This framework provides conceptual tools to rethink history and politics independent of individualistic and fusional identities. Overall, Nancy does not produce, though, a coherent analytical method but rather a fragmentary approach that refuses totalisation and any form of subsumption of reality into a greater whole (James, 2006: 2) whilst pivoting around the concepts of deconstruction, being and body.

Deconstruction, Being and Body

Deconstruction, here, is not (only) the philosophical analysis of language originally formulated by Derrida, as it is often understood in the Anglophone academic world. According to Nancy, deconstruction involves uncovering and addressing the ontological weakness of Western cultural foundations, confronting what Heidegger refers to as 'finitude' (Nancy, 1996/2000: 15). Finitude is human beings' existential state: the absence of any solid ground, the lack of a destiny other than this very groundlessness. This is what is inevitably shared by human beings; their most fundamental character is their being *thrown* into such a condition, whose ultimate horizon is death. However, Nancy maintains, this should not lead to a nihilistic position of passive acceptance of meaninglessness. Instead, because existence is never a solitary situation but necessarily a shared state, here arises a crucial communal task: addressing this groundless existence, treating it as humans' *sense*. Human beings are 'abandoned' to this condition and to this task (Nancy, 1986/1991: 18). Yet, again, abandonment is not a condition of doom but the collective experience of abyssal freedom, the very state of being human when any solid ground is withdrawing. Addressing such an experience means confronting something which cannot be appropriated, due to the fact that this is always already integral to human existence. Nevertheless, withstanding our groundless condition, when understood as the deliberate act of traversing to the end of this existential state, does lead to the positive affirmation of (and not a passive surrendering to) human abandonment, actively creating a world out of it.

From a normative perspective, this approach ultimately leads to bridging the gap between what Nancy calls *the political* (the fundamental condition of being-in-common) and *politics* (the forces conflicting over the representation and governance of social existence) (Nancy and Lacoue-Labarthe, 1983/1997). In fact, Nancy's ontological deconstruction is intrinsically a political examination of the sociality of being as abandoned being. Western ideas – of community as a common substance to be put to work, the subject as a self-positing atom, freedom as property, love as fusion and the body as bare flesh – once their ontological character (their shared finitude as the only ground in an otherwise groundless existence) has been deconstructed appear as necessarily relational.

Relationality entails the idea that politics is not rooted in any kind of higher moral authority which reproduces the logic of sameness by forcing people to comply with that very model of being. Nancy supports instead the idea of ontological sociality, embracing the dissolution of any metaphysical, religious and moral super-subject, as well as the connected ethical-political task of 'tying, untying and retying of the social bond', which characterises human existence (Libbrett, 1997: xxi).

Within this context, the concept of the subject as a self-grounding entity, with an interiority made of specific mental states, is rethought by Nancy as *body* – that is, as a stratification of worldly experiences which are necessarily social. Bodies, in fact, are inevitably exposed to each other, sharing a dynamic space – or 'spacing' (Nancy, 1986/1991: 19) – through which their common existence unfolds. Such a coexistence is at once *singular and plural* (Nancy, 1986/1991: 19): a unique flow of incommensurable events, of infinite value, which, however, are shared across human beings. This relational, singular-plural matter is human beings' most distinctive character. It is not a fixed nature, though, but an overflowing relation, an excess which cannot be fully signified or entirely organised because it is never fully realised (similarly to Agamben's idea of potential and Deleuze's concept of desire; see previous chapters). Therefore, any attempt at objectifying or appropriating humans' singular-plural character, forcing it into a preset identity or essence, leads to destroying relationality and reducing human beings to empty and senseless forms (Nancy, 1996/2000). From this perspective, being itself appears as a singular-plural bonding, a relation which is never settled but always potential, never predetermined but always free, always articulated in unforeseeable ways.

Along these lines, it is possible an original deconstruction of the concept of community. Nancy draws not only from Heidegger and Hegel but also from Bataille and Blanchot and their idea of *inoperativity* (in French *désœuvrement*) – that is, of a non-productive community (Nancy, 1986/1991). Community, here, is the being-with of singularities and not their synthesis on the basis of a shared identity. Their mutual exposure discloses their projection towards death, their finitude. Community is therefore essentially dislocated, an active loss, shared by human beings (James, 2006: 177). Within this framework, which in many respects influences Agamben's work as described in the previous chapter, community cannot be inscribed and exhausted into an objective institutional system (e.g. a totalitarian state). Community, instead, is a prepolitical relation which expresses both the most essentially political condition of politics and human beings' most human character (Smith, 2002: ix–x).

This conceptual framework has immediate political implications. In fact, in addition to a critique of identitarian communities and a contestation of the totalitarian state, it lends itself to produce a fundamental critique of capitalism (Nancy and Engelmann, 2015/2019). Capitalist techno-social devastation, from Nancy's perspective, is an expression of a non-social ontology. Capitalism, in fact, is built upon the idea of being as an essence instantiated in autonomous, self-grounding individuals, who are either consigned to infinite loneliness or objectified in organicist nations. Such entities are forced to compete as atomic individuals or fusional groups, negating their shared communal condition as beings exposed to death. Such ontological violence informs capitalism (and capitalist forms of justice), rendering it so destructive. Nancy denounces this denial of the human condition, suggesting a specific form of resistance. This involves a fundamental struggle – what Nancy calls 'justice' (1996/2000: 189) – to be carried out as an infinite task to affirm humanity. Nancy aims to uncover those (capitalist) myths which turn into substantive and objectifying narrations of the human condition (Nancy, 1986/1991: 26). The taken-for-granted ideas of sovereign subject, individual freedom, exclusive belonging, possessive individualism, infinite exchange and measurability ultimately lead to a colonisation of the cultural and political world, the denial of relationality and multiplicity, which are reduced to preset essential identities.

Against this backdrop, the only political and ethical duty is first recognising human finitude – that is, humans' intrinsic relationality and exposure to death – then engaging with the endless process of world-making, understood not as a theological generation from nothing but as the endeavour of addressing human groundlessness. This task is the fundamental way 'to do justice to the multiplicity and to the coexistence of singularities, to multiply thus, and infinitely singularize the ends' (Nancy, 2002/2007a: 61). In sum, the only effective way to counter capitalism involves denouncing and suspending its (non-relational) ontology, and this is the task of (a relational) justice.

Demythologising Restorative Justice

An ontological deconstruction of restorative justice involves identifying the *myths* that form the basis of this idea of justice, then uncovering their underlying ontology, the figure of being they imply and their connections with capitalism. The second part of this endeavour puts forth a *singular-plural* justice – that is, a reformulation of restorative justice based on Nancy's relational ontology, drawing out some ethical and political implications for a restorative justice to come.

Myths of Restoring Justice

In Nancy, *myth* refers to a narrative of origins and destinies, a specific mode of thinking characterised by a foundational fiction that engenders itself (1986/1991: 57). This self-generating narrative is an attempt to fill up the pure lack of ground which characterises human existence. Myth, in fact, produces 'the concepts or images that will form the basic vocabulary of the community by which that community will be able to name itself and the elements that comprise the world' (Morin, 2015: 165–6). Myths inject a substantive sense into human life, perpetuating a form of being-together which is essentialised. These mythic concepts and images are all rooted in the perception of the absence of foundation combined with the desire for an absolute ground. Myth arises as the result of this dynamic, though such foundational stories are always themselves necessarily without foundation (Nancy, 1986/1991: 57).

Restorative justice is itself a tangle of mythic narratives which found – that is, explain and justify – certain justice practices which blossomed at the margins of modern systems of formal social control. These narratives are built around specific subjects, their actions and relationships. The *victim* in restorative justice is an entity consistently in search of safety, of a physical and emotional space wherein to recover from the harm suffered, as a step towards healing and closure (Johnstone, 2011: 52). In this space, 'being heard' is a crucial need, to the point of appearing as the victim's most vital demand. Victims need to communicate their emotions and find answers to some fundamental questions as a condition for their sense of autonomy and safety to be restored (Van Ness and Strong, 2022). This individual, in search of safety and recognition, is the subject to whom restorative justice *responds*. However, more recently, other narratives around the victim in restorative justice have been generated and circulated. The natural environment (Ordóñez-Vargas, Peralta Gonzalez and Prieto-Rios, 2023; Pali, Forsyth and Tepper, 2022) and supra-individual groups (Gaddi and Rodríguez Puerta, 2022), for instance, are increasingly presented as possible harmed subjects. This emerging narrative has the potential to alter the idea of a necessarily embodied and discrete victim, opening up a space for thinking differently about stakeholders, harm and reparation.

The *offender*, routinely portrayed as lacking in emotional understanding of the crime's human costs, is another crucial subject in this narrative. The offender is a decision-maker who is required to take active responsibility for the harm caused. Restorative justice seeks to hold them accountable through moral-psychological processes of remorse and shaming, giving them an opportunity to 'own' their behaviour by making amends to the victim. This narrative has been more recently paralleled by innovative representations of this stakeholder. Critical criminological analyses have raised the issue of the role of marginal offenders who are further marginalised by mainstream restorative justice practices, demanding a thorough recognition of how an array of diffused subjects – ethnic minorities, socio-economically disadvantaged individuals, people affected by learning disabilities – experience their role as those who are required to repair (Aertsen and Pali, 2017). Similarly, non-living offenders, such as deceased settler-colonial slave traders or non-human offenders (e.g. state agencies or corporations), increasingly feature in accounts of how restorative justice could radically change current understandings of offending and how to respond to it (Spalding, 2015; Shackford-Bradley, 2023).

Lastly, the *community* is characterised by a few recurrent attributes: it is innocent, local, an alternative to the state and society, weak but resilient and fusional. The premise of this view is that crimes and crime responses are conceived of in terms of micro-social conflict (Christie, 1977) taking place in (and against) the wider community, understood as a cohesive social environment. It follows that community involvement and participation is an essential component of restorative justice and, as such, is a purportedly key difference with respect to criminal justice (Johnstone, 2011: 126). Often the involvement of this actor is considered a legacy of an Indigenous form of justice, an expression of First Nations peoples' traditional ways of dealing with wrongdoing (e.g. in the Americas, Australia and Aotearoa New Zealand). Against this conception of community as a smooth fabric of moral values and beliefs, embodied in family members or local professionals, new ideas of community have been produced by practitioners and scholars (Blagg and Anthony, 2019). The idea of community as a process of sharing power, not as a subject with a fixed identity, has been put forth as one of the main challenges for the future of restorative justice (Chapman, 2019; Maglione, 2017).

There are two other key components of the foundational narratives constituting restorative justice. The first is the notion of *harm*. In the literature, this has traditionally been conceptualised as either material or symbolic (e.g. Barnett, 1977; Eglash, 1977; Retzinger and Scheff, 1996). Material harms include physical damages to a direct or indirect victim or community. Symbolic harms refer to the breach of the interpersonal relationship between victim and offender, by creating a sense of fear and lack of safety.

Harm needs to be restored. *Restoration* involves a holistic process wherein symbolic and material, moral and psychological, individual and social elements coalesce. Restoration aims to meet the stakeholders' needs ingrained in their (supposed) human 'nature' (safety, justice, participation, empowerment) whilst healing social bonds in the community (Zehr, 2005). Again, harm and restoration appear as conceptualised differently over time. Whilst the representations outlined earlier are deep-rooted and widespread, other understandings of what has to be restored and how have recently emerged. Ideas of structural, socio-economic harms linked to microrelational harms have been proposed (Willis, 2020). Along the same lines, the idea of linking restoration to broader social processes of structural transformation has been formulated (Maglione, 2020).

Victims, offenders and community and their relationships are then cast against a polemical backdrop – *criminal justice*. This expression, here, designates a model of responses to wrongdoing rooted in a self-sufficient and individualistic idea of subjecthood (Leung, 2015: 130). Criminal justice is represented as a legal rationality implemented by public prosecution, trial process and individualised criminal punishment justified by retributivist or rehabilitative philosophies. This model is described as marginalising victims, inflicting pain on the offender and ignoring communities (Zehr, 2005). It is highly professionalised and, as such, removed from people's needs and interests, cold and distant. Restorative justice's foundational narratives contend that criminal justice has never been able to address victims' needs, opening the way for new forms of justice to emerge.

Overall, the mythical structure of restorative justice appears as an array of responses to materially or psychologically harmful behaviour involving a limited set of subjects, arising as a functional response to the failures of criminal justice. There are variations regarding who those actors are, their needs and interests and what restorative justice can offer them. This field appears as rather stable at its centre, though with increasing peripheral complications, and its margins as slowly but increasingly blurred due to the emergence of new understandings of restorative justice's origins and purposes. A recurrent aspect, though, is the conceptualisation of stakeholders as self-enclosed entities, whose relationships are often shaped as contingent psycho-social interactions (cf. Nancy, 1986/1991: 4).

From Myths to Mythologies

Myths serve a crucial role in providing individuals, groups and organisations with a story of their origins. The problem, here, is when myths turn into *mythologies*. In our case, this means that certain narratives constituting restorative justice acquire force at detriment of others. Certain myths, due to contingent contextual factors (e.g. the development of the capitalist state), become authoritative sources of identities and meanings, whilst others are marginalised. This process of self-institutionalisation and self-legislation characterises the present of restorative justice.

Myths become mythologies when multiple understandings of a historical phenomenon (e.g. the rise of restorative justice), which have emerged organically, are absorbed into a single fictional narrative that is then propagated through institutional means (Biro, 2019: 68–9). Mythological narratives crystallise the logos of restorative justice, stifling the modes of thinking that characterised restorative justice as a practice-based justice. This logos is ontologically divided since its singular articulations never voice the same origin (Fynsk, 1991: xxii–xxiii). Institutionalisation involves instead negating this fundamental historical plurality and denying the singularity of those voices.

The institutional narrative of restorative justice is built around essential subjects with predetermined identities (the disempowered and resilient victim, the morally immature offender and the fusional community) and preset relationships (the harm as material or psychological loss, restoration as healing and closure). In this context, restorative justice works as a penal mechanism which relies on the prior existence of a norm – restoration as the fulfilment of certain subjects' needs – and its enforcement (Daly, 2016).

This mythology excludes competing perspectives, perpetuating *sameness* – that is, the closing out of the diversity characterising marginal justice practices – through a distinctive form of epistemic violence. The generalisation and abstraction which define the institutional representations of restorative justice, described, for example, as a 'sanction' (as established in the French Law 2014–896), a 'rehabilitation requirement' (in the UK Offender Rehabilitation Act 2014) or a 'process' (in European Union Directive 2012/29/EU), express the solidification of restorative justice as a discrete tool or service integrated into existing systems of formal social control and enforcing preset ideas of 'just' actors and their relationships.

The risk here, therefore, is that restorative justice becomes a self-perpetuating mechanism for realising a specific, fixed model of being human. The adoption of distinctive ideas of victims, offenders and communities tends to re-engender a world populated by such subjects, and, in turn, *this* world becomes the destiny of restorative justice. The primal relationship with myth cannot be avoided; what is needed is awareness of the ways in which myths found fictionally and ideologically institutional restorative justice as the only restorative justice possible (Biro, 2019: 65–6).

Institutional restorative justice rests on the same ontology which underpins both atomistic individualism and communitarian philosophy. In fact, restorative subjects appear as self-sufficient and substantive entities, with firm identities around which justice is shaped. Institutional restorative justice's 'error' is that of oscillating between the individualistic legacy handed over by liberal criminal justice – the victim/offender dichotomy, individual responsibility, reliance on law enforcement, gender and race blindness – and the communitarian philosophy developed by Western informal justice movements, with its emphasis on a fusional community as an alternative to the state, even if this community works as another fixed cultural and social background.

Either way, restorative justice espouses a distinctive form of ethical sovereignty which foregrounds the reproduction of sameness – a preset idea of subjectivity which exempts itself from finitude, becoming the telos of justice, 'bringing the plurality of existence under the logic of unity . . . the phantasm of sovereignty, which is the non-shareable par excellence' (Gratton, 2015: 222). This is the logic of institutionalisation, the idea of stabilising marginal, fragmented mythical narratives, leading to the objectification and appropriation of singularity (Nancy, 2020/2021: 15).

Why this institutional-legal closure? One possible answer is to relate this dynamic to capitalism, understood as a process of establishing singularities as infinitely substitutable entities, producing a distinctive techno-social devastation by isolating individuals and denying their finitude. Capitalism disavows the possibility of exposing our lack of foundation, trying instead to appropriate it, turning it into a need to be filled or a fear to be removed (Fynsk, 1991: xvi).

As Nancy argues, 'Capital is something like the reverse side of co-appearance and that which reveals co-appearance. . . . One could say that capital is the alienation of being singular plural as such' (1996/2000: 73). The world produced and reproduced by capitalism is stripped bare of any signification, whilst human and non-human bodies are incorporated into a system where they are arranged and put to work according to capital's logic of infinite commensurability and exchange (Nancy, 2002/2007a: 33). For Nancy, capital is not an abstract ideology or a concrete economic programme but an ontological process which installs an idea of the world and of being that perpetuates the endless substitution of singularities and the distribution of ethical, political and material misery. This force destroys relationality, closing the space of mutual exposure to human beings (Hiddleston, 2015: 237), and so it opens the way to an essentialised model of restorative justice. Restorative justice, in fact, when institutionalised, reinforces the logic of capital by reproducing specific ideas of subjects and their relations, with stable features and functions, needs and interests, as if they were measurable and exchangeable commodities.

Institutionalisation as the Retreat of the Political

As seen earlier, Nancy distinguishes between politics and the political: the first is the clash, representation and government of social forces; the second is the relational and communal foundation of politics, its sense. Mythologies reduce restorative justice to a substance which can be taken up by political subjects and used as a tool of political programming. Restorative justice is subsumed under a general principle which imposes a fixed form and an external end, becoming a mere political instrument of law enforcement.

This process of institutionalisation is an expression of the *retreat of the political*, that is, of withdrawal from the ever-coming space where multiple singular beings unfold (Nancy and Lacoue-Labarthe, 1983/1997). As Nancy argues, 'The retreat presents itself in two ways at once: on the one hand, the theologico-political withdraws into the realm of law; on the other, it withdraws into a self-representation that no longer refers to an origin, but only to the void of its own specularity' (1996/2000: 47). This dynamic entails the institutionalisation of difference, the negation of the ontological condition of human beings. In this context, institutional politics endeavours to institute a community founded on an idea of justice as instrumental to a specific – individualist or communitarian – political ideal. Justice becomes the most prominent political apparatus whose aim is applying a normative code to found a polity with rigid boundaries.

The political exploitation of crime victims to generate consensus in a time when politics undergoes a crisis of legitimation, and the consequent transformation of restorative justice into victim-centred or victim-led justice (Kearon and Godfrey, 2007), is an example of the instrumental politicisation of this model of justice. The insertion of a non-political subject – the individual victim – at its core, individualises restorative justice, whilst the reference to community provides a shared socio-cultural backdrop. The institutionalisation of restorative justice consists of subsuming justice under an ordering principle – satisfying the victim in the community – turning restorative justice into a means to a political end. Institutionalisation, therefore, is informed by and perpetuates a distinctive archē, the *sovereign victim*, which endows restorative justice with a stable purpose, a sense. This means turning justice into a device to erase those variations which characterise the recent dissenting myths of restorative justice – the ideas of non-corporeal victims, vulnerable offenders, community as a power-sharing process, structural restoration – ensuring sameness.

Nancy suggests that behind this process lies the supposed impossibility of facing the mutual exposure and shared finitude that mark the human condition. The terror of addressing the existential abandonment and lack of ground that characterise human beings' ontological condition is countered by capitalist apparatuses through fixed meanings and identities. The retreat of the political is this denial of humans' abandoned condition and of what makes this condition bearable: that we are always already in-common.

Institutionalised restorative justice responds to the unbearable lack of foundation by constructing a static space which treats human beings as a united common substance, according to a specific political principle. This process superimposes the immanence of social reality, rejecting the plurality of narratives, ends and lives that is the condition for the generation of sense (Prozorov, 2018).

Yet the retreat of the political is not simply a critical event leading to social and political paralysis. In fact, it also demands the generation of different opportunities for collective existence, the development of new forms of political spacing to enable resistance to fusion and totalisation. The retreat of the political involves 'first, withdrawing the political . . . but also . . . re-tracing of the political, re-marking it, by raising the question in a new way which, for us, is to raise it as the question of its essence' (Nancy and Lacoue-Labarthe, 1983/1997: 112). Institutionalisation, thus, is not merely the demise of a justice aligned with our ontological condition but an opportunity to retrace a singular-plural justice.

Restorative Justice Singular Plural

According to Nancy, our task is to interrupt this mythologising process, thereby reaffirming the experience of finite being-in-common (James, 2006: 199–200). This involves suspending the institutional denial of difference generated by capitalist forces, reversing 'the insignificant equivalence . . . into an egalitarian, singular, and common significance. The "production of value" becomes the "creation of meaning"' (Nancy, 2002/2007a: 49). Interruption does not involve rejection or the erasure of myths but rather recognition of the existing plurality of foundational narratives and their possible degeneration into mythological material. This is only the first step towards countering the injustice which arises from the self-institutionalisation of restorative justice. The task, here, is opening up new possibilities for alternative and non-institutionalised forms of restorative justice, creating avenues for ontological, ethical and political praxis.

World, Multiplicity and Justice

Justice is a thing of this world, if by *world* we mean not the totality of facts, but the endless process of making sense of human existence, in which beings are constantly involved. This process is necessarily relational, for sense-making requires beings to be in contact with one another. This contact, the sharing of this relational space, is the condition of possibility for the world to be, for sense to take place. Creating the world, enabling sense-making, is a response, and an obligation for human beings, to the condition of being thrown into this relational existence. Abandonment thus consists in the obligation to make a world (Raffoul, 2012: 78) and the duty to enable its sense.

Institutionalisation, instead, solidifies myths and erases multiplicity, which reduces the participation of each multiple, singular being in the process of sense-making. It imposes transcendental models of hierarchy and sameness, limiting its possibilities of restoring relational bonds (Hiddleston, 2012: 151). Institutionalisation *is* injustice, the sovereign suppression of coexistence, the fictional erasure of abandonment and, as a consequence, the reduction of beings to passive entities.

Conversely, justice is the effort to enable the sharing of the world, exploring the freedom which is implicit in our condition of ontological abandonment and activating our ethical obligation to live in and address such relationality. This endeavour alone generates community, in contrast to the 'unworld' of institutionalisation (Hand, 2012: 136). Justice is this crucial world-forming activity which resists the totalising impulse of techno-social institutionalisation by refusing any transcendental abstraction of our being-in-the-world, offering instead a measure for what is necessarily unmeasurable – that is, our ontological condition. Justice does not provide specific moral rules. Instead, it is the condition of being obligated to interrupt the transformation of humans into essential identities and relations into codified practices, multiplying human beings' ends and relations (Marchart, 2012: 180; Heikkila, 2012: 54). Additionally, this being-obligated can never be itself institutionalised; justice cannot become a function of an institutional agency. Justice is not the mere task of producing a relational world, a fabrication that supposes a given object, a project and a producer (Hand, 2012: 134). To the contrary, justice is always *to come*, an endless resistance to any ontological reduction of the coexistence of singularities.

This is what Nancy designates as *inoperativity*, the condition of something never closed or completed, something which 'does not belong to the order of the achieved, or the unachieved; it lacks nothing while being nothing accomplished' (Nancy, 2014/2016: 8; cf. Agamben, 2014/2017: 1278). The community that justice creates is inoperative since it involves the binding and unbinding of social bonds, the undoing of subjectivities, always in progress and never turned into a completed work or a finished product. Justice's constitutive incompleteness is the root of resistance to institutionalisation and to any form of grounding justice in some total, unified identity. Inoperative justice counters the totalitarian political program of putting justice to work as an instrument to reproduce stable identities, marginalising any residual entity which does not comply with the chosen model, creating instead a non-unitary space of encounter. As Nancy poetically puts it, 'This is also why justice is always – and maybe principally – the need for justice, that is, the objection to and protest against injustice, the call that cries for justice, the breath that exhausts itself in calling for it' (1996/2000: 189).

Ontological Restoration

Restoration, in this context, acquires a new and distinctive meaning. As Nancy states, it refers to 'what needs to be rendered . . . [w]hat needs to be restored, repaired, given in return to each existing singular . . . in its coexistence with all other creations' (1996/2000: 186–7). Nancy describes the core of justice as the process of ontological restoration, the restoring of something which is given with the world, its sense, integral to our existence, and which has to be rendered (McMahon, 2011: 624). Justice does not come from the outside to fix the world; it is not external to existence but is the very expression of humans' singular-plural condition. Justice generates a restorative relation whereby humans actively take responsibility for the world and its sense. This restorative logic shapes justice as a world-forming task, as seen earlier, which enables our being-in-common.

Restoring the world thus involves restoring the subsistence of multiple singular beings. This entails responding to the elimination of relationality caused by institutionalised justice by enabling bodies to be exposed to each other and, in this way, restoring their condition of shared finitude. This justice, clearly, is not an abstract normative principle enacted by some 'objective' judgement delivered by a supposedly neutral, third-party and independent sovereign agency. Justice, for Nancy, is not just a question of giving something its due but of rendering and restoring what is always already there (James, 2012: 39). This restoration is an ontological responsibility which is at once political and ethical. The existential call for making sense of the world is what justice ought to secure. This responsibility is not a legal duty but a task intrinsic to human existence. Restoring this world requires recognising its incommensurability against any attempt to impose the logic of identity (James, 2006: 236–7).

The material form of this justice is that of *bodily encounters*. An encounter is not a space but a spacing, the unfolding of a relationship wherein listening (and not simply hearing), as conscious exposure towards the other, becomes possible (Nancy, 2002/2007b: 9). Justice develops a restorative relation whereby bodily encounters reactivate multiple singular relations across human beings objectified by external events. Harm, here, designates the *un-sharing*, the isolation of singularities as atomic individuals or as communitarian beings. Harm is the elimination of difference, the closure of the space wherein beings expose and share their finitude. Yet it is through these interrupting events that a possibility to address the world is offered: harms are openings to otherness. In this context, humans' world-forming task turns into an infinite endeavour, without a final product, an inoperative activity to address otherness and its excess. In such encounters, a non-identitarian bonding can be explored as a practice of resistance to the negation of human relationality.

The restorative encounter follows the scheme of *love*. Love is not an experience of fusion with another into a greater community but an open-ended relation with another singularity which leads to the shattering of one's self-images, narratives and relations. Love affirms itself as a *loss*, beyond any attempt to fill, erase or remove that experience (Nancy, 1986/1991). The encounter is a space of *touching* difference, wherein the other takes place in its naked abandonment: 'Touching is the taking-place of a relation: the proximity according to which forces encounter one another, one coming to another, feeling their powers, their resistances. Touch is the very act of the encounter of forces' (Nancy and Goh, 2021: 37). In this spacing, material or psychological harm is deconstructed as an existential loss, whilst human beings are allowed to rethink their experience of victimisation or offending as a process of touching the other as a broken, mutually exposed and codependent singularity. This is not a journey back to oneself but an opening to the broken constitution of the being-in-common (Nancy, 1986/1991: 99).

Love and touch are resistance to violence and power, objectification and appropriation, insofar as they are the release of a space for relating. This space does not produce community; it *is* community, the restored finitude, the incomplete process of interruption, the suspension of singularities, deactivating social, economic, technical and institutional arrangements (Nancy, 1986/1991: 31). The subject encountered, and loved, and touched, is a subject exposed, a subject sharing its finitude, traversed by the other. Rediscovering this subject's infinite potential is justice's sole aim.

Democracy and Justice

This ontological restorative justice is always already a democratic justice. Justice is the affirmation of the immeasurable and unexchangeable to be shared among people against the capitalist demands of absolute exchange and the necessary equivalence of beings. Democratic justice embodies the idea of difference, of singularities transcending themselves, of fragmentary social and political arrangements which resist the institutional-legal capture of human beings and their relations (Marchart, 2012: 176–8).

The democratic affirmation of what cannot be measured and exchanged can displace and suspend the domination expressed by the capitalist negation of difference. This means restoring community as a potentiality, recognising ontological relationality and repairing the world as an event, the surging up and sharing of sense. This democratic event has no end, no final completion, but it does need to be affirmed; it is an ongoing struggle for justice (Nancy, 2016/2020: 15).

Here, democracy is not a specific political system but an event without a preset form, a process of *anarchic* resistance, an excess which cannot be captured by a fixed, superimposed rule (cf. in this book the chapter on Jacques Rancière and his concept of democracy). Democracy is the disruption of existing social and political arrangements, not a political system. Justice is democratic when it serves as the ever-renewing endeavour to restore difference. This justice is a mode of action that does not abstract and generalise, subjecting beings to a higher figure of being, but rather 'gives to each evaluating gesture – a decision of existence, of work, of bearing – the possibility of not being measured in advance by a given system but of being, on the contrary, each time the affirmation of a unique, incomparable, unsubstitutable "value" or "sense"' (Nancy, 2008/2010: 24).

Democratic justice's underlying ontology is therefore distinctively anarchic: 'Democracy equals anarchy . . . the power to foil the *archē* and then to take responsibility, all together and individually, for the infinite opening that is thereby brought to light' (Nancy, 2008/2010: 31). To be anarchic means to be deficient by definition, defying any archē, any essential end or beginning (Marchart, 2012: 174). Anarchic democracy endeavours to defy sovereignty and suspend the institutionalisation of justice, the sovereign-capitalist grounding and crystallisation of justice into the law of sameness and its pre-existing norms.

Democracy entails the disconcealment of mutually irreducible means, ends and forms-of-life, the protection of their spacing, their emergence and transformation. A democratic justice is always a justice against totalising constructions, against the process of organising forces to impose upon multiple singular beings a global principle which would supposedly determine the course of their life, their ends and sense. Democratic justice deconstructs totalitarian forms of justice that impose commensurability and equivalence on singularities and defy difference (Nancy and Engelmann, 2015/2019: 89).

The goal is not picking an end or value to make it the overarching sense of a certain political organisation but the deconstruction of any total figure of being, any ultimate value, reopening the spacing of plurality by subtraction and detotalisation (Prozorov, 2018). Democratic justice therefore enables the ontological community to speak its own difference, instead of generating any form of consensus, to take responsibility for the absence of a supreme principle of political organisation, instead of covering over this void with individualistic or communitarian political arrangements.

Beyond Nancy

Encountering community, engaging with Nancy's thought, means undertaking a journey inside human existence, realising that its foundation is nothing but an infinitely withdrawing ground, the absence of a human nature or destiny understood as a form of ontological abandonment. This awareness may understandably suggest either melancholy, which translates into nihilism and passive deliverance to a senseless world, or an existential anxiety, which results in desperate attempts to conceal that void which is humans' common identity, by either a celebration of atomistic individualism or the rediscovery of primordial communities.

Nancy's deconstructive effort proposes a third way: an ethical-political post-foundationalism cast against any form of nihilist anti-foundationalism and fusional communitarianism (Marchart, 2012: 172). Nancy acknowledges that there is no absolute stable ground, no transcendent principle of legitimation, and that foundations cannot be instituted if not temporarily. But the acceptance of the absence of ground also inevitably uncovers a crucial dimension of human existence. This is the mere fact that we *share* this groundlessness, and this sharing-out is nothing but the result of the inevitable mutual, naked, mute, abandoned exposure of each and every being to the other.

Nancy does not deduce from this ontological consideration any ethical or political principle. Instead, his main point is that our ontological groundlessness, insofar it is shared, is always already ethical and political, an ethos and a praxis. This does not entail the existence of a normative ideal inherent in the 'nature of things', to be restored by some political program. The only human task, instead, is to make sense of this world we are thrown into, enabling our shared finitude, our community.

Justice, in this scheme, plays a crucial role. Justice is the endeavour to enable such a community to resist being put to work and instituted (Watkin, 2012: 20–1). It is not an 'ultimate justice' founded on human nature but the never-completed, always-coming endeavour to resist the political closure and ethical violence of totalising our being, radically displacing any form of institutionalisation.

This conceptual apparatus provides profound insights into the development, present conditions and possible futures of restorative justice. From this angle, restorative justice appears as a tangle of myths – foundational narratives constituted around specific subjects and their relationships cast against a background represented by liberal criminal justice. These myths turn into (institutional) mythologies when contingent historical conditions – aggregated around the development of capitalist state – lead to the enforcement of certain myths to the detriment of others. Institutional restorative justice is constructed ontologically on the same self-engendering and self-perpetuating subject which underpins both atomistic individualism and communitarian philosophy. This development reduces the ethical-political potential of human relationality, turned into organised sameness against difference, prioritising unification against fragmentation and stability against temporal unfolding. Restorative justice becomes an *instrumentum regnii* meant to implement an essential, self-engendering polity around the idea of a sovereign victim.

A restorative justice singular plural, instead, is the endeavour to restore the world shattered by the closure of difference. It interrupts the mythologies which reduce justice to one voice and then opens up new possibilities for forming the world, reactivating our responsibility, our infinite task and endless duty to restore multiplicity. This is a justice of the encounter, an encounter of encounters wherein a dynamic space – a spacing – for sharing is reconstituted. This ontological spacing is always already a democratic task, an ethical-political process of contesting the imposition of an archē upon justice, an anarchic spacing which rejects the subjection of justice to law and encounter to judgement.

In this way, restorative justice is not any more a way of covering over the shattering and groundlessness uncovered by a crime but the endeavour to create a more hospitable form of abandonment, as a spacing delivered from criminal justice. In this spacing, the loss of coexistence is addressed instead of denied, explored instead of filled.

Nancy's delicate exploration of our being-in-the-world as being-with, which demonstrates that the ontological question is always already an ethical-political issue, demands that we rethink the very core of justice as ontological restoration. His post-foundational thought does not leave us with ready-to-use solutions but with openings, broken assumptions and shattered certainties. It is by addressing this debris that a new possibility of justice may arise.

References

Aertsen, I. and Pali, B. (2017) (eds.) *Critical Restorative Justice*. Oxford: Hart.

Agamben, G. (2014/2017) *The Use of Bodies*. In *The Omnibus Homo Sacer*, vol. 4.2. Stanford, CA: Stanford University Press.

Barnett, R. (1977) 'Restitution: A New Paradigm of Criminal Justice'. *Ethics*, 87(4): 279–301.
Biro, S. (2019) 'Disrupting Symmetry: Jean-Luc Nancy and Luce Irigaray on Myth and the Violence of Representation'. *Eidos*, 3(2): 62–74.
Blagg, H. and Anthony, T. (2019) *Decolonising Criminology: Critical Criminological Perspectives*. London: Palgrave Macmillan.
Braithwaite, J. (1989) *Crime, Shame and Reintegration*. Cambridge, UK: Cambridge University Press.
Chapman, T. (2019) 'Searching for Community in Restorative Justice'. *Verifiche*, 48(2): 179–204.
Christie, N. (1977) 'Conflicts as Property'. *British Journal of Criminology*, 17(1): 1–15.
Daly, K. (2016) 'What is Restorative Justice? Fresh Answers to a Vexed Question'. *Victims & Offenders*, 11(1): 9–29.
Eglash, A. (1977) 'Beyond Restitution: Creative Restitution'. In Hudson, J. and Galaway, B. (eds.) *Restitution in Criminal Justice*, 91–100. Heath, UK: Lexington Books.
Fynsk, C. (1991) 'Foreword to Nancy, J.-L'. In *The Inoperative Community*, vi–xli. Minneapolis: University of Minnesota Press.
Gaddi, D. and Rodríguez Puerta, M. J. (2022) 'Towards a Restorative Justice Approach to White-Collar Crime and Supra-Individual Victimisation'. *International Journal of Restorative Justice*, 5: 215–25.
Gratton, P. (2015) 'Sovereign/Sovereignty'. In Gratton, P. and Morin, E.-M. (eds.) *The Nancy Dictionary*, 221–2. Edinburgh: Edinburgh University Press.
Hand, S. (2012) 'Being-in-Common, or the Meaning of Globalization'. In Hutchens, B. (ed.) *Jean-Luc Nancy: Justice, Legality and World*, 131–45. London: Bloomsbury.
Heidegger, M. (1927/1962) *Being and Time*. Oxford: Blackwell.
Heikkila, M. (2012) 'Doing Justice to the Particular and Distinctive: The Laws of Art'. In Hutchens, B. (ed.) *Jean-Luc Nancy: Justice, Legality and World*, 47–59. London: Bloomsbury.
Hiddleston, J. (2012) 'Nancy, Globalization and Postcolonial Humanity'. In Hutchens, B. (ed.) *Jean-Luc Nancy: Justice, Legality and World*, 146–59. London: Bloomsbury.
Hiddleston, J. (2015) 'World'. In Gratton, P. and Morin, E.-M. (eds.) *The Nancy Dictionary*, 236–7. Edinburgh: Edinburgh University Press.
James, I. (2006) *The Fragmentary Demand: An Introduction to the Philosophy of Jean-Luc Nancy*. Stanford, CA: Stanford University Press.
James, I. (2012) 'The Just Measure'. In Hutchens, B. (ed.) *Jean-Luc Nancy: Justice, Legality and World*, 35–46. London: Bloomsbury.
Johnstone, G. (2011) *Restorative Justice: Ideas, Values, Debates*, 2nd ed. London: Routledge.
Kearon, T. and Godfrey, B. S. (2007) 'Setting the Scene: A Question of History'. In Walklate, S. (ed.) *Handbook of Victims and Victimology*, 11–36. London: Routledge.
Leung, G. (2015) 'Jurisfiction'. In Gratton, P. and Morin, E.-M. (eds.) *The Nancy Dictionary*, 130–1. Edinburgh: Edinburgh University Press.
Libbrett, J. (1997) 'Between Nihilism and Myth: Value, Aesthetics, and Politics in The Sense of the World'. In Nancy, J.-L. (ed.) *The Sense of the World*, vii–xxvi. Minneapolis: University of Minnesota Press.
Maglione, G. (2017) 'Communities at Large: An Archaeological Analysis of the "Community" within Restorative Justice Policy and Laws'. *Critical Criminology*, 25: 453–69.
Maglione, G. (2020) 'Restorative Justice and the State: Untimely Objections against the Institutionalisation of Restorative Justice'. *British Journal of Community Justice*, 17(1): 5–22.
Marchart, O. (2012) 'Being with Against: Jean-Luc Nancy on Justice, Politics and the Democratic Horizon'. In Hutchens, B. (ed.) *Jean-Luc Nancy: Justice, Legality and World*, 172–85. London: Bloomsbury.
McMahon, L. (2011) 'Jean-Luc Nancy and the Spacing of the World'. *Contemporary French and Francophone Studies*, 15(5): 623–31.

Morin, M.-E. (2015) 'Myth'. In Gratton, P. and Morin, E.-M. (eds.) *The Nancy Dictionary*, 164–6. Edinburgh: Edinburgh University Press.
Nancy, J.-L. (1986/1991) *The Inoperative Community*. Minneapolis: University of Minnesota Press.
Nancy, J.-L. (1996/2000) *Being Singular Plural*. Stanford, CA: Stanford University Press.
Nancy, J.-L. (1997/2002) *Hegel: The Restlessness of the Negative*. Minneapolis: University of Minnesota Press.
Nancy, J.-L. (1973/2001) *The Speculative Remark: One of Hegel's Bons Mots*. Stanford, CA: Stanford University Press.
Nancy, J.-L. (1976/2007) *The Discourse of the Syncope: Logodaedalus*. Stanford, CA: Stanford University Press.
Nancy, J.-L. (2002/2007a) *The Creation of the World or Globalization*. Albany: SUNY Press.
Nancy, J.-L. (2002/2007b) *Listening*. New York: Fordham University Press.
Nancy, J.-L. (2008/2010) *The Truth of Democracy*. New York: Fordham University Press.
Nancy, J.-L. (2014/2016) *The Disavowed Community*. New York: Fordham University Press.
Nancy, J.-L. (2016/2020) *Doing*. Calcutta: Seagull Books.
Nancy, J.-L. (2020/2021) *The Fragile Skin of the World*. Cambridge, UK: Polity.
Nancy, J.-L. and Engelmann, P. (2015/2019) *Democracy and Community*. Cambridge, UK: Polity.
Nancy, J.-L. and Goh, I. (2021) *The Deconstruction of Sex*. Durham, NC: Duke University Press.
Nancy, J.-L. and Lacoue-Labarthe, P. (1978/1988) *The Literary Absolute: The Theory of Literature in German Romanticism*. Albany: SUNY Press.
Nancy, J.-L. and Lacoue-Labarthe, P. (1973/1992) *The Title of the Letter: A Reading of Lacan*. Albany: SUNY Press.
Nancy, J.-L. and Lacoue-Labarthe, P. (1983/1997) *Retreating the Political*. London: Routledge.
Norris, A. (2015) 'Schmitt, Carl'. In Gratton, P. and Morin, E.-M. (eds.) *The Nancy Dictionary*, 211–12. Edinburgh: Edinburgh University Press.
Ordóñez-Vargas, L., Peralta Gonzalez, L. and Prieto-Rios, E. (2023) 'An Econcentric [*sic*] Turn in the Transitional Restorative Justice Process in Colombia'. *International Journal of Transitional Justice*, 17(1): 107–22, https://doi.org/10.1093/ijtj/ijad003.
Pali, B., Forsyth, M. and Tepper, F. (2022) *Palgrave Handbook on Environmental Restorative Justice*. Cham, Switzerland: Springer.
Prozorov, S. (2018) 'A Thousand Healths: Jean-Luc Nancy and the Possibility of Democratic Biopolitics'. *Philosophy & Social Criticism*, 44(10): 1090–1109.
Raffoul, F. (2012) 'Abandonment and Categorical Imperative of Being'. In Hutchens, B. (ed.) *Jean-Luc Nancy: Justice, Legality and World*, 65–81. London: Bloomsbury.
Retzinger, S. and Scheff, T. (1996) 'Strategy for Community Conferences: Emotions and Social Bonds'. In Galaway, B. and Hudson, J. (eds.) *Restorative Justice: International Perspectives*, 315–36. Monsey, NY: Criminal Justice Press.
Shackford-Bradley, J. (2023) 'Legal Violence and Restorative Justice'. *Hastings Women's Law Journal*, 34(2): 103–32.
Smith, J. (2002) 'Introduction: Nancy's Hegel, the State and Us'. In Nancy, J.-L. (ed.) *Hegel: The Restlessness of the Negative*, ix–xxix. Minneapolis: University of Minnesota Press.
Spalding, A. B. (2015) 'Restorative Justice for Multinational Corporations'. *Ohio State Law Journal*, 76(357): 41–9.
Van Ness, D. and Strong, H. (2022) *Restoring Justice*, 6th ed. Cincinnati, OH: Anderson.
Watkin, C. (2012) 'Being Just? Ontology and Incommensurability in Nancy's Notion of Justice'. In Hutchens, B. (ed.) *Jean-Luc Nancy: Justice, Legality and World*, 19–34. London: Bloomsbury.
Willis, R. (2020) '"Let's Talk about It": Why Social Class Matters to Restorative Justice'. *Criminology & Criminal Justice*, 20(2): 187–206.
Zehr, H. (2005) *Changing Lenses: A New Focus for Crime and Justice*, 3rd ed. Scottsdale, PA: Herald Press.

Legislation

France

Loi n° 2014–896 du 15 août 2014 relative à l'individualisation des peines et renforçant l'efficacité des sanctions pénales [Law 2014–896 of 15 August 2014 on the Individualisation of Punishment and Strengthening the Effectiveness of Penal Sanctions], JOURNAL OFFICIEL DE LA RÉPUBLIQUE FRANÇAISE [J.O.] [Official Gazette of France], No. 0189, 17 August 2014.

United Kingdom

Offender Rehabilitation Act 2014, 2014 c. 11.

International

Directive 2012/29/EU of the European Parliament and the Council of 25 October 2012 Establishing Minimum Standards on the Rights, Support and Protection of Victims of Crime, and Replacing Council Framework Decision 2001/220/JHA [The Victims' Directive], OJ L315/57.

5 Encountering Identity

Identity, Violence and Justice

'Doing justice' entails preliminary decisions regarding who can seek justice, who is worthy of achieving it and who cannot. These decisions are often deeply woven into the very fabric of a society and therefore assumed to be natural and unchangeable.

Adopting a relational political ontology similar to Jean-Luc Nancy's, this chapter delves into the intricate relations between identity, violence and restorative justice. It draws on the work of Judith Butler, a contemporary American philosopher who has developed innovative thinking on the conditions and effects of those crucial decisions about what counts as a 'person' and its implications for a just society (Lloyd, 2007). Butler started her career engaging with Hegelian concepts, such as recognition, desire and dialectic. Working through feminist scholars and drawing on psychoanalysis and Michel Foucault's theory of power, Butler produces an eclectic body of work on an extensive range of issues, from gender to non-violence (Brady and Schirato, 2011). Butler notably problematises the boundaries which traditionally separate sex from gender, paving the way for the emergence of queer studies (Butler, 1990, 1993, 2004b). Her ethical and political philosophy, then, offers a subversive view of human agency as intimately tied to vulnerability, serving as the foundation for egalitarian and non-violent political obligations (Butler, 1997b).

The following sections creatively appropriate Butler's theories to rethink restorative justice and then to formulate a space for new strands of political thought and action within it. In so doing, this chapter draws on Butler's entire intellectual journey, from her early Hegelian studies to the most recent reflections on non-violence, focusing on aspects relevant to the critical scrutiny of restorative justice.

Central to Butler's work is her endeavour to challenge the reifying effects of discourses in the production of subjectivities (1987, 1997b). Notably, she posits that not only identities but also bodies, not only gender but also sex, are an effect of cultural constructs. Individuals perform their gender and sex by repeating existing rules of behaviour influenced by heteronormative discourse. Such constant iteration creates the 'naturalness' of sex, gender or any other essential identity. This dynamic is not only a personal matter but also an ethical and political issue since it entails marginalising certain identities, bodies or lives as non-natural whilst imposing others as normal (Butler, 1990, 2004b). The strategic response to this predicament is to

DOI: 10.4324/9781003298359-5

re-signify those taken-for-granted discourses, rewriting their meaning to produce new inclusionary and emancipatory arrangements that recognise human beings' shared vulnerability (Butler, 1997a).

Encountering this wide-ranging, transdisciplinary perspective prompts a critique of key claims surrounding restorative justice: Who is restorative justice for? How can restorative justice be a space wherein to perform different identities or even defy the very category of 'identity'? What are the implications of a form of justice which recognises vulnerability? Butler furnishes elements to complicate certain aspects of restorative justice – the focus on interdependence, the critique of state justice, non-violence – whilst raising a number of objections that can stimulate a political reimagining of restorative justice.

Encountering Judith Butler

Butler's work could be described as a series of intellectual efforts to develop original readings of a wide range of texts across disciplinary boundaries, from political theory to psychoanalysis, from Anglo-American literature to legal theory.

Her philosophical training encompasses German idealism, French phenomenology and Frankfurt School critical theory. A pivotal theme running through her work is the idea of humans' constitutive relation to *alterity* – we become who we are by encountering and engaging with the other. In her debut monograph, Butler (1987) elaborates on the idea of a subject that is necessarily social, drawing on Hegel's idea that self-consciousness depends on the desire to be recognised by the other, and that this in turn binds individuals in complex ways. Similarly to Nancy, she reads Hegel not as the philosopher who aims to resolve difference into identity but as the proponent of a subject who 'neither has nor suffers its desire, but is the very action of desire as it perpetually displaces the subject' (Butler, 1987: xxi).

In the early 1990s, Butler publishes probably her most well-known intervention – *Gender Trouble: Feminism and the Subversion of Identity* (1990). This work aims to liberate feminism from the still-reifying idea that gender is a social construct and sex a predetermined biological entity (Butler, 1990: 11). In this period, Butler develops the key idea of *performativity*. We do not have a sex or gender; instead, we perform them – that is, we comply (more or less creatively) with existing social rules about sex and gender over time. Butler emphasises the role of repetition as the core of performativity, rejecting simplistic ideas of doing gender/sex as mere theatrical practice or as voluntaristic choice. The formation of a gendered/sexed identity results from embodying consistently those rules of being and becoming – they become part of our body, as Butler argues in a distinctively Foucauldian (and Nietzschean) manner (1993: 6). It is for exactly this reason that it is possible to construct different genders, sexes and bodies via the creation of different rules and different behaviours. These themes are lately redeveloped in *Undoing Gender* (Butler, 2004b), which again contests the idea of 'choosing gender', reflecting on the contextual challenges posed by the encounter with the other and existing social arrangements when performing oneself. Butler's point, here, is to underscore the crucial importance of recognition, repeated performance and interdependence for the formation of one's – fundamentally social – self.

In the late 1990s, Butler utilises the theory of performativity to describe a specific type of symbolic violence – hate speech. *Excitable Speech* (Butler, 1997a) insists on the issues of symbolic violence, of how 'words wound' (ibid.: xvi), influencing reality, creating, modifying or erasing the conditions for certain acts or subjects to be and become. Unlike those analyses that see hate speech as mere conduct and the only way to stop it is via censorship, Butler maintains that this repressive approach reinforces those legal-political structures that enable hate speech. Censorship, in her view, is predicated on an individualistic notion of symbolic violence, which limits hate speech to an individual and responsible act. Hate speech is instead imbricated in large (state) power structures, and legal censorship can do nothing to alter them; in fact, censorship feeds their violent/punitive logic. Butler's alternative approach involves *subversively re-signifying* hate speech – reclaiming violent words to strip them of their hateful charge. Just as the word *queer*, once a derogatory term, is now used to assert the freedom to be oneself, other forms of hate speech can serve as instruments for emancipation when wielded by those harmed by them, without resorting to repressive state interventions (Butler, 1997a: 159).

During this phase, Butler also refines her theory of subjectivity by combining Foucault and psychoanalysis (1997b). Butler reflects on how psychic life is generated by the entanglement between individual and social processes, active subjectivation and passive subjection, how social power is introjected and forms one's psyche. Her main argument here is to highlight the paradoxical structure of becoming a subject – what subjects us, power, is also what constitutes our individuality; we never choose such dependency, and yet 'that paradoxically initiates and sustains our agency' (Butler, 1997b: 2). Butler draws on psychoanalysis to describe this socio-individual dynamic. The Freudian concept of *melancholy* – that is, the formation of the ego through the incorporation of the lost object – helps explain how social prohibitions become part of our psyches. Butler argues that the same-sexed parent is desired by the child and that such desire is repressed by (heteronormative) society. Repressed homosexual desire is then incorporated as a lost object into one's ego, becoming a constitutive part of our (melancholic) identity.

The early 2000s mark a more explicit political and ethical turn in Butler's work, although building on her previous writings on performativity, normative violence and subjectivity. Critiquing United States' response to terrorism as a missed opportunity for fostering collective mourning, Butler introduces the key concepts *of precarity/precariousness*, *vulnerability* and *grievability* (2004a, 2009). At the heart of her argument, once again, lies a Hegelian premise: human beings are necessarily interdependent; we develop self-consciousness first by being recognised by the other. Yet this 'fundamental dependency' (Butler, 2004a: xii) is fraught with complexities, implying exposure and vulnerability. We are exposed to each other for recognition as much as susceptible to the potential violence of the other. This inevitable vulnerability (or *precariousness*, as Butler terms it) is an integral part of human existence, shaping individuals as both dependent on and dispossessed by the other (Butler, 2004a: xviii). In *Frames of War* (2009: 2), Butler, drawing on Emmanuel Levinas and Foucault, reflects on how social, economic and political contingencies lead to a differential distribution of vulnerability (what she calls *precarity*) and an uneven allocation of the possibility of death and grievability. Some lives count as life and can be grieved; others are categorised as non-lives and are ungrievable (like the 'terrorist's' or the 'immigrant's' lives), and this, in turn, justifies lethal politics of revenge. Cultural frames have the potential to dehumanise individuals and groups, negating humans' shared relationality and fundamentally vulnerable condition (Butler, Gambetti and Sabsay, 2016).

This ethical-political shift is accompanied by a further development in Butler's idea of subjectivation. *Giving an Account of Oneself* (Butler, 2005) elaborates on the theory of power/subject to define a distinctive ethical approach which, in turn, could guide actual interventions in social and political matters. If the subject is constitutively paradoxical, and constantly in the making, socially dependent and vulnerable to the other (i.e. beyond one's own control), the very premise of individualistic ethics – the notion of the responsible 'I' – collapses. This 'I' is a pure narrative fiction meant to cohere and make sense of human deeds. Instead, the ethical address should account for our limited self-knowledge, incomplete self-constitution and fundamental interdependence (a theme that we will find in this book also in the chapter on Gayatri Chakravorty Spivak). As a consequence of this socialisation of the 'I', social and political critique are placed at the core of ethical practice, rejecting the notion of individualising responsibility and advocating for social accountability when harms occur (see also Butler and Athanasiou, 2013).

Butler's more recent body of work (2015, 2020) applies her conceptual and methodological apparatus to some contemporary political and social controversies, like the power of public gatherings as exemplified by Black Lives Matter and Occupy movements, focussing on the struggle against racialising and gendering state violence. *Notes Toward a Performative Theory of Assembly* (Butler, 2015) reflects on the performative power of spontaneous, bottom-up assemblies as crucial sites for radical democracy. Public gatherings are instances where bodies materialise as both precarious and resistant, vulnerable entities and yet conditions for democratic action. Likewise, *The Force of Nonviolence* (Butler, 2020) reimagines non-violence as a militant and relational practice rather than a passive one. It reflects on the crucial role of the apparatuses which define what counts as violence whilst linking non-violence to the struggle for radical and democratic equality.

Butler's Approach

The core of Butler's theoretical work, as previously mentioned, is her exploration of how culture contributes to the forming of the human world (Lloyd, 2007; Brady and Schirato, 2011). Cultural formations – that is, context-bound chains of symbols, such as words or images – create the conditions for certain existing configurations of things to receive meaning and, in this way, to play a significant social role in people's lives. Conversely, cultural formations can strip those arrangements of meaning, consigning them to meaninglessness and therefore to the impossibility of a socially relevant existence. Queer, for example, became a socially relevant identity only when people experiencing the oppression of the heteronormative discourse were able to understand their existential condition not as a natural state of things but as a man-made form of subjugation. This awareness emerged through the development of a new – queer – discourse which could make sense of and legitimise their non-heteronormative preferences and needs. Butler's primary concern is to unearth this discursive-material dynamic, adopting a socially and historically deconstructive approach. Her focus is consistently on the normative power – or normative violence – of cultural frameworks: how symbols establish what is right or wrong, good or bad, but also liveable or unliveable and even existing and non-existing lives. Butler is interested in the materiality inherent in discourses as much as the discursivity of the material realm, in the fluid transactions between 'nature' and 'culture' taking place within specific contexts traversed by multiple social forces. Her innovative claim, in fact, is that not only can identities be generated or effaced by cultural frameworks but that material bodies are socially formed as well. Bodies are always already signified, always imbued with symbols which, congealing over time, become natural and taken for granted.

Butler addresses this constellation of issues by piecing together epistemological, ontological, anthropological and ethical-political elements. The normativity of epistemic practices – that is, the idea that cultural frameworks are entangled with power relationships and manufacture both subjectivities and social reality – is Butler's fundamental argument, derived from Foucault (1975/1977). Butler's approach elaborates on this claim by incorporating key ideas from Georg Wilhelm Friedrich Hegel (1807/1977), Louis Althusser (1970/1971), John L. Austin (1962) and Jacques Derrida (1967/1974).

The starting point here is Foucault's well-known idea that no one is born a subject, but we become one through epistemic-political operations. 'Becoming subject' is a process whereby social forces produce the field within which cultural formations create the conditions for developing self-consciousness (Foucault, 1975/1977). This dynamic is both active (people engage with these discourses, selecting or contesting them) and passive (ultimately, people subject themselves to existing discourses), both social (it is inevitably a shared process) and individual (it requires individuals' context-bound choices) resulting in the constitution of a subject incomplete and ambiguous. The first phase of this process is when individuals are 'interpellated' (Althusser, 1970/1971: 110) – that is, addressed by existing discourses, called upon not merely as acceptable or unacceptable but as existing entities. Naming and creating a subject are concurrent operations. Yet, through a synthesis of Austin (1962) and Derrida (1967/1974), Butler contends that becoming a subject requires necessarily the active participation of those who are interpellated. Subjectivation entails a performative process – the daily and active work of acting upon those frames, repeating those deeds which cast the doer as the deeds' retrospective shadow, within existing social contexts. Being subjected to discourses and then performing them over time produces a naturalising effect: subjects look at and evaluate themselves and others through this process, as if it were normal and unchangeable. Human beings are not simply (and naturally) 'women' or 'men', 'national citizens' or 'immigrants'. They become these categories by simultaneously being subjected to cultural frameworks that convey those conditions and performing them in compliance with existing social rules.

Recognition and Subjectivation

What needs to be explained, at this point, is how individuals become attached to discourses and how they end up embodying those meanings which then solidify as their identities. Butler's main suggestion is to draw on Hegel's theory of the dialectical development of self-consciousness. Hegel (1807/1977) posits that one attains self-consciousness through *recognition* – that is, by seeing oneself through the eyes of another. The very development of an 'I' can happen only through this (mutual) recognition – that is, through a social relation (Butler, 2005: 8). This perspective underscores the fact that human beings are fundamentally dependent on each other. However, this is anything but a linear and harmonious process, since social recognition entails being subjected to the other. We need the other to establish ourselves: 'the "I" is invariably implicated in the "we"' (Butler and Athanasiou, 2013: 107). Similarly, human beings' social existence depends on existing discourses, even though such discourses inevitably constrain their possibilities of being and becoming – as if it were better to be consigned to oppression than not to exist.

This position has significant implications for our understanding of both agency and resistance (Butler, 1997b: 6). Butler claims that our agency, exactly like the process of becoming a subject through recognition, is socially conditioned and ambivalent yet never obliterated by subordination. The other never completely determines our existence, as much as culture never completely forges our identity. From this angle, Butler contests both the idea of a self-sufficient and autonomous (liberal, masculine and rationalist) subject and the nihilistic conceit that humans are doomed to passivity in the face of the world. If we need each other in order to become ourselves, and if we are never entirely determined by this process, then human beings are endowed with autonomy, though this must be conceived of as a conditioned social practice.

Butler famously applies this conceptual framework to the discourse of compulsory heteronormative gender identity. This theory emerges when she incorporates into her Hegelian framework a reference to the feminist critique that women only become women because of the circumstances of their society (Butler, 1990). Butler argues that sex is always gendered and that cultural formations shape sexed bodies by signification – that is, by making them meaningful. Moreover, there is a hierarchy of cultural formations, with the heteronormative discourse being the most powerful when it comes to gendering (in a binary way) individuals. Butler insists on the exclusionary effects of such discourses, focusing on how they produce seemingly natural sexes and accepted genders whilst foreclosing others. She emphasises how such mechanisms work at individual level, claiming that both gender and sex are performed. This means that the language we use actually has the potential to bring into existence what it names when enacted by adhering to socially available (heteronormative) rules (Butler, 1990: 185).

More recently, Butler has shifted the focus onto other ethical and political matters, from hate speech to the War on Terror, from Black Lives Matter to the COVID-19 pandemic. Although the core of her philosophical approach largely remains unaltered, one major integration is worth noticing: an increasing reference to vulnerability and interdependence (Butler, 2004a, 2009). The main theoretical reference here is Emmanuel Levinas (1961/1969), combined with Hegel's concept of recognition. The resulting ethical approach revolves around the project of responding to the demand made by the very encounter with the other in ways which honour interdependence. This encounter does not reduce otherness to sameness (like in Nancy; see previous chapter) but keeps otherness as an incessant demand to be reckoned with, the source of an endless responsibility towards the other.

Overall, Butler's eclectic approach seems animated by recurrent perspectives and concerns: a non-dualist, relational ontology whereby matter and discourse are mutually constituted, a fundamental concern with the intertwinement of epistemic and political operations in the creation of subjectivities, and a crucial commitment to explore resistance to oppressive epistemic-political regimes through recourse to the ideas of interdependence and vulnerability.

Troubling Restorative Justice

Troubling, here, refers to the critical examination of taken-for-granted notions in restorative justice, aiming to unearth and destabilise those understandings which tend to captivate scholars, advocates and practitioners' imagination. This process has the potential to generate new areas for critical political engagement with doing justice by scrutinising how interdependence, precarity, subjectivity and vulnerability are conceptualised in restorative justice. It also involves considering the political implications of these engagements and pointing towards new avenues for a radical restorative praxis.

From Interconnectedness to Interdependence

Restorative justice has frequently been characterised as resting on a vague concept of *interconnectedness* (cf. Johnstone and Van Ness, 2007: 17). This designates the assumed pre-existing social connection between those who have been harmed and those who have harmed, set against the backdrop of an imagined community (e.g. Zehr, 2005). Here, interconnectedness entails the presence of relations between crime stakeholders to be restored and, as a consequence, the need for 'victims', 'offenders' and 'communities' to actively participate in dealing with the harmful consequences of the crime. The restorative encounter is typically seen as a time and space where the different issues at stake can be addressed, restoring emotional, social, symbolic and material relations, with a specific emphasis on the victim's needs. This view challenges the retributive concept of 'hard treatment', as the deliberate infliction of pain disrupts existing social bonds that tie stakeholders together. This viewpoint is rooted in a communitarian perspective on human nature (Christie, 1977; Braitwaite, 1989), emphasising the significance of the interpersonal links upon which communities are built, which can be hindered by destructive behaviours. Restorative interventions aim, therefore, to restore such interconnectedness, addressing positively the consequences of actions which undermine those relations.

Interconnectedness is also what renders restorative justice a paradigm of personal transformation which can lead people to act upon themselves and others relying on dialogue and peacebuilding (Sullivan and Tifft, 2001). Transformation involves victims' healing, offenders' reintegration and community building; it entails the stakeholders' inclusion in a community-based, prosocial moral order (Van Ness and Strong, 2022) to be reactivated through the restorative encounter. This discourse is intertwined, as far as its principles and goals are concerned, with a range of philosophical speculations and ethical doctrines (both secular and religious) around the spiritual dimensions of crime and justice (Consedine, 1995; Richards, 2005; Liebmann, 2007).

In summary, restorative interconnectedness appears as a link between autonomous individuals, eventually broken by harm, to be then fixed. Crime equates to a social and moral pathology, an accident affecting the prosocial link which binds people together.

On closer examination, this understanding appears as predicated on functionalistic and political liberal assumptions. Interconnectedness is shaped as a tacit social pact (similar to the one that forms the basis of liberal criminal justice) which presumes autonomous subjects, instead of as a constitutive element of the human condition which can be disavowed but never completely erased. Restorative justice, through the idea of interconnectedness, acknowledges social *interdependence* yet not its constitutive role for the creation of one's self. There is no appreciation of the entanglement of individual and social dimensions characterising interdependence, which is reduced to a purely external relation between autonomous and premade subjects. Interconnectedness is limited to the idea that the victim and offender shared some moral values, knew each other, perhaps had common worldviews and were part of the same community.

Even more, restorative justice appreciates only the prosocial side of such a condition, ignoring its destructive dimension. This destructiveness derives from the fact that human beings are inevitably exposed to each other. Interdependence, in fact, embodies an ambivalence related to its violent potential, which needs to be reckoned with and addressed. There is a need, in restorative justice, to acknowledge the necessity to provide, on the one hand, spaces for recognition and, on the other, the resources to address the possible destructive effects integral to this condition of mutual dependency. From this perspective, harm is not a breach of interconnectedness but a moment of misrecognition of social interdependence. Being harmed is not simply an accident to be overcome or naturalised as a social and moral pathology but a tragic opportunity to reckon with the destructiveness which characterises any relation to the other, its impact on the constitution on one's subjectivity and the hallmark of the constitutive ambivalence of the social formation of personhood.

Justice Precarity

From a socio-cultural perspective, restorative justice consists of a variety of discourses that inject meaning into objects, actions or bodies. Examples of these cultural frameworks include concepts like victim-centredness, the notion of morally immature offenders, the importance of prosocial and innocent communities and the concept of relational harm. Butler reminds us that there is a specific type of violence integral to discourses like these: their power to establish not just what is acceptable or unacceptable but also what actually exists or does not, which experiences are meaningful and thus socially relevant, and which are irrelevant and therefore unworthy of consideration.

The frequent emphasis on victim-centredness in restorative justice makes restorative encounters implicitly adhere to the needs of individuals victimised by a specific and clearly identifiable offender, rather than by social structures or organisations (cf. Maglione, 2017). The insistence on the victim's need to listen and be listened to, as well as the focus on healing, closure, forgiveness and reconciliation, engenders a model of victim that revolves around emotions, moods and feelings. Similarly, restorative justice adopts a concept of the offender not as bad, depraved or wicked but as morally immature, needing to encounter the victim's pain in order to realise the impact of their actions. This offender is assumed to be a clearly identifiable and definite individual able to directly harm the victim and community, a flesh-and-blood offender and not a corporation, state or any other disembodied entity. Lastly, restorative justice conceives of the community as an innocent entity that envelops the immediate stakeholders of a crime and uses language which underscores physical proximity and even intimacy, positioning it as a (partial) alternative to the state.

These discourses define restorative justice as a penal mechanism that underscores the responsibilisation of the offender whilst idealising the victim. This approach embraces essentialist binary oppositions (e.g. law-breaker/law-abiding, offender/victim, guilty/innocent) associated with individual categories (e.g. responsibility, subject, intent), which tend to diminish the significance of social, cultural, economic and political interactions in shaping human relationships. Crimes are seen as exceptional behaviours committed by morally imperfect individuals.

These cultural frameworks are essentially normative – they preset stakeholders' categories, defining acceptable ways of doing and being in restorative encounters. They produce simplifications which are always instrumental, standardised and, as such, fictitious and possibly violent. These epistemic-political operations, in fact, embody and contribute to perpetuating social relations which are unbalanced and hardly negotiable, defining victims and offenders as natural entities characterised by permanence, homogeneity and stability and carved out of the social world.

Applying these frameworks to people and social relations can lead to the generation of *justice precarity*. As seen earlier, Butler distinguishes between precariousness and precarity. Precariousness designates a generalised human condition related to the mere fact that human beings are interdependent, exposed to each other and therefore vulnerable. Precarity, instead, is unequally distributed vulnerability, affecting only marginalised people regularly exposed to insecurity, injury and violence. In the context of restorative justice, those excluded from the idealisations generated by the prevailing epistemic frameworks are likely to be prevented from partaking in restorative encounters or to experience them as non-ideal victims or offenders (Maglione, 2017). Powerful victims, victim-offenders, weak offenders and non-prosocial communities are not entirely suited to restorative justice. The functioning of restorative encounters could render non-ideal stakeholders unable to benefit from such spaces. This would entail depriving certain groups of the possibility to seek justice outside the criminal justice world, or would at least limit their capacity to engage meaningfully with restorative encounters.

Interpellating Subjects

Restorative justice discourses create specific conditions for people to 'become subject'. This process does not consist in deferential subordination to existing discourses or in acts of voluntaristic self-constitution. Instead, it is the incomplete result of the interaction of both cultural and material arrangements, the psyche and the body, within the context of restorative spaces. Becoming a subject hinges on socially specific and historical frames of intelligibility, like the discourses outlined earlier, which make possible or impossible the emergence of certain ideas of who one is. This claim, however, does not imply that subjects are passively shaped by almighty cultural formations. Becoming a subject is a performative activity – that is, a process of engaging with those frameworks, repeating authoritative behavioural rules, within a pre-existing social context and along with other subjects.

Restorative justice favours the constitution of subjects who are intensely responsible for their destinies, foregrounding certain ideas of subjectivity whilst foreclosing other possibilities of being. Discourses of victim-centredness, offender's moral transformation, community prosociality and relational harms *interpellate* participants in restorative encounters, exerting pressure on their ideas of themselves. Such discourses stress, at the same time, the moralising role of the community and the agentic responsibility of individual actors, the need for protection and transformation, the necessity of distance but also operational proximity to criminal justice. Victims and offenders are deemed to have the necessary psychological, moral and practical resources to engage in restoration, which is the outcome of their decisions. Individual agency is the only necessary and sufficient 'site' for the regulation of criminal harms. Individual actors are fashioned as responsible subjects, yet restoration can happen only against the backdrop of a community. Somehow paradoxically, the restorative subject appears as both agentic and disempowered, in search of participation, acknowledgement and empathy (cf. Maglione, 2019).

This subject ultimately emerges from a process that is inherently ambiguous and unfinished. One fundamental ambiguity arises from the fact that subjects become attached to those discursive frameworks even though they may limit their capacities. This is because people's existence as suitable participants in restorative encounters hinges on embracing those pre-existing ideas of subjectivity. Butler (1997b: 7) refers to 'passionate attachment' as the attachment through dependency that leaves the subject open to subordination and exploitation. The subject only emerges through a process of affective bonding to the very discourses that subordinate them.

Yet restorative subjects are not mere abstract entities; they are embodied beings. The body, here, is not simply a mass of cells determined by genetic makeup. The body is the effect of discourses on people who become meaningful entities capable of action upon themselves and the world. The material body, therefore, is the process of materialisation of cultural frameworks into self-consciousness, the injection of meaning into pre-existing, silent cells.

Against this background, participants' gender equates with the gendering dynamics affecting their bodies during restorative encounters. Gender is not a static attribute but a dynamic process, a result of ongoing gender performances. Thus, the focus on gender in restorative encounters should shift onto gendering dynamics, on the performative activities participants and facilitators engage with, rather than solely relying on their declared genders. The point is that this embodied and gendered subject only remains a subject so long as they are able to reiterate themselves as an identifiable, intelligible and hence governable subject. Governability, here, depends on the subject's ability to perform themselves according to authoritative discourses. What would happen if a victim performed their gender without complying with the script of an individually vulnerable and 'feminine' victim? What if the offender acted as vulnerable and passive, against the 'masculine' assumptions related to offending? In such a scenario, they would position themselves beyond the boundaries of accepted modes of being, potentially encountering practitioners' reluctance to allow such unscripted reactions.

However, it is important to note that the ambivalent nature of subjectivation also provides the conditions for resistance to take root. It is in the gaps characterising subjectivation's paradoxes that spaces of contestation (and active subjectivation) will likely arise as opportunities for individuals and groups to seize (see the final sections of this chapter).

Institutionalisation and Vulnerability

Vulnerability ultimately consists in being 'undone' by the presence of the other (Butler, 2004b: 19). Whilst the constitution of one's subjectivity is a daily 'doing' within a certain social, cultural, political and economic context, vulnerability can be understood as the process of being undone when facing the other.

Yet vulnerability is frequently disavowed, countered by the fantasy of self-sufficient subjects and individual autonomy. Criminal justice, often portrayed as the 'constitutive outside' (Butler, 1993: x) of restorative justice, is such a fantasy – not simply and only a collection of agencies but an imagined constellation of symbols which revolve around a rational, self-grounding and thus individually responsible subjectivity: the defendant/offender. Within the criminal justice fantasy, the subject is an individualistic entity – a category predicated on the

Hobbesian rejection of vulnerability. Vulnerability is criminal justice's *lost object*, melancholically incorporated as the core of the Hobbesian fantasy. Every crime is a 'narcissistic wound' (Butler, 2004a: 7) in Leviathan's flesh, to be denied by a violent response – punishment.

In this context, the institutionalisation of restorative justice consists in the restorative justice movement giving up to the criminal justice fantasy of standardising restorative practice, ultimately resulting in capturing and constraining vulnerability. Within institutionalised restorative justice, vulnerability appears primarily as a psychological disposition, rather than as 'a relation to a field of objects, forces and passions that impinge on or affect us in some way' (Butler, Gambetti and Sabsay, 2016: 25). The emphasis on victims' vulnerability – that is, on their essential condition of being psychologically/materially harmed – within restorative encounters does not reflect the vulnerability that is shared by both victims and offenders, particularly within deprived and marginalised communities. In this way, institutional restorative justice foregrounds a fixed conception of vulnerability distributed unevenly and relying on criminal justice gatekeepers' separation of (vulnerable and feminine) victims and (powerful and masculine) offenders.

Furthermore, there appears to be a limited recognition of vulnerability's 'creative' side, the fact that one can be vulnerable and yet resist power. The emergence of a trauma-informed approach within restorative justice, particularly when it extends beyond addressing the victim's psychological trauma to consider the possibility of shared trauma among all participants, is an incipient acknowledgement of the intricate nature of vulnerability in this context (cf. Randall and Haskell, 2013). Yet recognising trauma could readily turn into a tool for paternalistic control and disempowerment of participants in restorative encounters. If participants are represented as passive, weak or unable to cope, someone else will have to decide for them or at least direct their decisions. This poses the question of how to recognise vulnerability without erasing the persistence and resistance that are integral to it, or at least how to create space for the expression of one's capacity to resist.

Vulnerability is not synonymous with passivity; instead, it signifies exposure to the other, a social condition which encompasses the possibility of resistance and even violence against the other, influenced by specific cultural and social factors. Resistance is not a matter of heroic individualism but results from the fact that we are never fully subjected to the other, and yet we are dependent on the other's recognition. Vulnerability and resistance, therefore, are not opposites, and hence vulnerability does not require state protective capture and the strengthening of its paternalistic power, as often proposed by both conservative and neoliberal political discourse. Yet there is a need to address the fact that this primary social bond is not immune to violence: 'violent potential emerges as a feature of all relations of interdependency' (Butler, 2020: 105). The issue becomes reckoning with such ambivalence without denying it through institutional controls. This requires collective efforts to limit the destructive potential of vulnerability while nurturing its capacity for resistance. Even more so, there is a need to oppose the uneven distribution of vulnerability. Existing social arrangements unjustly burden certain populations with economic and social vulnerability, exposing already-marginalised groups to a concentration of violence and a lack of protection. Institutionalised restorative justice obliterates this condition, treating participants in a way which is largely precarity-blind, denying, like liberal criminal justice, the existence of obstacles to social equality (Willis, 2020).

The challenge for a critical restorative justice lies in addressing this ambivalent entanglement without oversimplifying vulnerability as an essentially psychological fact, as the emphasis on trauma in restorative justice sometimes seems to entail. Restorative justice would need to embed an idea of agency that is social, conditioned and ambivalent, yet never completely erased by subordination.

Restorative Justice Otherwise

What is needed is a critical theory of restorative justice which integrates the psychic-individual and socio-political dimensions of power, recognising the mutually constitutive links between vulnerability and resistance, subjectivation and subjection.

Restorative Justice, Precariousness and Precarity

Restorative justice should acknowledge the presence of unevenly distributed vulnerability, recognising it as a political and social phenomenon rather than merely a psychological disposition (Butler, 2009: 25). This entails the recognition of structurally deprived groups and individuals as actors whose agency is denied by specific political, cultural and economic processes. As Butler suggests, there is a need to address this condition of precarity as a form of contextual vulnerability imposed on certain individuals and groups whilst also avowing the fundamental vulnerability which pertains to every human being (i.e. precariousness) (Butler, 2009). The attempt to foreclose vulnerability – as liberal criminal justice does – produces violence, since subjects 'immunize [themselves] against the thought of [their] own precariousness' by asserting 'their own righteous destructiveness' (Butler, 2009: 48). Conversely, accepting vulnerability can help prevent violent responses to crime, understood as a narcissistic wound in the body politic, from taking place. In this way, vulnerability can become the basis of non-violent interventions.

From this perspective, restorative justice would combine moral theory with social and political critique, promoting the mobilisation of precariousness against precarity and emphasising the recognition of human vulnerability in the face of socio-economic marginalisation. Thus far, the restorative justice movement has done little to engage with social precarity, often relying on criminal justice gatekeepers and, in this way, reproducing their biases and the forms of justice precarity described earlier. Only very recent, in fact, are the examples of scholarship on the role of social factors in affecting the functioning of social encounters and practices which aim to bridge the socio-structural, not only the socio-relational, dimensions of harms and conflicts (e.g. Willis, 2020; Gavrielides, 2022). Denouncing the structural factors which possibly impact on restorative justice requires the integration of a further critical element – that is, the normative critique of social precarity is strengthened by the affirmation and recognition of human precariousness. Embracing precariousness means opposing politics that aim at achieving stability for select groups whilst structurally disavowing the needs of others. It then entails favouring the recognition of what is common across individuals and groups as a foundation for a liberating moment, which can help reimagine what we mean by justice and how we try to achieve it (Butler, 2004a).

This critical perspective necessitates the development of a new cultural framework (Butler, 2009) that problematises the binary divisions between victims, offenders and communities whilst contesting criminalisation. The goal is to shift the focus away from individualistic responsibility and, instead, highlight people's experiences of precarity, as influenced by factors such as wealth, gender and race. Within restorative encounters, individuals would be encouraged to rethink their relationships, beyond juridical frameworks, and recognise them as related also to wider social, economic and political vulnerabilities. In this way, the criminalisation process (and not just crime), its precedents and effects, would become the object of discussion. The recognition of human vulnerability would be the fundamental common ground, the starting point for a reflection on the possibility of violence (which is integral to being exposed to the other) and on how to recognise and address the grief caused by it. This could be the first step to appreciating how violence has contributed to creating subjectivities, altering one's psychic reality, modifying daily behaviours, sedimenting in one's very body, affecting the other bodies to which one is exposed and producing broader social ripple effects.

Through the rejection of securitarian notions of total immunity from others as the sole means of preventing and addressing conflicts and harms, restorative justice can pursue a more extensive objective – nurturing a culture centred on mutual recognition whilst addressing violence without resorting to further violence. This implies criticising institutionalised restorative justice insofar as it individualises conflicts by downplaying their intertwined political, social and cultural drives. It then requires denouncing how restorative encounters constitute parties as individual victims and offenders involved in microsocial harms, who are in need participants of personal reconciliation and psychological healing, detached from the broader social context.

Restorative Justice and Injurious Discourses

As argued earlier, cultural frameworks can wound and produce a distinctive type of (symbolic) violence. Yet discourses are also *excitable* – that is, their effects are beyond the control of the speaker, shaped by context and power structures (Butler, 1997a).

Institutionalised restorative discourses, often embedded in policy, have the potential to generate subjugating effects on people caught in their symbolic nets during restorative encounters. They can also be reappropriated, though, and reinterpreted according to progressive ideals and turned into potentially emancipatory discourses. Can 'better' policy serve as a means to redress those oppressive effects and unlock the emancipatory potential of restorative discourses? Policy is a product of state power, and to use it as the regulative framework of violence is problematic. When the policy at stake is the (liberal) criminal law, then, a certain (individualistic) notion of personhood and responsibility is foregrounded, and as a consequence, conflicts and harms are individualised and interdependence is denied. Instead, we should explore alternative methods for cultivating peaceful social structures, placing our focus on the process of 'subversive re-signification' (Butler, 1997a: 159). Language, in fact, even when replete with constraining policy labels, can be used to talk back; legal speech can reinforce power structures, but it can also be reinterpreted in ways that separate language from its injurious potential (as Jacques Rancière also argues; see the next chapter). Language's oppositional power resides in its insubordinate and dynamic nature, the fact that it belongs to everyone and no one at once, in its being appropriable by those who are subjected to it to generate new and unpredictable counter-effects. Re-signification means altering the meanings of those terms and categories which bring the subject into social existence. This is possible since words are fundamentally unstable and, without being adopted and ritually repeated over time, will never be able to construct fully what they name.

Here, restorative justice should strive for a subversive re-signification of the authoritative discourses that tend to confine participants within rigid categories during encounters. The victim-centeredness of restorative justice can be reappropriated by people harmed, who may reclaim the power to define themselves not only as relationally harmed but possibly as socially, politically and culturally injured. This is particularly the case for harms such as environmental, hate and gendered harms. More so, it can be adopted by offenders to highlight their being situated in a wider social, political, economic and cultural context and not simply (and always) necessarily autonomous individuals who choose to harm through rational deliberation. Rejecting or negotiating the label of victim or offender can be emancipatory, and it can offer new ways of *re-storying* the harm which brought participants to restorative encounters. Other times, instead, people may need those labels to fully conceptualise their experience as a way forward to restoring just relations.

Similarly, harm can be redefined, allowing participants to link their specific relational harms to the broader socio-structural conflicts that frequently precede or contextualise such harms. The problem is not language as such but how it is performed, what constrictions it materialises through repetition and its possibly injurious consequences for people. In restorative encounters, problems arise when people experience a limitation of their possibilities to restore justice due to the discursive limitations imposed on them, and when such limitations work as violent and unequally distributed injuries. Any reappropriation, though, requires restorative practitioners' active involvement in creating spaces for rethinking non-negotiable oppositions, challenging the mentality that restorative justice inherits from state apparatuses, particularly liberal criminal justice.

This critical restorative justice should ultimately disengage from the state, understood as both a formal, centralised, legal-political entity and a hierarchical, non-negotiable and inherently violent social construct that negates vulnerability

(Maglione, 2020). The aim is to create a decentralised way of dealing with conflicts and harms, outside a legal framework, presenting opportunities to rethink social relations and political obligations, instead of re-establishing identity hierarchies rooted in justice precarity. This approach involves challenging institutionalised restorative justice by turning restorative encounters into spaces where facilitators support participants in reflecting upon and re-signifying fixed identities (e.g. victim and offender) according to values of inclusion, equality and non-violence. Encounters would provide cultural capital to contest the very institutional framework and underpinning values – the state – they are inserted into when relying on criminal justice's processes and mentalities. This involves discussing the commonalities and differences, opportunities and constraints, at both the individual and societal levels, that people experience in their pursuit of justice when their needs are unmet.

However, re-signification, in itself, does not always lead to a subversive transformation of the existing arrangements. Re-signification must be situated within the framework of radical democratic and non-violent praxis. The negotiation of restorative discourses can produce further harm if it is not grafted onto a normative framework which privileges the inclusion of all voices, as well as equality and non-violence.

Restorative Justice, Non-violence and Identity

A non-violent restorative justice aims to generate discourses to intensify resistance by promoting practices which recognise and cultivate interdependence and equality. The encounter itself should become an 'embodied form of calling into question the inchoate and powerful dimensions' (Butler, 2015: 9) of state-mediated conflict resolution, the site wherein that critical disarmament of violence may commence. In this context, restorative encounters may work like micropolitical assemblies, public arenas for debate wherein people performatively challenge precarity, re-signify relationships and establish novel strategies to address harms. Restorative encounters may become spaces where the performative enactment of new subjectivities, built around the recognition of vulnerability, is possible, and a new 'we' is generated (Butler, 2015: 169). Justice, here, is not merely a judgement about how to treat people or constitute a society but concerted 'decisions about what a person is, and what social norms must be honoured and expressed for "personhood" to be allocated' (Butler, 2004b: 58).

Along these ethical-political lines, it is possible to *disidentify* restorative justice – that is, to provide a new *gendering* (and not just *gendered*) critique of restorative encounters. In fact, traditional gender-based analyses of restorative justice seem based on a largely essentialist conception of gender as fixed identity and a binary dichotomy of sex/gender. The focus thus far has predominantly fallen on the potential gendered benefits or risks of restorative justice to improve practice on the micro level (Österman and Masson, 2018). Policy, instead, often oscillates between complete erasure of the issue of gender in restorative justice and paternalistic protection of females as passive victims against males as active offenders (Hudson, 2002; Ptacek, 2009; Goodmark, 2018).

All this amounts to a form of gender essentialism: the assumption that the experiences of all women and men could be distilled into that of a woman model (premised on injury, passivity, blamelessness) or a man model (premised on domination, control, lack of emotion), whilst completely neglecting non-binary subjects and their experiences in restorative encounters. Gender relations, when addressed in restorative justice, appear mainly as structured by relations of 'coerced subordination', as if this condition constituted the social meaning of being a 'woman' (Butler, 1994: 7). As a consequence, state regulation of gender dynamics in restorative processes is geared towards alleviating that coerced subordination, incorporating a phallocentric narrative that conceptualises women as weak and disempowered and therefore unable to take care of themselves (Hudson, 2002).

Non-violent restorative justice should actively confront this normalisation of fixed identities, highlighting the process through which individuals are shaped by their interactions with others. The categories of woman and man, as well as non-binary gender categories, are contingent, never completely stable and unified. It is *difference* rather than identity which should be embraced, and gendering, as a specific subjectivation process, should be reckoned with in all its ambiguity, expressed by both its performative character and the passionate attachment to subjection. Restorative justice, rather than criminal justice arrangements, has the potential to create space for remedies that undermine essentialist conceptions of what people are and how they should respond to harm. Instead of reinforcing the ontological divisions between identities, restorative justice should create an environment for those who seek to engage with the other and to define the terms of a future non-violent relationship. The condition for taking this step is the further development of a self-critical consciousness within the restorative justice movement – that is, a steadier awareness of the dependency, conformism and instrumental character of the institutionalisation of restorative justice. This would lead to putting resources in diffused networks of performing 'just relations' which emphasise solidarity. This very process embodies non-violence and thus presents an immediate challenge to institutionalised restorative justice, as well as, more broadly, to the state.

Beyond Butler

Butler's thought-provoking work, with its emphasis on the ontological effects of cultural frameworks, the production of subjectivity as inevitably bound to subjection and interdependence, and vulnerability as a shared human condition, is a powerful theoretical lens through which to critique restorative justice. Her work on performative politics as subversive re-signification, the recognition of precarity and the struggle for empowering ambivalent subjectivities to resist symbolic violence helps us to sketch out a different, critical restorative justice.

By adopting a relational political ontology and constructivist epistemology, one can appreciate restorative justice as marked by complex interplays between subjectivity and identity, as well as subjection and agency. This approach has been applied to scrutinise the widely accepted notion that restorative justice derives its rationale and legitimacy from human interconnectedness – a contingent social bond between autonomous individuals, disrupted by harm, to be subsequently restored. Highlighting its functionalistic and liberal background, this chapter has contested the idea of interconnectedness as a social pact (like the one which underpins criminal justice), arguing instead for social interdependence as an ontological condition which precedes individuality, to the point that self-consciousness is itself a social practice.

The restorative subject emerges as being called forth by a dynamic array of contradictory discourses, setting the stage for an incomplete, fluid and ambivalent process of subjectivation within restorative encounters. However, this process can give rise to a unique form of (symbolic) violence when it forcefully ascribes to individuals fixed and hierarchical identities. Yet discourses are also excitable – that is, their effects are beyond the control of the speaker, influenced by context and power structures. A non-violent restorative justice embraces the ethical-political operation of disidentifying individuals and groups whilst generating competing frameworks to intensify resistance by situating and naming practices which cultivate interdependence and equality.

This is possible, though, only if the oppressive effects of the authoritative discourses which inform restorative justice are unearthed. The victim-centredness of restorative justice and its emphasis on psychological healing, closure, forgiveness and reconciliation; the offender as a morally defective individual but one willing to earn their social redemption through reparation; the idea of community as a moral stabiliser and as the background of restorative interventions; and the conceit of harm as relational accident, all appear as discourses producing specific subject positions to which a passionate attachment can develop, sometimes with problematic effects. Certain 'types' of people who have been harmed or people who have harmed can appear as non-ideal participants and can therefore be excluded by restorative justice. This produces a situation of justice precarity – that is, of uneven (and unjust) distribution of access to and participation in restorative encounters.

The restorative justice movement has thus far made limited efforts to acknowledge and confront social precarity. There is significant work to be undertaken in addressing this condition, emphasising that while precariousness, defined as human exposure to the other, is unavoidable, precarity itself is a product of regressive political strategies.

Butler's work helps denaturalise the reifying effects of discourses imbricated with power over the production of subjectivities. The most innovative insight here is that not only identities but also bodies are an effect of cultural formations. Actors in restorative encounters meet cultural formations, whose natural appearance is the mere effect of a series of acts whose constant repetition creates the 'naturalness' of their position: as such, essentialised. The strategic response to this apparent naturalisation is to promote subversive re-significations of those discourses, reappropriating exclusionary categories to rewrite their meaning and produce inclusionary and emancipatory arrangements.

Restorative encounters can serve as spaces where individuals can enact different identities informed by equality and non-violence. This perspective extends an invitation to explore forms of justice which recognise vulnerability and address uneven distributions of cultural and material capital, all the while acknowledging that human existence is ontologically marked by social interdependence. It is for the restorative justice movement to accept this invitation, or not.

References

Althusser, L. (1970/1971) 'Ideology and Ideological State Apparatuses'. In *Lenin and Philosophy and Other Essays*, 85–126. New York: Monthly Review Press.

Austin, J. L. (1962) *How to Do Things with Words*. Oxford: Clarendon.

Brady, A. and Schirato, T. (2011) *Understanding Judith Butler*. London: Sage.

Braithwaite, J. (1989) *Crime, Shame and Reintegration*. Cambridge, UK: Cambridge University Press.

Butler, J. (1987) *Subjects of Desire: Hegelian Reflections in Twentieth-Century France*. New York: Columbia University Press.

Butler, J. (1990) *Gender Trouble: Feminism and the Subversion of Identity*. New York: Routledge.

Butler, J. (1993) *Bodies That Matter: On the Discursive Limits of "Sex"*. New York: Routledge.

Butler, J. (1994) 'Against Proper Objects'. *Differences*, 6(2–3): 1–26.

Butler, J. (1997a) *Excitable Speech: A Politics of the Performative*. New York: Routledge.

Butler, J. (1997b) *The Psychic Life of Power: Theories in Subjection*. Stanford, CA: Stanford University Press.

Butler, J. (2004a) *Precarious Life: The Powers of Mourning and Violence*. London: Verso.

Butler, J. (2004b) *Undoing Gender*. New York: Routledge.

Butler, J. (2005) *Giving an Account of Oneself*. New York: Fordham University Press.

Butler, J. (2009) *Frames of War: When Is Life Grievable?* London: Verso.

Butler, J. (2015) *Notes Toward a Performative Theory of Assembly*. Cambridge, MA: Harvard University Press.

Butler, J. (2020) *The Force of Nonviolence*. New York: Penguin Random House.

Butler, J. and Athanasiou, A. (2013) *Dispossession: The Performative in the Political*. Cambridge, UK: Polity.

Butler, J., Gambetti, Z. and Sabsay, L. (2016) *Vulnerability in Resistance*. Durham, NC: Duke University Press.

Christie, N. (1977) 'Conflicts as Property'. *British Journal of Criminology*, 17(1): 1–15.

Consedine, J. (1995) *Restorative Justice: Healing the Effects of Crime*. Lyttelton, New Zealand: Ploughshares.

Derrida, J. (1967/1974) *Of Grammatology*. Baltimore, MD: The Johns Hopkins University Press.

Foucault, M. (1975/1977) *Discipline and Punish*. London: Penguin.

Gavrielides, T. (2022) *Power, Race, and Justice: The Restorative Dialogue We Will Not Have*. London: Routledge.

Goodmark, L. (2018) 'Innovative Criminal Justice Responses to Intimate Partner Violence'. In Renzetti, C. M., Edleson, J. L. and Bergen, R. K. (eds.) *Sourcebook on Violence against Women*, 253–70. London: Sage.

Hegel, G. W. F. (1807/1977) *Phenomenology of Spirit*. Oxford: Oxford University Press.

Hudson, B. (2002) 'Restorative Justice and Gendered Violence: Diversion or Effective Justice?' *British Journal of Criminology*, 42: 616–34.

Johnstone, G. and Van Ness, D. (eds.) (2007) *Handbook of Restorative Justice*. London: Willan.

Levinas, E. (1961/1969) *Totality and Infinity: An Essay on Exteriority*. Pittsburgh, PA: Duquesne University Press.

Liebmann, M. (2007) *Restorative Justice: How It Works*. London: Jessica Kingsley.

Lloyd, M. (2007) *Judith Butler: From Norms to Politics*. Cambridge, UK: Polity.

Maglione, G. (2017) 'Imaging Victims, Offenders and Communities: An Investigation into the Representations of the Crime Stakeholders within Restorative Justice and Their Cultural Context'. *International Journal of Law, Crime and Justice*, 50: 22–33.

Maglione, G. (2019) 'The Restorative Justice Apparatus: A Critical Analysis of the Historical Emergence of Restorative Justice'. *Social & Legal Studies*, 28(5): 650–74.

Maglione, G. (2020) 'Restorative Justice and the State: Untimely Objections against the Institutionalisation of Restorative Justice'. *British Journal of Community Justice*, 17(1): 5–22.

Österman, L. and Masson, I. (2018) 'Restorative Justice with Female Offenders: The Neglected Role of Gender in Restorative Conferencing'. *Feminist Criminology*, 13(1): 3–27.

Ptacek, J. (ed.) (2009) *Restorative Justice and Violence against Women*. Oxford: Oxford University Press.

Randall, M. and Haskell, L. (2013) 'Trauma-Informed Approaches to Law: Why Restorative Justice Must Understand Trauma and Psychological Coping'. *Dalhousie Law Journal*, 36(2): 501–33.

Richards, K. (2005) 'Unlikely Friends? Oprah Winfrey and Restorative Justice'. *Australian and New Zealand Journal of Criminology*, 38(3): 381–99.

Sullivan, D. and Tifft, L. (2001) *Restorative Justice: Healing the Foundations of Our Everyday Lives*. Monsey, NY: Willow Tree Press.

Van Ness, D. and Strong, K. (2022) *Restoring Justice*, 6th ed. Waltham, MA: Anderson.

Willis, R. (2020) '"Let's Talk about It": Why Social Class Matters to Restorative Justice'. *Criminology & Criminal Justice*, 20(2): 187–206.

Zehr, H. (2005) *Changing Lenses: A New Focus for Crime and Justice*. Scottdale, PA: Herald Press.

6 Encountering Equality

Equality, Democracy and Justice

Restorative encounters are spaces wherein people articulate their experiences by narrating their deeds, feelings and needs, asking questions and giving answers. We learnt from Judith Butler that in these spaces participants are also faced with assumptions about who they are (e.g. 'victims' or 'offenders'), which they may adjust to or resist. This chapter, drawing on French philosopher Jacques Rancière, argues that such discursive dynamics should be considered as distinctively political processes. People caught in those interactions, in fact, find themselves provided with or lacking rights and duties to perform particular kinds of meaningful actions, such as negotiating or rejecting assigned identities. This approach poses the problem of whether and how restorative encounters ensure equality between participants or instead enforce an unequal distribution of those rights and duties.

Rancière's figure emerges from the Marxist French philosophical milieu, during the post-1968 struggles for social justice. His fundamental contention is that *equality* must be assumed as a point of departure and not a destination, a presumed condition and not a promised land. Politics, in his view, is the *verification* of this axiom – that is, the cultural and material struggles of marginalised groups to assert their equality by exercising the very capacities they are said to lack and by claiming the rights they are not entitled to.

From this (agonistic) perspective, this chapter widens and deepens the discussion on the politics of restorative justice, connecting broad issues of institutionalisation and deinstitutionalisation with the specific functioning of restorative practices. It reflects on the risks of both imitating criminal justice and appealing nostalgically to a cohesive ethical community and on how these diverging political aspirations impact on the dynamics taking place when 'victims' and 'offenders' meet. Rancière's radical approach suggests viewing restorative encounters as instruments for a political transformation which goes beyond individual harm repair, questioning broader social and political distributions of resources, roles and powers. This transformation is fuelled by *dissensus* (Rancière, 2000/2004), a preliminary confrontation over which/whose speech counts in a community. This idea could assist in re-examining who is included in and excluded from

DOI: 10.4324/9781003298359-6

restorative encounters and in rethinking the meaning of harm as a political wrong. This (democratic) politicisation requires interrupting the *police order* (Rancière, 1995/1999) which sometimes informs restorative encounters – that is, the rigid allotment of rights and duties which produces fixed roles, positions and identities whilst limiting people's intellectual and moral capacities.

How can we rethink preset rights and duties associated with participants' positions within restorative justice encounters, enabling people to articulate their own *logos*? How can we generate restorative spaces wherein people can openly discuss criminalisation (and not only crime) and conflict (and not only harm)? How can restorative facilitators promote social equality? Rancière offers some answers worthy of meditation whilst also raising related challenges in relation to such key questions.

Encountering Jacques Rancière

Rancière's intellectual profile defies rigid disciplinary classifications. His career starts with a breakthrough when he co-authors *Reading Capital* (Althusser, Balibar, Estable, Rancière and Macherey, 1965/1970) with the Marxist philosopher Louis Althusser. In the following years, he comes to develop an original and radical body of work largely motivated by a critique of Althusser's perspectives and more broadly of the standard concept of political philosophy (Rancière, 1995/1999: viii).

From 1975 to 1981, Rancière writes in the journal *Les Révoltes logiques*, interrogating the historiographic and political norms around the representation of workers' social history. Rancière endeavours to reveal the complexity, contradictions and diversity of workers' thought 'from below', countering the tendency in academic historiography to discard working class writers and writings as insignificant, exploring the archives wherein workers' words were buried. In this period, Rancière grows increasingly critical of Althusser's idea that masses are victims of ideological obfuscation and that only an intellectual and political avant-garde can enfranchise them. This idea is seen by Rancière as yet another way of subjugating the proletariat to intellectual hierarchy and, therefore, as a betrayal of social equality (Deranty, 2010: 5). In *Proletarian Nights* (1981/2012), *The Philosopher and His Poor* (1983/2002), *Staging the People: The Proletarian and His Double* (2011) and *The Intellectual and His People* (2012), Rancière articulates this critique of the Althusserian orthodoxy, describing the history of those who contested their identities as 'workers', challenging the predefined space given (or denied) to them to speak (Tanke, 2011: 25).

The Ignorant Schoolmaster: Five Lessons in Intellectual Emancipation (1987/1991) represents a development of Rancière's archival work. The story of a teacher, Joseph Jacotot, who taught French to Flemish students without knowing Flemish himself is used to dismantle the idea that (intellectual) equality is a destination. Teachers need not know anything; rather, their role is to motivate students to realise their intellectual capacities. By denying his own knowledge, in fact, Jacotot creates space for students to express their intelligence. This radical view challenges the taken-for-granted idea of teachers injecting knowledge into students and, metaphorically, of oppression predicated on the reliance on experts. We find similar remarks in a later work, *The Emancipated Spectator* (2008/2009), wherein Rancière disputes the depiction of cinema or theatre audiences as passive, arguing that the spectator has to be thought of as an active agent and the work of art as a performance which removes barriers for that agency to express itself and flourish.

During the 1990s and early 2000s, many of Rancière's essays are translated into English, and his work becomes more widely known in the Anglophone world. Namely, his writings on *political aesthetics* – that is, on the redefinition of the sensible space as a common aim of both politics and aesthetics – reach a growing audience. *Dis-agreement: Politics and Philosophy* (1995/1999) is a slender manifesto of Rancière's ideas in this period. Starting from a critique of Plato's political philosophy, Rancière argues that politics has no foundation, being only the agonistic process instantiated at the very moment 'the people' (*demos*) disrupts the order of things, bodies and language created by existing authorities. Politics is the unfolding of this disruption, the contestation of the logic which naturalises arbitrary social arrangements.

Dissensus: On Politics and Aesthetics (Rancière, 1988/2010) and *The Politics of Aesthetics: The Distribution of the Sensible* (Rancière, 2000/2004) collect a number of works revolving around the conceptualisation of the politics of aesthetics and the aesthetics of politics. Rancière argues that politics is ultimately an aesthetic phenomenon, if by 'aesthetics' we mean the original Greek word *aisthesis* – sensory perception of the world and our place in it. Politics, in fact, is the endeavour to set boundaries between visible and invisible bodies, audible and inaudible words, thinkable and unthinkable experiences, possible and impossible lives. Similarly, artistic production is an effort to reorganise our perception of the surrounding world and our position in it, generating new images, thoughts and words or re-signifying old ones. As Rancière writes in *On the Shores of Politics* (1990/2007), democratic politics and art ultimately defy 'consensus', what is accepted as natural, whilst letting subjugated voices speak by themselves, creating a space for their expression.

From the 2000s onward, Rancière develops this approach further, analysing artistic practices, particularly in cinema and literature, to reveal their intrinsic political dimension. Again, this is not related to any explicit political function assigned by the writer or the director to their works. Instead, art's political essence depends on its very capacity to influence our perception of ourselves. *Mute Speech: Literature, Critical Theory, and Politics* (Rancière, 1998/2011), *Mallarmé: The Politics of the Siren* (Rancière, 1996/2011) and *Aisthesis: Scenes from the Aesthetic Regime of Art* (Rancière, 2013) exemplify this recent development, offering a critique of the representational hierarchies of established modernist understandings of figurative arts and literature. Rancière's aim is to reveal the democratic nature of artistic performances and their capacity to be appropriated, activated and used by audiences in order to change their perception of reality, producing new behaviours and conjuring up new subjects.

Rancière's Approach

Rancière's intellectual journey coheres around a few interlinked themes underpinned by a distinctively anti-materialist stance. This approach entails the upturning of Marx's idea that the economic and social structure determines people's culture and habits (Rancière, 2011). Material reality does have a bearing upon individuals, yet people's culture (or logos), how they make sense of (and so modify) themselves and the world through language, is not a simple projection of their position in the empirical world – for example, whether they are poor or wealthy. Language, in fact, is *fatherless* and (similarly to Butler's theory of re-signification; see previous chapter) can be appropriated by anyone; anybody can use it. This means that words can deviate from their author's intention, be injected with new meanings and produce unintended material effects (Lane, 2013: 39). This understanding is derived from Aristotle's affirmation (widely referenced by Giorgio Agamben as well; see Agamben's chapter in this book) that language is the defining feature of human beings (Rancière, 1995/1999: 1). However, whilst Aristotle argues that the foundation of politics is the natural fact that all men are endowed with meaningful speech (whilst all animals produce only meaningless sound), Rancière contends that all political activity is a conflict meant to distinguish between who can speak and who cannot. The fact that words can be appropriated by everyone and can alter reality implies the possibility that certain individuals or groups may use them to silence others. Politics, within this context, is the endeavour to uncover and disrupt the marginalisation of voices and bodies, employing discursive means to denounce and counter oppressive arrangements (Rancière, 2000/2004: 35).

Against this backdrop, Rancière contests traditional (Platonic, Aristotelian, Marxist and postmodern) political philosophies for speaking on behalf of the masses, which ultimately results in suppressing their voices (Gayatri Chakravorty Spivak argues something similar; see next chapter). He insists that intellectuals' focus should be placed on unearthing how spaces and resources for people to speak and be heard are generated or erased. Rancière terms this allocation of positions the 'distribution of the sensible' (in French *partage du sensible*) (1995/1999: 26). When a distribution of the sensible is informed by equality, then it can be described as *democratic*. Equality, however, is the premise of political action, not its goal: Rancière invites us to assume we are all equal in our capacities and that the unequal manifestations of them depend on obstacles put in place by social and economic contingencies (1983/2002: 223). Undocumented migrants today, for instance, like workers in the nineteenth century, can and should effectively participate in political life, yet the lack of legal arrangements activating their capacities renders them politically irrelevant. A distribution of the sensible is democratic only when it is informed by a willingness to realise our presumed equality and to make it real. This effort entails a contestation of (or 'disagreement' with) social arrangements which silence certain groups, imposing inequality (Rancière, 1995/1999: x). Rancière defines as a 'police order' this non-egalitarian partitioning the social world, the imposition of rigid identities, which democratic politics aims to disrupt

(1995/1999: 28). *Dissensus* (or active conflict) is the logic of politics, while *consensus* (or passive conformity) is the logic of the police, and their clash is the agonistic game which gives rise to the demos – the only truly political subject (Rancière, 1988/2010).

Regimes, Distributions and Equality

This theoretical background informs Rancière's methodological approach. This is characterised by three interconnected aspects: firstly, a meticulous attention to the historical unfolding of the subject analysed; secondly, a distinctive analysis of the positions occupied by the subject at stake in given distributions of the sensible; and lastly, a normative evaluation of such positions, opening up spaces for new political engagements.

Rancière reconstructs the history of his subjects of interest in different ways at different stages of his career. Early archival works centring on rediscovering workers' voices from below have been more recently complemented by abstract frameworks – *regimes* – when analysing the historical development of art (Rancière, 2000/2004).

Rancière employs the concept of a 'regime of the arts' as a tool to systematise historically different ways of understanding how certain practices ordering the sensible – that is, instituting relations between the world, language, artefacts and community – could be defined as art. Such regimes are not fixed structures but heuristic instruments which isolate, abstract and generalise certain features from long-term historical contexts (Tanke, 2011: 77). Rancière identifies three different historical regimes: 'ethical', 'mimetic' and 'aesthetic' (2000/2004: 10). The *ethical regime* refers to the Platonic understanding of arts as practices which establish an ethical-political relation with the normative core of the polity. Art is subordinated to the ethical values and political principles of a community, and only those images and words which express those values and principles will be judged as art. Within the Aristotelian *mimetic regime*, practices to be qualified as art do not need to express any ethical-political value but only mirror the social nature of a community, its rules, roles and hierarchies. Such social reality is an inert matter that art can vivify by representing it. Lastly, the *aesthetic regime* captures a split in the correspondence between ethical-political or social nature and art. What counts as art here is an operation of dissensus against representation (Guerlac, 2017: 165). Practices to be defined as art must saturate things with meaning, beyond their standard connotations. In this way, they can then be taken up and used in possibly unlimited ways by individuals, allowing infinite configurations of the sensible.

Within each given regime a different distribution of the sensible will take place. 'Distribution of the sensible' (Rancière, 1995/1999: 26), as previously mentioned, refers to the process of making visible and audible certain bodies and voices. It works by classifying and separating certain roles, powers and positions from others and then distributing them across people, based on whether they are valuable or not according to those operating the partitioning. As a consequence, some actions, thoughts and bodies become sensible – that is, visible and audible – others insensible, excluded from the possibility of being perceived. Impeding the capacity of certain groups (e.g. slaves, the mentally insane or women) to articulate political claims (e.g. voting) or censoring certain words or thoughts, are examples of this partitioning. Along these lines, this process sets the very preliminary boundaries of a community, defining the threshold between what and who counts and can be included and what and who is irrelevant and should be kept at the margins. This process is at once discursive, since it assigns a certain meaning to people and things; phenomenological, by generating a certain political reality; aesthetico-political, since it orientates the perceptual basis of a shared world; and ultimately material, since it directly impacts on people's lives (Panagia, 2010: 100).

The evaluation of whether a certain distribution, within a certain regime, enables or obliterates equality completes the two previous methodological steps (Rancière, 1995/1999: 28). In fact, distribution of the sensible is a neutral concept, neither good nor bad. It is possible to qualify normatively a distribution based on whether it is informed by *equality* or *inequality*. This means that in Rancière, both politics and police order have a fundamental relation with the distribution of the sensible – police is simply one example of such partitioning, informed by inequality, whilst politics is the disruption of a police partitioning through a reorientation of the sensible based on the idea of giving voice to those muted by police. Thus, the division between sensible and insensible becomes the crucial site of political struggle, the virtual space wherein the boundaries of a political community are drawn, modified and erased (Panagia, 2010: 97). Police create communities with rigid identities passed on as natural, whilst politics disidentifies such communities, modifying the criteria of political participation.

Equality, within this context, is a crucial (both normative and methodological) concept. Rancière, however, does not provide a direct definition of it. Looking at how he uses this term, we can infer that equality designates a virtual field wherein capacities and possibilities are generated and coexist (Davis, 2013: 9). On this plane, human beings are assumed to be provided with the same capacities but hindered by non-egalitarian, oppressive social structures. Equality is thus a virtual condition to be enacted in order to verify itself, realising a remodulation of the sensible which is the condition for the constitution of the demos. This antagonistic force can never be instituted as a fixed entity; it is always moving, unsettled and unsettling. Rancière's work aims to unearth how this force works and gets captured, serving as a methodological-normative tool for the affirmation of (egalitarian) politics.

A Political Aesthetics of Restorative Justice

Writing a political aesthetics of restorative justice means looking at the development of restorative justice as a combination of historical regimes, then analysing the distribution of the sensible inherent in each regime and lastly evaluating such distributions (Rancière, 2000/2004: 3). Historical regimes are not diachronic phases but coexisting dimensions of a certain phenomenon which expand or contract over time, representing, in our case, the richness of restorative justice as a historical entity. Exploring how, within each regime, certain voices are foregrounded or silenced involves uncovering how socio-discursive spaces are created and shaped, limiting or expanding people's possibilities of articulating their logos and becoming a demos. Evaluating such milieus involves expressing a normative stance towards those partitionings, based on their affirmation or denial of equality, as a preliminary step towards democratising restorative justice.

Communitarian Restorative Justice

Values such as informality, victims' empowerment and offender rehabilitation in the community led to the early inception of modern restorative justice, which was shaped originally as a range of non-adversarial, community-based practices in North America, Australia, Aotearoa New Zealand and parts of Europe. This *communitarian* restorative justice grew out of criminal justice practitioners' endeavours to disentangle themselves from liberal criminal justice and its failures, during the 1970s.

Victim-offender reconciliation programs (VORPs), victim-offender mediation (VOM) and family group conferences (FGCs) are examples of these early practices which only in the early 1980s were bundled together under the overarching label of 'restorative justice'. They reflected the emergence of several informal and alternative justice approaches in the late 1960s and 1970s as a part of a growing movement to de-institutionalise and deformalise responses to social conflicts and harms (Christie, 1977). The first recognised case of a VORP was documented in a small Canadian town, Elmira, in 1974 (Zehr, 2004). VORPs bring together victims and offenders to address the facts and feelings regarding an offence from the point of view of each of the principal participants. VORPs are based on the idea that following a criminal offence, the victim and the offender have a common interest in responding to the offence in a way that leads to reconciliation and closure. The emphasis is placed on assisting victims to overcome the consequences of the crime, helping offenders to change their lives and, more generally, humanising the criminal justice system. VOM, a typical European form of restorative justice, similarly involves a face-to-face encounter between victim and offender. With the assistance of a neutral third party – a trained mediator – parties are provided with an opportunity to talk about what has happened and express their feelings. Victims can tell offenders how crime has affected them and ask questions. Then the parties may decide together what needs to be done about what happened and reach a mutually satisfying agreement. This agreement may include the offender's making financial restitution, working for the victim or community, undertaking to behave in a particular way or attending some form of rehabilitation programme.

FGCs originated in Aotearoa New Zealand as a form of Western appropriation of local (Māori) community-based justice practices. They consist of a mediated meeting between family members and other officials (e.g. social workers and police) in regard to a crime committed by a young person. The process includes a meeting where professionals inform the family of the concerns they have, followed by private family time, where the family can develop a plan that addresses the concerns related to the offending. The plan is then presented to the professionals, who should support it if the concerns have been addressed. FGCs are described by their proponents as aiming to realise 'the transfer of power from the state, principally the courts' power, to the community; the [generation of] a negotiated, community response; the involvement of victims as key participants, making possible a healing process for both offender and victim' (McElrea, 1998: 527).

The 'ethical' dimension of this regime is exemplified by the fact that such practices are often described as driven by a return to community values, from civic responsibility to an emphasis on local traditions, leading to the enhancement of individuals' social connections (Bazemore and Griffiths, 1997). Here, the community appears as a cohesive subject, 'obsessed with its own unification' (what Rancière calls *ochlos*) (Rancière, 2000/2004: 92) – a non-conflictual homogeneous entity (similar to Jean-Luc Nancy's idea of fusional community; see the chapter on Nancy in this book). This transcendental 'one' provides a normative reservoir from which individuals will draw meaning, to make sense of themselves and the surrounding world. The other ethical component of this regime is the idea of personal transformation or reconciliation. This element resonates with a range of religious belief systems, particularly Mennonite and Quaker doctrines (Liebmann, 2007). The belief that humans are naturally good capable of recognising right and wrong, the emphasis on non-violent responses to wrongdoing and on spiritual reform (Immarigeon, 1994; Marshall, 1999) still constitute a crucial ethical dimension of restorative justice, often starkly opposed to the dehumanising effects of criminal justice.

Communitarian Distribution of the Sensible

The spaces of early restorative justice have certain characteristics, which to some extent still inform current ways of doing restorative justice. From a socio-relational viewpoint, the communitarian regime reflects the need for change in the 1970s in the way of doing justice, emphasising the significance of community reintegration against the backdrop of the crisis of criminal justice structures. These spaces are presented as embodying culturally significant practices related to traditional conflict resolution methods and community building (Hobson, Payne, Bangura and Hester, 2022). Materially, the communitarian regime largely revolves around a circular structure characteristic of both VORPs and FGCs, constituted by the trained practitioner, the victim, the offender and their supporters. Such spatial organisation is meant to generate a physical and conceptual closeness between participants. However, it also gives rise to subtly hierarchical and rigid relational processes and structures (particularly in the VOM case).

This regime, in fact, establishes relatively neat subject positions, each incorporating taken-for-granted conceptual repertoires. As a result, participants in restorative encounters are encouraged to adopt the perspective associated with their position, using certain images, metaphors and concepts which are relevant within the particular discursive space in which they are located (cf. Harré and Moghaddam, 2003). Victims, offenders and sometimes families or supporters represent self-evident subject positions laden with images and storylines that constitute a preset discursive space. Within this space, the scope for individual manoeuvring is significantly limited. The victim position assumes a higher moral ground, shaping the encounter as a space to enable them to speak and to be heard. The offender, by contrast, is required to listen and answer questions, to be held accountable and responsibilised. The expression of remorse becomes a key performance required of this actor. Remorse, in this context, involves the offender's self-assessment of their own failure in understanding the immorality and material consequences of their actions (Maglione, 2023). This failure has ultimately resulted in a breach of the moral bonds which tie the offender to the victim within a supposedly shared community. Within this context, another negative moral emotion – shame – is often expected from the offender. Such rigidification of positions and associated expectations can be conceptualised as a *police order.* As seen earlier, for Rancière, the term 'police' does not refer to specific law enforcement institutions but to the opposite of politics, to which it is tied by an unmediated relation. Police order refers to any hierarchical organisations enfolded by the veil of consensus, the imposition of a certain arrangement of bodies and words, naturalised as essential and necessary.

From an ethical perspective, this regime foregrounds certain voices whilst silencing others, presenting this distribution as obvious or natural. Victims and offenders are typically the only stakeholders legitimised to actively participate in early restorative processes. Additionally, such subject positions reflect criminal justice gatekeepers' – mainly law enforcement's – criminalisation choices (cf. Maglione, 2020). The selective framing of certain issues as worthy or unworthy of attention and the foregrounding of certain voices are complemented by the exclusion of individuals who do not fit the choices of officers and prosecutors who make referrals to restorative justice services. This happens in the case of victims who are also offenders, systemic victims (e.g. ecosystems or populations) or non-ideal victims, who hardly can adopt the identities preformed by criminal justice gatekeepers. By excluding these voices and bodies, the police order manifests itself as an instantiation of social inequality. This order greatly limits the possibility of disagreement with existing procedures, roles and powers. This vertical organisation hinders the emergence of any genuinely political subjectivity, depoliticises human relations, enforces cohesion and stabilises identities (Tanke, 2011: 45; Clarke, 2013: 16).

Institutional Restorative Justice

The *institutional* regime refers to another dimension of the history of restorative justice – its institutionalisation. Here, the development of restorative justice imitates the nature of criminal justice – its rules, roles and hierarchies. This dimension is exemplified by the legalisation of early restorative practices, which involves altering, but not necessarily erasing, their communitarian roots.

FGCs were legislated in the late 1980s, becoming the foundation of the Youth Justice system in Aotearoa New Zealand in 1989. Through a top-down approach, FGCs were integrated in state-delivered youth justice practices, often in serious cases of youth offending. The Children, Young Persons, and Their Families Act 1989 institutionalised this measure (which was not explicitly defined as restorative justice at the time). The aim was to address high custody rates for young people, as well as the lack of inclusion of young people's families in decisions regarding youth justice.

In England and Wales, early policy on 'reparation' activities involving offenders and victims dates back to the Labour governments of the 1990s, specifically the Crime and Disorder Act 1998 and the Youth Justice and Criminal Evidence Act 1999, followed by the Criminal Justice Act 2003 and the Criminal Justice and Immigration Act 2008. In particular, the Crime and Disorder Act 1998, which introduced the reparation order for youth offenders, and the Youth Justice and Criminal Evidence Act 1999, which established referrals orders and youth offenders panels, paved the way for the institutionalisation of restorative justice in England and Wales as a legislated, state-organised and quasi-professionally run system.

In Europe, Belgium has always been at the forefront of the legalisation of restorative justice. Here, a legal provision on penal mediation (Code of Criminal Procedure, art. 216ter) was introduced in 1994. In 2006, the Belgian Youth Protection Act recognised and encouraged mediation and sentencing circles in juvenile cases. In 2005, a federal law provided that every person who has 'a direct interest' can request mediation at any stage of the criminal procedure (Code of Criminal Procedure, art. 553[2]). Similarly, Norway has an established tradition of alternative measures to criminal prosecution, with pioneering legislation on mediation introduced in 1991. The National Mediation Service (in Norwegian *Konfliktrådet*) handles both civil and criminal cases 'restoratively' (The Mediation Service Act: §1) – that is, aiming to enable the parties and others concerned by an offence or a conflict to jointly decide, helped by non-professional mediators, how its harmful effects should be handled. The Mediation Service Act was significantly amended in 2014 through the introduction of the 'youth monitoring and follow-up measure' (§1), a restorative sanction for young people who have not committed serious or repeated crimes which aims to prevent reoffending. This measure, among other things, introduced the figure of a professional facilitator with powers to restrict the young person's freedom (Holmboe, 2017).

France and Italy represent more recent European cases of VOM absorbed by or integrated into novel legislation on restorative justice. In France, early practices of penal mediation were supplemented in 2014 by the right to obtain, at any stage of the criminal justice process, 'reparation of the consequences of crime', which may involve 'a restorative justice measure' (Law 2014–896). This law also introduced a new penal sanction – the 'penal restraint' – conceived of as the suitable legal framework within which to propose a restorative measure. In Italy, Law 2021–134 introduced a systematic reform of restorative justice for adults, in the past minimally regulated by provisions scattered across multiple statutes. This new law provided a new definition of restorative justice as any programme which enables victim, offender and community to freely participate in the resolution of the issues arising from the crime, with the help of an impartial third party. It also enacted a wide range of legal safeguards regarding, for example, access, confidentiality and rights to information and established that the outcome of restorative encounters, which may have an impact on the judicial process, will be evaluated by a judicial authority.

Finally, it is worth noting that many national efforts to institutionalise restorative justice have been prompted by international policy. Examples of these early prompts are the United Nations Economic and Social Council 'Basic Principles on the Use of Restorative Justice Programmes in Criminal Matters' (2002), the Council of Europe Committee of Ministers Recommendations R(99)19 and CM/Rec(2018)8 and European Union Directive 2012/29/EU on victims' rights (The Victims' Directive).

This cursory overview illustrates the tendency to turn early restorative practices, which emerged at the margins of Western criminal justice systems, into codified processes expressed in the language of criminal justice. This progressive and gradual imitation is a long-term historical dynamic, although recently the pace and spread of this process have significantly increased (see González, 2020 for a critical overview of this process in the United States).

Institutional Distribution of the Sensible

Institutionalising restorative justice involves creating a policed space that confines voices and bodies into legal-bureaucratic positions. This space is populated by victims, offenders, (sometimes) communities and a fourth entity – the state. The state occupies a crucial position, being often represented by authorities who make referrals to restorative services, supervise their provision and certify their outcomes. This organisational structure is designed to exclude or significantly limit the possibility of conflict. For example, if the offender does not acknowledge responsibility, they will not be allowed to partake in encounters, and if the restorative facilitator rejects the control of the state, no referrals will be made. A logic of consensus underlies the assumed legitimacy of legal procedures, roles and powers. The arbitrariness of this distribution of the sensible – dichotomic, abstract, functionalist – is concealed by the state, presented by large sections of the restorative justice movement as a necessary instrument for scaling up restorative interventions. Additionally, this institutionalised arrangement is hypertrophic and self-replicating. Its aim is to saturate the sensible with policy, leaving increasingly less space for other, spontaneous organisation of bodies and words, creating a solid and smooth, apolitical space. Hence, the creation of political subjects is impeded, replaced by non-political legal entities.

This discursive closure relies on the use of liberal criminal justice language to regulate restorative justice (Clarke, 2013: 24). The dichotomy victim/offender and the concept of community exemplify this perspective. Restorative justice policy neatly establishes individuals as either victims (or 'persons who have been harmed') or offenders (or 'persons who have harmed'), with little room for (social, personal, cultural) overlaps between these positions. When community (infrequently) features in policy, it is often described as a collection of professionals who play a supporting role to the primary stakeholders (i.e. victims, offenders and criminal justice representatives). This is the case for youth offender panels in England and Wales or the new Norwegian youth justice restorative measure. These initiatives involve the youth offender's 'professional network' and possibly (but not necessarily) the victim and their network. These discursive choices reflect the same functionalist understanding of crime which underpins criminal justice (Walgrave, 2017: 97). Crime is an individual moral deficiency which needs to be neutralised, and restorative justice is presented as a way to address this pathology, giving victims' voice and responsibilising the offender whilst neglecting the unbalanced power relations which contribute to the definition of behaviours as crimes. This functionalist language can also lead to the development of a bureaucratic 'tick the box' approach to justice interventions with culturally colonising effects when restorative justice programs are imposed as standardised commodities on non-Western communities (Blagg, 1998, 2017; see also next chapter).

Overall, institutional restorative justice appears as a discrete, standardised process informed by criminal justice concepts. Penal policy reduces restorative justice to a transparent object: a sequence of codified steps which supposedly lead from crime to social order. Restorative justice becomes a state-run technical device, a means to achieve victims' satisfaction and reduce reoffending (Shapland, Robinson and Sorsby, 2011). In this way, it loses much of its radical potential to address human interactions. This is a consequence of the policing of bottom-up informal justice practices and of the immobilisation of their ethical roots. This situation is exacerbated by the fact that policy generates its own demand, making itself necessary even when it does not deliver on its promises of efficient regulation. Policy generates more policy, relentlessly, legitimising the police order of the sensible, which is integral to the institutionalisation of restorative justice.

Democratic Restorative Justice

Democratising restorative justice requires infusing equality into both communitarian and institutionalised forms of justice, although without imposing another regime which would yet again restrain people's capacities. Democratic restorative justice is, in fact, a process and not an end product, an active challenge which does not demand the abolition and then replacement of existing distributions of the sensible. Instead, it promotes an ongoing process of uncovering the limitations of existing forms of justice, questioning their foundations and effects, establishing new relations, allowing new voices to emerge and politicising what is at stake (Sachs, 2017: 71).

Miscounts

As mentioned earlier, politics is the human activity that aims to realise equality. Restorative justice becomes a political force when it enables the contestation of the consensual logic which neutralises conflict and naturalises inequality (Rancière, 1988/2010). This can be achieved by supporting individuals to question the positions assigned to them within restorative encounters (Deranty, 2010: 10). Politicising restorative justice entails creating spaces for reflecting critically on pre-established subject positions, such as 'victim' and 'offender', or non-legal labels (such as 'person who has been harmed' and 'person who has harmed'), all influenced by a simplifying dichotomous logic. In fact, whilst imposing such positions creates a rigid discursive space, characterised by fixed rights and duties, questioning this arrangement aims to allow unheard voices to affirm their needs and interests. This process may well include the appropriation of such labels, yet only as one option available to participants, not as their predetermined personas. This implies providing parties with opportunities to contextualise their actions, to narrate not only their personal stories but also their *social histories*, considering not only the crime and the harm but also criminalisation and its conditions (cf. Rancière, 2001). Broader social, cultural and economic factors surrounding participants could be included as possible material for reflection. Along these lines, taken-for-granted ideas of individual responsibility and individual victimisation become questionable. Again, this does not mean denying them but creating spaces for a dialogue around these concepts that are considered abiding in existing regimes of justice.

A related form of politicisation consists in providing participants with resources within restorative encounters to reframe interpersonal harms as 'miscounts' (Rancière, 1995/1999: x). *Miscounting* designates the process of reflecting on which voices count, who is allowed to speak and about what issues, with the aim of questioning the very preconditions of restorative encounters. Discussing who should participate in such arenas, with which role and powers, under which circumstances, amounts to instituting relations, convening new populations and creating new subjects through discursive acts. For example, this process can involve extending the reach of restorative encounters to include as direct stakeholders the agencies which both criminalise individuals (often on gendered, classist or racialised grounds) and are supposed to protect them (e.g. police). Exploring such agencies' power to 'name' victims and offenders, inviting them to reflect on the human consequences of their work and the complex conditions and legacies of wrongdoing, has the potential to lead to the expansion of the concept of harm within restorative encounters.

Within this context, 'democracy is neither a form of government nor a form of social life' (Rancière, 1988/2010: 50) but what is at stake in restorative encounters: the altering of the socially and legally accepted order built around the 'natural' separation between victim and offender and the individualisation of responsibility as much as the distinction between person who has been harmed and person who has harmed and the privatisation of conflicts. This does not imply abolishing *tout court* those labels but turning them into objects for open yet safe discussion and disagreement. Democratic restorative justice opposes dissensus to taken-for-granted partitioning (Rancière, 1988/2010), demanding a critical reflection on the effects of abstracting harms from their social context and on the political implications of individualising responsibility and victimisation. Yet a paradox should be noted here. As an interpreter of Rancière has sharply noticed, 'democracy ungrounds itself when spreading democratisation, since micropolitical practice which enables the egalitarian distribution of the sensible also engenders anti-political resistance, that is, policing order' (Apter, 2017: 12). This means that in democratising restorative justice there is a risk of recreating a new fixed, unequal order, which simply replaces the imposition of certain voices with others. Democratic restorative justice is therefore always already *impure* – never fully democratic, never a stabilised distribution of rights and duties, always set to question its own foundations (Chambers, 2013). This is because democracy is not a regime but a disrupting force supporting marginalised voices, preventing human encounters from immobilising people's potential to reimagine themselves and their relations.

Expanding Boundaries

Political action produces emancipation first of all discursively, and this is intrinsic to the fact that human beings are 'literary animals' (Rancière, 2000/2004: 35). Politics, in fact, relies upon the capacity of language to create, modify or erase reality, assigning new meanings, authorising new ways of relating to the surrounding world and forging new subjects. This is fundamentally the aesthetic driver of politics and, in our context, of restorative justice.

As said earlier, politics and the arts are always contingent and precarious attempts to reorder the sensory community, subverting and reconfiguring hegemonic social arrangements. Democratic art is art that, once freed from the task of representing social nature or political communities, is able to create 'possibilities of life by refusing to be part of the settled sensible, shattering meanings and shared appearances' (Tanke, 2011: 85). Art pushes the boundaries of what can be thought and said, dismantling self-evident facts, defying any hegemonic social order and ultimately inventing new forms of life (Chanter, 2017: 158).

For democratic restorative justice to embody this aesthetic core and its emancipatory potential means accepting the idea that 'everything speaks' (Tanke, 2011: 86–90). Not only individuals and groups but also non-human and more-than-human entities, such as ecosystems or social movements, should be able to participate in encounters, whose boundaries should be extended. Very recent, albeit still marginal, examples of this expansive process are environmental restorative justice and restorative cities.

Environmental restorative justice, understood as an ecocentric approach to harm to human and non-human entities, can create space for alternative narratives which have the potential to redefine and challenge notions of harm and justice (Pali, Forsyth and Tepper, 2022). Here, stakeholders can define themselves as victims of environmental harm even if they are not legally defined as such by the criminal justice system. It is possible to narrate a type of harm that is not legally acknowledged, imagining ways of making the ecosystem speak of the harms it suffers, whilst politicising their causes and effects.

The idea of restorative cities involves producing cultural change by expanding some of the values characterising restorative justice to inform wider social processes within spaces as wide as entire political communities (Mannozzi, 2019). From this angle, it consists of a movement, rather than a process, advocating for a range of strategies – from dialogic decision-making processes to architecture, to social networks to deal with vulnerability – which contain a political potential, promoting a 'logical revolt' insofar they extend the bounds of restorative justice beyond the limiting spaces of face-to-face encounters (cf. Rosenblatt and Adamson, 2023).

What unites these different processes is their common foundation: the non- anthropocentric acknowledgement and inclusion of new restorative actors. These are not embodied subjects, but complex entities constituted by physical matters as much as moods, memories and sensory impressions, sensating interfaces of social space and individual needs (Rancière, 2000/2004: 35). Expanding the boundaries of restorative encounters amounts to creating new spaces wherein to articulate new configurations of the real and conjure up new subjectivities.

Restoring Subjects

The concepts of *subject* and *subjectification* are central to Rancière's idea of democratic politics (Rancière, 1992, 1995/1999). Rancière challenges the common-sense relation between politics and subjectivity, arguing that politics is itself a subjectivation process, a dynamic through which political subjects are formed, and thus that no political subjects exist before politics. This process begins when a non-political subject – that is, an individual or group who in the current hegemonic arrangement is considered unable to speak and to be heard – realises and then publicly denounces their subjugation, or, in Rancière's words, declares a 'wrong' (1995/1999: 39).

Democratic restorative justice should create the conditions to enable non-political individuals – that is, victims and offenders, persons who have been harmed and persons who have harmed – to become political subjects and to articulate their disagreement with current justice arrangements as a wrong, a political injustice. Declaring a wrong involves politicising their condition and connecting their harms with wider and deeper social, economic and cultural conflicts. It involves challenging the idea of individual responsibility by connecting people's choices with contextual processes, letting emerge the fluid transactions between agency and structure that restorative encounters, largely informed by a dichotomous mentality, neglect. It also calls for contesting the absorption of one's individuality into the nostalgic horizon of communitarian justice, making conflicting voices and their claims audible.

Subjectivation consists in detaching oneself from one's natural and predefined social roles, producing new spaces and possibilities for becoming, new realms of experience, generating a new 'we' (May, 2010: 78). Against this backdrop, victim and offender, as well as person who has been harmed or person who has harmed, can transition from predetermined identities to active subject positions. This requires assisting people in restorative encounters to critically reflect on those labels and to decide together whether they are appropriate or not to name their conditions and fulfil their needs. This implies that the process of becoming a subject is not the same as taking up an identity but entails questioning an identity imposed by others upon us. Subjectivation requires disidentification, the 'creation of a space between identities in police orders' (Chambers, 2013: 104) and never passive submission to a pre-existing ethos.

Predetermined identities, in fact, tend to 'objectify social attributes whilst elevating them to constituents of an ideal identity which determines in advance what people are and what they can do' (Lane, 2013: 29). In contrast, democratic restorative justice assumes that individuals or groups have the capacity to articulate their voice, generating something different than a pre-established ethos. The challenge lies in removing barriers to these capacities, transforming restorative justice into a political movement that assists people in recognising and then distancing themselves from externally imposed social positions (Mecchia, 2010: 45). The ultimate aim of this ongoing process is the generation of the demos, an 'excessive' – that is, undetermined due to its permanent self-renewal – subject, rather than a community obsessed with its own unification (Rancière, 2000/2004: 92).

The foundation of this polemical and open-ended notion of political subjectivation is, once again, Rancière's idea of language's inherent openness to deviation from its intended meaning (Lane, 2013: 42). Subjectivation is always and only a linguistic process, relying on poetic devices which dislodge fixed arrangements by naming them as wrongs, injecting equality into them (Chambers, 2013: 20).

Politicising Facilitators

There is at least one other way to democratise restorative justice, by focusing on the role of the facilitator and drawing on Rancière's pedagogy. The educational approach described in *The Ignorant Schoolmaster* revolves around the concept of equality of intelligence. We are all provided with intelligence, and the variations in its manifestations simply depend on external factors. Rancière's pedagogy thus requires teachers to remove those obstacles, beginning with their own idea that students need someone to explain subjects to them. Explaining is an act grounded in inequality, on the presumed intellectual inferiority of learners, which reproduces inequality by 'stultifying' people and perpetuating a distribution of the sensible characterised by the subordination of one intelligence to another (Rancière, 1987/1991: 13).

A democratic restorative facilitator should avoid rigidly 'scripting' encounters, imposing fixed positions on parties and erasing, in a directive way, anything deemed irrelevant or inconsistent with the script. Such rigid structuring of the process is not a simple means towards an end but the condition for transforming an emancipatory process into a stultifying one. In fact, this hierarchical pedagogy ultimately rationalises and legitimises its own practices and institutions whilst it defers the emancipation it promises (Davis, 2013: 4). In this way, it accepts inequality, which is simply transferred from criminal justice to restorative justice.

A radical political-pedagogical approach, inspired by Rancière, assumes that everyone has the capacity to effectively participate in these democratic encounters and everyone can engage with this task, based on the presumption of equality of intelligence. In other words, people involved in harms or conflicts are deemed to have the competence and skills to deal with their own problematic situations. Yet some contingent obstacles can arise, from a lack of linguistic resources to participants' special needs. These circumstances are unrelated to intelligence, being instead factors that a democratic restorative praxis must remove, upholding the axiom of intellectual equality (Rancière, 1987/1991: 27). This approach ultimately leads to uncovering and supporting everyone's existing intellectual power, creating the conditions for realising human potential.

From this perspective, restorative facilitators should become political activists playing a role in removing obstacles both within and outside encounters that hinder the expression of participants' intellectual power and the affirmation of their equality (Citton, 2010). Emancipation, in this context, designates the process of supporting participants to engage with the meaning-making process that underlies encounters, providing space for them to translate into their own language what they have seen, heard or felt. When restorative encounters exceed the determinations of any preset narrative, only then they can produce a dissensual reconfiguration of the sensible, letting participants confront and rewrite the meanings of reality. In this way, restorative justice becomes a form of dissensus, empowering marginal voices to manifest themselves, disrupting the sense of self-evidence with which we approach the sensible and generating a space antagonistic to the hegemonic order.

Beyond Rancière

This chapter has engaged with Rancière's political theory to unpack and then rethink restorative justice as a democratic force. Rancière's method helps reconstruct restorative justice history as characterised by different regimes, which, although emerging at different times, end up coexisting in the present. The communitarian regime refers to ethical elements characterising the early, practice-based development of restorative justice: informality and an organic and participatory nature, aiming to reform criminal justice from outside. The institutional regime captures other aspects of restorative justice – namely, its imitation of criminal justice. The institutionalisation of restorative justice involves the transformation of those early practices into structured and codified processes relying on criminal justice authorities and often subordinated to their logic.

Both regimes ultimately create a police order – rigidified structures which confine participants' identities by 'scripting' their stories and limiting their possibility of expressing their voices beyond pre-existing labels. The communitarian regime anchors restorative justice to nostalgic communitarian values of return to an informal, humanised justice, whilst the institutional regime binds restorative justice to the criminal justice concepts of crime and individual responsibility. Rancière's political theory prompts a radical democratic reimagination of restorative justice. This approach does not aim to replace the existing regimes and then to solidify as a new authoritative model but to unsettle ethical and mimetic identities, creating spaces for subjugated practices, processes, bodies and voices to be seen and heard. Democratic restorative justice *is* this anarchic disruptive force seeking to reconfigure relations that communitarian and institutional representations tend to conceal.

This reconfiguration requires uncovering and challenging the criminal justice identities of victim and offender, expanding the boundaries of restorative encounters, like in restorative cities and environmental restorative justice. It also involves rethinking harms as political disagreements and wrongs, producing spaces for expressing one's capacities by removing obstacles to the affirmation of equality, enacting subjectivating processes and pushing facilitators to become political activists willing to assist parties to realise their equality. Overall, this restorative justice is democratic because it is founded on dissensus; it is an attempt at politicising what criminal justice and institutionalised versions of restorative justice depoliticise, contesting any order of the sensible based on inequality. In this context, restorative encounters become agonistic spaces which support people to rethink their social positions, providing cultural resources to connect private troubles with public issues.

Democratic restorative justice does not aim to find a stable space in the social world, becoming a hegemonic form of justice. It needs instead the existence of other regimes in order to produce that impure social space wherein new voices and bodies can count. This view highlights the fundamental connection between politics and justice – a depoliticised justice is a justice which implicitly succumbs to subjugating police orders. Democratic restorative justice, instead, is an open challenge to the seductive illusions of an objective, third-party and independent justice, as well as their implicit endorsement of hegemonic orders of the sensible. It underscores the importance of maintaining a disruptive and politically engaged approach to justice, one that continually challenges and questions existing power structures.

References

Althusser, L., Balibar, E., Estable, R., Rancière, J. and Macherey, P. (1965/1970) *Reading Capital*. London: Verso.

Apter, E. (2017) 'The Hatred of Democracy and "The Democratic Torrent": Rancière's Micropolitics'. In Bray, P. (ed.) *Understanding Rancière, Understanding Modernism*, 11–32. New York: Bloomsbury.

Bazemore, G. and Griffiths, C. T. (1997) 'Conferences, Circles, Boards, and Mediations: The "New Wave" of Community Justice Decisionmaking'. *Federal Probation*, 61(2): 25–37.

Blagg, H. (1998) 'Restorative Visions and Restorative Justice Practices: Conferencing, Ceremony and Reconciliation in Australia'. *Current Issues in Criminal Justice*, 10(1): 5–14.

Blagg, H. (2017) 'Doing Restorative Justice "Otherwise"'. In Aertsen, I. and Pali, B. (eds.) *Critical Restorative Justice*, 61–78. Oxford: Hart.

Chambers, S. (2013) *The Lessons of Rancière*. New York: Oxford University Press.

Chanter, T. (2017) 'Feminist Art: Disrupting and Consolidating the Police Order'. In Bray, P. (ed.) *Understanding Rancière, Understanding Modernism*, 147–60. New York: Bloomsbury.

Christie, N. (1977) 'Conflicts as Property'. *British Journal of Criminology*, 17(1): 1–15.

Citton, Y. (2010) 'The "Ignorant Schoolmaster": Knowledge and Authority'. In Deranty, J.-P. (ed.) *Jacques Rancière: Key Concepts*, 38–56. Durham, UK: Acumen.

Clarke, J. (2013) 'Rancière, Politics and the Social Question'. In Davis, O. (ed.) *Rancière Now: Critical Perspectives on Jacques Rancière*, 13–27. Cambridge, UK: Polity.

Davis, O. (2013) 'Editor's Introduction'. In Davis, O. (ed.) *Rancière Now: Critical Perspectives on Jacques Rancière*, 1–12. Cambridge, UK: Polity.

Deranty, J.-P. (2010) 'Introduction'. In Deranty, J.-P. (ed.) *Jacques Rancière: Key Concepts*, 1–14. Durham, UK: Acumen.

González, T. (2020) 'The Legalization of Restorative Justice: A Fifty-State Empirical Analysis'. *Utah Law Review*, 5(3): 1027–67.

Guerlac, S. (2017) 'Rancière and Proust: Two Temptations'. In Bray, P. (ed.) *Understanding Rancière, Understanding Modernism*, 161–77. New York: Bloomsbury.

Harré, H. R. and Moghaddam, F. M. (eds.) (2003) *The Self and Others: Positioning Individuals and Groups in Personal, Political, and Cultural Contexts*. Westport, CT: Praeger.

Hobson, J., Payne, B., Bangura, K. and Hester, R. (2022) '"Spaces" for Restorative Development: International Case Studies on Restorative Services'. *Contemporary Justice Review*, 25(2): 143–62.

Holmboe, M. (2017) 'Norwegian Youth Punishment – Opportunity or Trap?' *Bergen Journal of Criminal Law & Criminal Justice*, 5(1): 37–58.

Immarigeon, R. (1994) *Reconciliation between Victims and Imprisoned Offenders: Program Models and Issues*. Akron, OH: Mennonite Central Committee.

Lane, J. (2013) 'Rancière's Anti-Platonism: Equality, the "Orphan Letter" and the Problematic of Social Sciences'. In Davis, O. (ed.) *Rancière Now: Critical Perspectives on Jacques Rancière*, 28–46. Cambridge, UK: Polity.

Liebmann, M. (2007) *Restorative Justice: How It Works*. London: Jessica Kingsley Publishers.

Maglione, G. (2020) 'Restorative Justice and the State: Untimely Objections against the Institutionalisation of Restorative Justice'. *British Journal of Community Justice*, 17(1): 5–22.

Maglione, G. (2023) 'Remorse and Restoration: The Role of Remorse in Constructing the "Ideal Offender" of Restorative Justice'. In Field, S. and Tata, C. (eds.) *Remorse and Responsibility in the Constructions of the 'Ideal' Defendant: Comparing Cultural Expectations in Criminal Process*, 239–60. London: Hart.

Mannozzi, G. (2019) 'The Emergence of the Idea of a Restorative City and Its Link to Restorative Justice'. *International Journal of Restorative Justice*, 2(2): 288–92.

Marshall, T. (1999) *Restorative Justice: An Overview*. Report by the Home Office Research Development and Statistics Directorate, United Kingdom. London: Home Office, Information & Publications Group, http://www.homeoffice.gov.uk/rds/pdfs/occ-resjus.pdf. Accessed 12 December 2022.

May, T. (2010) 'Wrong Disagreement, Subjectification'. In Deranty, J.-P. (ed.) *Jacques Rancière: Key Concepts*, 80–94. Durham, UK: Acumen.

McElrea, F. W. M. (1998) 'The New Zealand Model of Family Group Conferencing'. *European Journal on Criminal Policy and Research*, 6: 527–43.

Mecchia, G. (2010) 'Philosophy and Its Poor: Rancière's Critique of Philosophy'. In Deranty, J.-P. (ed.) *Jacques Rancière: Key Concepts*, 57–68. Durham, UK: Acumen.

Pali, B., Forsyth, M. and Tepper, F. (2022) *Palgrave Handbook on Environmental Restorative Justice*. Cham, Switzerland: Springer.

Panagia, D. (2010) '"Partage du Sensible": The Distribution of the Sensible'. In Deranty, J.-P. (ed.) *Jacques Rancière: Key Concepts*, 104–15. Durham, UK: Acumen.

Rancière, J. (1987/1991) *The Ignorant Schoolmaster: Five Lessons in Intellectual Emancipation*. Stanford, CA: Stanford University Press.

Rancière, J. (1992) 'Politics, Identification, and Subjectivization'. *October*, 61: 58–64.

Rancière, J. (1995/1999) *Dis-Agreement: Politics and Philosophy*. Minneapolis: University of Minnesota Press.

Rancière, J. (2001) 'Ten Theses on Politics'. *Theory & Event*, 5(3): 1–16.

Rancière, J. (1983/2002) *The Philosopher and His Poor*. Durham, NC: Duke University Press.

Rancière, J. (2000/2004) *The Politics of Aesthetics: The Distribution of the Sensible*. London: Bloomsbury.

Rancière, J. (1990/2007) *On the Shores of Politics*. London: Verso.

Rancière, J. (2008/2009) *The Emancipated Spectator*. London: Verso.

Rancière, J. (1988/2010) *Dissensus: On Politics and Aesthetics*. London: Bloomsbury.

Rancière, J. (1996/2011) *Mallarmé: The Politics of the Siren*. New York: Continuum.

Rancière, J. (1998/2011) *Mute Speech: Literature, Critical Theory, and Politics*. New York: Columbia University Press.
Rancière, J. (2011) *Staging the People: The Proletarian and His Double*. London: Verso.
Rancière, J. (1981/2012) *Proletarian Nights*. London: Verso.
Rancière, J. (2012) *The Intellectual and His People*. London: Verso.
Rancière, J. (2013) *Aisthesis: Scenes from the Aesthetic Regime of Art*. London: Verso.
Rosenblatt, F. F. and Adamson, C. (2023) 'Non-Encounter Restorative Justice Interventions – Now What?' *Contemporary Justice Review*, 26(1): 93–110.
Sachs, L. (2017) 'The Ignorant Schoolmaster: Intellectual Emancipation in Circular Form'. In Bray, P. (ed.) *Understanding Rancière, Understanding Modernism*, 52–72. New York: Bloomsbury.
Shapland, J., Robinson, G. and Sorsby, A. (2011) *Restorative Justice in Practice: Evaluating What Works for Victims and Offenders*. London: Routledge.
Tanke, J. (2011) *Jacques Rancière: An Introduction. Philosophy, Politics, Aesthetics*. London: Bloomsbury.
Walgrave, L. (2017) 'Restorative Justice Is Not a Panacea against All Social Evils'. In Aertsen, I. and Pali, B. (eds.) *Critical Restorative Justice*, 95–110. Oxford: Hart.
Zehr, H. (2004) 'Commentary: Restorative Justice: Beyond Victim-Offender Mediation'. *Conflict Resolution Quarterly*, 22(1-2): 305–15.

Legislation

Belgium

Code d'Instruction Criminelle/Wetboek van Strafvordering [Code of Criminal Procedure], art. 216ter.
Code d'Instruction Criminelle/Wetboek van Strafvordering [Code of Criminal Procedure], art. 553(2).
Loi modifiant la loi du 8 avril 1965 relative à la protection de la jeunesse, du Code d'instruction criminelle, le Code pénal, le Code civil, la nouvelle loi communale et la loi du [24 avril 2003] réformant l'adoption [Belgian Youth Protection Act 2006], M.B., 15 May 2006.

England and Wales

Crime and Disorder Act 1998, 1998 c. 37.
Criminal Justice Act 2003, 2003 c. 44.
Criminal Justice and Immigration Act 2008, 2008 c. 4.
Youth Justice and Criminal Evidence Act 1999, 1999 c. 23.

France

Loi n° 2014–896 du 15 août 2014 relative à l'individualisation des peines et renforçant l'efficacité des sanctions pénales [Law 2014–896 of 15 August 2014 on the Individualisation of Punishment and Strengthening the Effectiveness of Penal Sanctions].

Italy

Legge 27 settembre 2021, n. 134, Delega al Governo per l'efficienza del processo penale nonché in materia di giustizia riparativa e disposizioni per la celere definizione dei procedimenti giudiziari [Law 2021–134 of 27 September 2021 on the Efficiency Of The Penal Process and in the Area of Restorative Justice and Dispositions for the Efficient Conclusion of Judicial Proceedings].

Aotearoa New Zealand

Children, Young Persons, and Their Families Act 1989.

Norway

Lov om konfliktrådsbehandling (konfliktrådsloven) [The Mediation Service Act], LOV-2014-06-20-49.

International

Council of Europe Committee of Ministers, Recommendation CM/Rec(2018)8 of the Committee of Ministers to Member States Concerning Restorative Justice in Criminal Matters (Adopted by the Committee of Ministers on 3 October 2018 at the 1326th Meeting of the Ministers' Deputies).

Council of Europe Committee of Ministers, Recommendation No. R(99)19 of the Committee of Ministers to member States Concerning Mediation in Penal Matters (Adopted by the Committee of Ministers on 15 September 1999 at the 679th Meeting of the Ministers' Deputies).

Directive 2012/29/EU of the European Parliament and the Council of 25 October 2012 Establishing Minimum Standards on the Rights, Support and Protection of Victims of Crime, and Replacing Council Framework Decision 2001/220/JHA [The Victims' Directive], OJ L315/57.

United Nations Economic and Social Council (ECOSOC) Resolution 2002/12, 'Basic Principles on the Use of Restorative Justice Programmes in Criminal Matters', UN Economic and Social Council, 37th Plenary Meeting, 24 July 2002, New York, Annex, ESCOR, 2002, suppl. no. 1, E/RES/2002/12 (24 July 2002).

7 Encountering Subalternity

Colonialism, Subalternity and Justice

Judith Butler and Jacques Rancière remind us that justice does not happen in a vacuum. Searching for, obtaining or being denied the experience of justice always takes place in specific contexts wherein human beings encounter each other. These contexts are often marked by struggles between those who are left at the margins, disenfranchised and suffering, and those who have the power to oppress both materially and culturally.

This chapter encounters Gayatri Chakravorty Spivak, a literary critic whose work has been informed by feminist concerns, Marxist analysis and deconstruction. Spivak has dedicated her career to engaging with *subalternity*, the condition of being at once politically disempowered, economically deprived and culturally silenced (1985/2020). This condition particularly affects those who live in the postcolonial world. Postcoloniality, in fact, does not merely refer to the end of colonialism but to its lingering, intergenerational and multidimensional effects. Spivak's work on the representation of subaltern voices, and on the risks of benevolent speaking on behalf of the other, is a powerful tool to criticise both identity politics and multicultural pluralism. The challenge, taken by Spivak as her lifelong mission, is to create spaces for the subalterns to reaffirm their life.

This critical stance unfolds through an itinerary in which biographical and intellectual spheres intertwine. Born in India, Spivak discovers Jacques Derrida's deconstruction during her postgraduate studies in the United States, leading to her breakthrough translation (1976) of Derrida's *De la grammatologie* (1967/1976), which introduced the French author to an American audience. Here, Derrida's deconstruction serves as a source of insights rather than a methodology, revealing how language generates domination through *masterwords* – 'workers', 'women', 'the other' – that collapse difference into identity. For Spivak, deconstruction is an ethical endeavour, as it challenges the authority of these masterwords. This intellectual ethic becomes more explicitly political when combined with Marxism and radical feminism.

While Spivak shares Marx's fundamental insights into alienation and the exploitation of labour, she adds a further dimension to this perspective. She explicitly highlights, and addresses, Marx's Eurocentric lack of reckoning with non-Western

DOI: 10.4324/9781003298359-7

socio-economic contexts, criticising his humanistic assumption that human beings are the same everywhere (Spivak, 1990, 1999).

Feminism then allows Spivak to criticise both Derrida, for his lack of genuine engagement with the gendered subject, and Marx, for his total absence of interest in the relationships between gender and social class (Spivak, 1985/2020). At the same time, deconstruction and Marxism add fundamental epistemic-normative dimensions to her feminism. Spivak's feminism, in fact, goes beyond (like Judith Butler; see the chapter on Butler in this book) the idea that 'sex is natural, gender social'. Using a deconstructive approach, Spivak challenges this binary opposition, producing an intersectional reading of gender which connects labour exploitation with the oppression of female bodies.

Encountering Spivak means not only enriching the political vocabulary of restorative justice but also reflecting on the positionality of such vocabulary, incorporating a further crucial layer into our analysis. How can restorative justice practitioners unlearn their cultural and material privileges when engaging with marginalised subjects? Can their well-intended words and actions perpetuate political and cultural exploitation? How can restorative justice reckon with its own widely acclaimed past as an ancient form of justice without collapsing cultural differences into Western identities? How can a decolonised, ethical restorative justice be developed? Ultimately, Spivak may serve as a catalyst for restorative justice to become an active force towards the re-establishment of a justice that is more than Western justice.

Encountering Spivak

Spivak's work follows a trajectory which is marked by recurrent themes – the entanglement of cultural and material struggles, the importance of a gendered focus, the acknowledgement of one's inevitable situatedness. Nevertheless, it is possible to observe significant shifts in emphasis over time, such that some of those overarching motives appear as more prominent at different stages of her career.

In the 1970s, after some early works on William Butler Yeats (1974), Spivak publishes her breakthrough translation of Derrida's *De la grammatologie* (1967/1976), including her introduction (1976), giving her an immediate reputation as a key interpreter of deconstruction. Her introduction is still considered a key entrance into this field, whilst at the time, it initiated the debate on Derrida in Anglo-American academia. Spivak understands deconstruction as a critique of Western thought, an endeavour to problematise the Western intellectual tradition by engaging with it as if reading a complex text.

'French Feminism in an International Frame' (1981) and 'Displacement and the Discourse of Woman' (1983) mark Spivak's first attempts at approaching deconstruction with a feminist lens. These works make visible the connections between deconstruction and the exploitation of women within the economy of property and international capital. They also provide insightful commentaries on French feminist thinkers, like Julia Kristeva, Luce Irigaray, and Hélène Cixous.

The 1980s see Spivak further developing her deconstructive-feminist critique, and also the beginning of her gendered critique of the effects of colonialism. In

Can the Subaltern Speak? (1985/2020), Spivak critiques colonialism's epistemic violence and its implications for the gendered subject. In this essay, she famously objects to the benevolent yet epistemically violent attempt, made by European intellectuals (such as Michel Foucault and Gilles Deleuze), to create an essentialised subject – the masses – supposedly able to represent itself (Spivak, 1985/2020: 8). In this way, an anonymous *other* is generated and, despite the anti-essentialist premises of Foucault's and Deleuze's works, objectified.

This Eurocentric approach is particularly problematic when considering marginalised women from the Global South. These women are unable to represent their own interests mainly because colonialism has changed the status of the precolonial subject, causing their 'pure' and 'innocent' voices to be irreparably lost. The *subaltern* (a word coined by Marxist philosopher Antonio Gramsci) is the position occupied by those who are at once politically disempowered, economically deprived and epistemically silenced (Spivak, 1985/2020: 28). Women occupy a distinctive subaltern position as gendered postcolonial subjects, and Spivak's aim is to access their subjectivity by deconstructing their identity, understood as the product of the colonialist Eurocentric representation of non-Western women. This approach inaugurates postcolonial studies and specifically postcolonial feminism as a response to Western feminist movements, which focused almost exclusively on the experiences of Western women. Instead of offering a neat theory or a discrete methodology, this perspective deconstructs the impacts of colonialism and globalisation on female bodies in the Global South, unearthing the intertwining of epistemic-cultural violence and capitalism.

These crucial themes are further developed in *In Other Worlds: Essays in Cultural Politics* (1987/2006), which includes essays refining Spivak's deconstructive reading of Marx and feminism, tied to a critique of them as lacking context-specific sensitivity to the condition of the proletariat in the Global South.

During the 1990s, Spivak first gathers her major contributions to the postcolonial field in *The Post-Colonial Critic* (1990) and then attempts to critically distance herself from some of the developments of postcolonial studies (1999). *The Post-Colonial Critic* consists of a selection of interviews and discussions that took place in the late 1980s. Here, Spivak reflects on questions of representation and self-representation, the politicisation of deconstruction, the situation of postcolonial critics, intellectual responsibility and political strategies. *A Critique of Postcolonial Reason* (Spivak, 1999) examines how European culture has turned non-Western subjects into 'native informants' (ibid.: ix), that is, commodified objects of knowledge without ethical substance. Spivak charges postcolonial scholars with adopting this simplifying viewpoint when, in good faith, they try to represent non-Western cultures. This book reflects on what a responsible postcolonial critic would look like, working on a wide range of authors and subjects, from Kant to Marx, from the concept of the sublime to child labour in Bangladesh.

In this same period, Spivak starts engaging directly with pedagogical questions, drawing on her experience as a teacher in Bangladesh. In the collection *Outside in the Teaching Machine* (Spivak, 1993/2009), she presents critical analyses of works of literature as a starting point for questioning power structures and reflecting on the political function of pedagogy.

The 2000s see Spivak returning to the relationship between language, women and culture and further expanding on themes of pedagogy and of the responsibility and complicity integral to every act of communication. This is the case for the essays collected in *An Aesthetic Education in the Era of Globalization* (Spivak, 2013), which propose to read the present by drawing on the idea of an aesthetic education for implementing global justice and democracy.

Overall, Spivak's itinerary is marked by the dynamic interrelations between deconstruction, feminism and Marxism. A constant theme is to use the resulting approach to read critically postcoloniality as a condition to improve the subaltern's life. Spivak's confrontation with the entanglement of economic conditions, cultural representation (or lack thereof), and political organisation outlines a cultural politics that leads us to rethink (restorative) justice by drawing on a combination of unexpected sources, ideas and theories.

Spivak's Approach

Spivak's background is characterised by a fundamental tendency to cross disciplinary boundaries, sometimes producing puzzling effects in readers who might instead expect epistemological, methodological and conceptual consistency. Spivak deliberately pursues such effects, not only by engaging with disparate cultural spheres but also by inventively addressing Derrida, Marx and feminist scholars.

Spivak (1976) starts off from Derrida's metaphysical understanding of deconstruction. This highlights how the Western philosophical tradition and culture are built on a series of binary oppositions – for example, male/female and writing/speech – that entail a hierarchy of one of the binary terms over the other (Spivak, 1987/2006: 103). Deconstruction aims first to displace and then to reverse such binary pairs by reinscribing the 'inferior' term (e.g. female or speech) as the origin of the opposition and the hierarchy itself (Spivak, 1996: 30). This approach is meant to show that the meaning of any word is nothing but a play of difference with other words, and therefore, a stable meaning is never achieved. For instance, our comprehension of 'speech' arises from its distinction from 'writing', our understanding of 'good' is shaped by its opposition to 'bad', and so forth. Consequently, meaning is in a perpetual state of postponement. This situation of differing and deferral of meaning is what Derrida calls '*différance*' (Spivak, 1976: xliii). From this angle, linguistic meaning is created rather than given, fluid instead of fixed, and hierarchies are always culturally determined.

Spivak uses deconstruction inventively, as an intellectual ethic that proposes to resist the institutionalisation of culture through authoritative and apparently neutral truths (1996: 27). She looks at the world as a text to be read, paying attention to its multiple and endless possibilities, destabilising the Western tradition of establishing a (Western) centre as a parameter to understand ourselves and the world we inhabit. In this way, Spivak examines and contests conventional theoretical concepts that have historically rationalised the exploitation and colonisation of non-Western societies, such as sovereignty, citizenship and individual rights (Morton, 2008: 54). Deconstruction allows Spivak to unpack not only these concepts but also the supposedly emancipatory terminologies employed by political movements. She highlights how terms like 'workers', 'women' and 'colonised' tend to encapsulate and oversimplify the experiences of minorities. Spivak contends that such words represent a misuse (or *catachresis*) of multifaceted struggles, reduced to cohesive and universal entities, with supposed material referents, which often conceal their (Western) origin and (Westernising) effects (1990: 104).

Clearly, this creative use of deconstruction carries an ethical dimension, since it challenges all supposedly universal frameworks that cause epistemic harm to non-Western subjects as a precondition of material oppression. Spivak, following Derrida (and Emmanuel Levinas), seeks ways of encountering *the other* as an ethical singularity, as *others* not reduced to a chain of universal labels. This encounter is never risk-free: there is always the risk of inadvertently silencing others' voices, and the awareness of such a limit is the key condition for an ethical encounter.

Spivak grafts Marxism and feminism onto this idea of ethical deconstruction. She reassesses Marxism by keeping the fundamental aspects of capitalist alienation and exploitation of labour while criticising Marx's neglect of non-Western economic and social realities. There is a strong Eurocentric bias in Marx's thoughts, expressed by his attempt to fit non-European contexts (e.g. the Asiatic mode of production) into a Eurocentric narrative. Spivak challenges Marx's idea that the working-class struggle for economic equality represents the political interest of all humanity, regardless of place or time. This perspective, in fact, overlooks other marginalised constituencies, such as women and the colonised, and their unique needs. Spivak argues that contemporary economic exploitation requires a context-sensitive and gendered analysis of the relations of production.

Radical anti-essentialist feminism enriches the Marxist analysis of production and its effects. The idea that 'one is not born but becomes a woman' is certainly a good starting point, but, Spivak maintains, there is a need to contextualise this claim historically and geographically. Working on Kristeva, Irigaray and Cixous, Spivak reclaims the experience of the female body, insisting that Western feminism must recognise the material, embodied experiences of 'Third World' women. She criticises European feminism for, much like Marxism, adopting a Eurocentric perspective that uses the Western woman as its paradigm, underscoring how modern transnational capitalism exploits women's productive bodies (Spivak, 1987/2006). This critique prompts a re-examination of Marxism that moves away from the conventional, androcentric and European definition of the working class and acknowledges the exploitation of disenfranchised working women in the Third World.

The relationship between Marxism, feminism and deconstruction is circular. Spivak, in fact, not only uses Marxism and feminism to politicise deconstruction but also utilises Derrida's intellectual ethics to uncover the inherent presumptions and omissions in both Marxism and feminism and their claims to represent and speak on behalf of all oppressed individuals.

In the first case, she deconstructs the binary opposition between capitalism and socialism, claiming that socialism cannot exist independently of the capital relation. She thus challenges simplistic notions of political and economic autonomy, highlighting the complex interplay of global economic forces and structural inequalities. Similarly, Spivak argues that the conventional definition of woman is often rooted in the word man. From a deconstructive point of view, it is necessary to move beyond this limiting and binary framework by proposing a more epistemically aware understanding of gender (Spivak, 1990: 70). It is necessary to challenge the universal feminist subject by calling for a more inclusive (intersectional) understanding that transcends Western-centric perspectives.

From Postcoloniality to Subalternity

The result of these transdisciplinary combinations is a critical approach concerned with creating a space wherein epistemic-political challenges related to Western truths, and their material effects, are unearthed and addressed in order to encounter the ethical singularity of the other (Spivak, 1995). Operating from the margins of central discourses, Spivak interrogates the mechanisms that generate and sustain these truths, foregrounding *subalternity* as the position wherein multiple forms of oppression intersect, removing people 'from the lines of social mobility' (2004: 531).

Deconstruction helps Spivak displace and reverse the effects of masterwords such as woman, worker and colonised. It highlights the normative and epistemic challenge posed by colonial exploitation which imposes a fixed representation of the oppressed. Drawing on Marx, she suggests that Western representations of the colonial and postcolonial world conflate two distinct meanings of representation: 'speaking for', in the sense of political representation, and the aesthetic sense of 'speaking about' (Spivak, 1985/2020: 19). Speaking on behalf of 'the masses', as benevolent Western intellectuals often do, further silences the colonial others, whilst aesthetic representation, if ethically aware of its inevitable othering effects, can generate some spaces for reactivating the political agency of the represented.

The concept of subalternity, here, provides Spivak with the sufficient flexibility to describe moments of subordination which cut across epistemic, political, economic and gender spheres to indicate the multidimensional effects of colonisation. Subalternity signifies not only economic exploitation but also the process of censoring voices (for instance, by marginalising local literature or negating access to historical records) whilst creating narratives that legitimise the capitalist-colonialist uneven distribution of resources. This dynamic particularly affects gendered subjects, who are more than others unable to represent themselves. Representation is the point of suture between the political, economic and epistemic spheres, to be contextualised geographically and with regard to gender (Spivak, 1985/2020).

This approach ends up being critical of postcolonial studies itself and the classical Marxist methodology that underpins it. Whilst Spivak greatly contributed to the birth of postcolonial studies, as seen earlier, at one point she distanced herself from it. The classical Marxist postcolonial approach is too rigid to accommodate the diverse and complex social history of Third World realities, and it is too restrictive since it is geared only to class politics. Instead, there is a need to incorporate liberation struggles, such as peasants' and women's movements (Spivak, 1987/2006). Additionally, postcolonial studies portray the colonised as 'sovereign' subjects, able to articulate their oppressed voice, neglecting the intertwinement of the colonised's voice and coloniser's violence. The subalterns' voices are inevitably contaminated, as impure as their consciousness is fragmented and contextual (Spivak, 1985/2020).

Expanding and complicating her own initial perspective, Spivak aims to show that when the subalterns attempt to speak, their voice is not recognised in the dominant political systems of representation. The challenge, therefore, is to acknowledge the power relationships imbricated with any form of cultural exchange, generating spaces for inclusive and expansive cross-cultural communication and an ethics that is aware of the limits of encountering and knowing others (cf. Spivak, 1996: 142).

Deconstructing Restorative Justice

A deconstructive critique combines an engagement with restorative justice masterwords and a Marxist-feminist analysis of their premises and effects, particularly within the postcolonial world. This approach reveals that restorative justice is largely a postcolonial endeavour, with significant epistemic and material limitations that demand philosophical consideration.

Masterwords and Institutionalisation

Restorative justice relies on a set of masterwords that form its conceptual foundations. These words are rooted in a *logocentric* bias – that is, in the idea that there exists an authoritative and transcendent foundation to ensure the fixed meaning of language (Derrida, 1967/1976: 43). These words function as oversimplifications of unique, fluid and contextual social relations, which are ossified as binary oppositions. Deconstruction challenges the dualistic thinking and assumed hierarchies that form the foundation of restorative justice, opening up possibilities for reinterpretation grounded in the openness of language.

Crime and *harm* are two fundamental concepts in restorative justice, bound by a binary hierarchical opposition. Crime, within restorative justice theory, is interpreted as the legal manifestation of an interpersonal conflict, while harm refers to the material and psychological consequences of a crime (cf. Zehr, 2005). The classification of behaviour as criminal wrongdoing remains in the hands of criminal justice agencies. Harm, instead, is defined by the victim and acknowledged by the offender upon admitting their responsibility. The concept of crime serves as a framework supporting the definition of harm. Crime, in fact, establishes the conceptual boundaries of harm, from the outside. It operates as a backdrop against which harm is described, thereby endorsing criminal justice agencies' definitional power (since they decide what a crime is). In this way, restorative justice is positioned as a response to the needs arising from supposedly dysfunctional social relationships, with harm being parasitic on a legal definition of crime.

Similarly, *victim* and *offender* as well as *state* and *community* are masterwords, denoting the primary subjects that populate restorative justice. They refer to entities with predefined characteristics rather than subject positions constructed within discourses through practices like classification, norm-setting, and foregrounding/backgrounding. The victim is the embodied recipient of material or psychological reparation, while the offender is the wrongdoer who harms a specific victim, often due to a lack of emotional understanding and moral maturity (Maglione, 2017b). The community is a law-abiding collective subject functioning as the fusional context within which crimes take place. Community serves as the local alternative to the state, understood as the 'cold monster' that steals crimes from the rightful owners.

Lastly, *restoration* and *punishment*. The concept of restoration encompasses and goes beyond the idea of reparation; it is not solely the material fixing of the consequences of a crime but a process that serves innovative functions and fulfils different needs triggered by harm. Restoration is characterised by recurring traits: it is holistic, needs-based and emotionally intelligent (cf. Van Ness and Strong, 2022). This view suggests the intimate interconnectedness of various aims within restorative justice, the combination of symbolic and material, moral and psychological elements around the ideal restorative outcome. This is envisioned as transcending cultural, social and personal differences since it can satisfy needs (apparently) rooted in human nature – such as safety, justice, participation and empowerment. This position underscores the (supposedly) universal needs of the individuals or communities harmed by a crime.

Overall, such masterwords reduce multifaceted relationships and conflicts to binary, cohesive and universal entities that often conceal their (Western) origin and (Westernising) effects. Spivak proposes to displace and reverse these binary oppositions and their implied hierarchies, questioning the privileged status of one term in a pair over the other – victim over offender, restoration over punishment, community over state. Meaning, in fact, is continuously deferred and differentiated within a chain of signifiers, with each signifier referring to others in an endless process of deferral. Displacing these words means focusing on the inherent impossibility of establishing meaning definitively, and therefore on the arbitrariness of immutable hierarchies. Consequently, this approach demands ethical and political thought to address the contextuality of those hierarchies.

Victim/offender, restoration/punishment and community/state are oppositional pairs in which the first term is assumed to be hierarchically superior to the second, with an ontological differentiation of meaning between them. These oppositions, and implied hierarchies, are instead socially constructed through language. Such constructions have powerful material effects, impacting on people's lives and destinies. This perspective highlights the instability of restorative justice, ultimately pointing to the fundamental undecidability – that is, openness and variability – of language, the absence of an absolute fixed meaning. Those masterwords instead seem to propose a 'closure' of the restorative language, which is problematic insofar as they do not reflect universal needs but context-specific interests.

This closure is further strengthened by the process of institutionalising/legalising restorative justice. From a deconstructive standpoint, institutionalisation can be interpreted as the ossification of speech into writing and the transformation of masterwords into law. Historically, Western culture has favoured written language over speech, a preference seemingly mirrored in the legalisation of restorative justice over its informal and organic nature. 'Writing' restorative justice involves the creation of laws, delineating a separation between the 'natural' origin of justice and its institutionalisation in writing. However, Spivak's interpretation does not seek to prioritise 'nature' over 'culture', or speech over writing, since these would be yet another set of binary hierarchical oppositions. Instead of considering nature (restorative justice) and institution (law) as existing independently, deconstruction proposes an understanding in which nature itself is constructed in relation to the institution. Law is not a direct representation of restorative justice; rather, our comprehension of both restorative justice and law is shaped by their dynamic interplay. This perspective blurs the rigid separation between them, rejecting the notion that restorative justice is an objectively pre-existing organic phenomenon that was at one point rediscovered by scholars and practitioners. Similarly, viewing law as a direct embodiment of the natural origin of restorative justice overlooks and conceals other potential interpretations of justice that are not explicitly represented in the law.

This approach challenges the idea that institutionalising restorative justice entails an ontological mutation of justice, rejecting the transcendental origin of law and the idea that one can go beyond the institution to discover something external – an autonomous origin, an 'outside of the text'. The dominant concept of restorative justice as a discrete victim-oriented process legitimises itself as a way of legislating the natural order, suppressing competing interpretations that nevertheless persist as traces within this dominant meaning. The still-existing debates around the definition of restorative justice among scholars reflect the existence of such traces (see Rosenblatt and Mazzucato, 2023).

Marxist-Feminist Analysis

From a classical Marxist perspective, restorative justice appears to be based on implicit class factors and characterised by the privatisation/commodification of harms and the neglect of social conflicts. Restorative justice foregrounds privatised notions of harm and restoration as opposed to crime and punishment. Harm is a relational phenomenon, opposed to the state-centric concept of crime, to be addressed through a holistic process which embodies both procedural and substantive justice elements. Privatisation refers not only to the exclusion of the state from the handling of social harms but also to the fact that harms are a private matter detached from larger social and economic factors. Restorative justice, in fact, biographises social harms and neglects their social history, focusing only on victims' and offenders' personal stories. The only transindividual element here is represented by the community, understood as an affective and functionalist entity characterised by social equilibrium (Koen, 2005). The harm alters this equilibrium, appearing as a social disturbance and a pathology to be cured within this community (cf. Maglione, 2017a).

This view overlooks the fact that social conflicts are the 'contexts' of relational harms. Restorative justice tends to disregard structural class conflict and its role as motor for social change because it is underpinned by a distinctively functionalist epistemology and individualising morality (Koen, 2005). The community portrayed in restorative justice appears as a unified, natural entity representing only one class, ignoring the reality of diverse social constituencies within it. Restorative justice seems to neglect that crime, criminalisation and harm are related to social conflict. Additionally, when positing the restoration of community harmony as its aim, restorative justice indirectly encourages stakeholders to accept the structure of capitalist exploitation (cf. Maglione, 2017a). In this way, the restorative process becomes a mechanism of class domination, disguised behind the façade of promoting social peace. The idea of restoration through empowerment and healing fails to recognise that these notions can vary significantly across different social classes (cf. Willis, 2020). Whether stakeholders have access to material resources or not is crucial to addressing the harm they have been involved in. Their capacity to actively participate in the process is contingent on their social conditions. Similarly, without such contextualisation, the reintegration process risks merely imposing conformity to the capitalist social structure, concealed by the veneer of a harmonious, affective-functional community (Koen, 2005). This mechanism turns social harms and their underpinning conflicts into a privatised commodity exchanged among the stakeholders. These are deemed to be formally equal, though formal equality can mask substantive inequality.

Overall, from a classical Marxist perspective, restorative justice works as a negation of the social antagonisms and economic conflicts that linger below social harms, desocialising and depoliticising them. In the consensus-based restorative justice process, the personal story of harm takes over the social history of conflict, inadvertently reproducing unequal social relations that perpetuate capitalist structures.

Radical anti-essentialist feminism, as employed by Spivak, enhances this socio-economic analysis, unearthing its affective-gendered dimension. The production of gender, in fact, is a process inextricably linked to relations of economic production. When restorative justice practices structurally neglect social conflict, they implicitly endorse and legitimise the gender roles implied by those conflicts – namely, the subordination of women to men and the complete silencing of non-binary genders. This process is fraught with uneven distributions of socio-economic and cultural resources, which make it particularly oppressive. The emphasis on restoring a harmonious community sidesteps issues of social accountability, institutional power and the creation of relationships that could rectify structurally uneven gendered relations. To truly promote equality within restorative processes, it is crucial to prioritise substantive equality over formal equality, acknowledging and challenging deeply entrenched societal structures, which affect the access to and participation in restorative encounters (Jülich and Thorburn, 2017).

The feminisation of restorative justice – that is, the idea of restorative justice as a form of 'emotionally intelligent' justice – is stereotypical and essentialised too (cf. Sherman, 2003). The stereotype that women are more emotional than men perpetuates harmful gender norms, restricting women's agency and contributing to inequality. Moreover, harmful gender stereotypes, when combined with other biases, can have a disproportionately adverse impact on specific groups of women. The idealisation of victims as powerless is also problematic since it essentialises a subject position which may not fit many actual people harmed.

This situation raises concerns about the potential of restorative justice to perpetuate and worsen unequal power dynamics marked by gender-based inequalities. In short, there is a need to consider whether the feminisation of restorative justice might intensify the marginalisation of women in society (Hodgson, 2022).

Spivak's crucial contention is that whilst a Marxist-feminist scrutiny empowers us to bring to light the gendered socio-economic conflicts underpinning harms, deconstruction helps make this analysis epistemologically and normatively more searing.

Postcolonial Restorative Justice

Deconstruction, Marxism and European feminism are informed by a Eurocentric bias. They either overlook non-European realities of cultural silencing, labour exploitation and gender oppression or attend selectively to such contexts, ultimately imposing a European perspective, with colonising effects. Spivak contextualises deconstruction, the Marxist analysis of labour alienation and the feminist concern for the exploitation of female bodies, placing them into the framework of colonisation and its consequences. The result is a gender-sensitive cultural politics of capitalist colonialism which uses deconstruction to critique those intersecting forms of exploitation and creating spaces for new epistemic-normative arrangements. The final aim is not the retrieval of the colonised's pure and innocent voice but an expansive, intersectional critique which captures a new subjectivity – *subalternity*. Subalternity is the product of this analysis, the intersection of multiple positions of cultural/material oppression, subsumed under a common yet flexible subject position which demands critical reckoning and ethical-political action.

From this angle, whilst criminal justice seems to reflect a typical colonial mindset, restorative justice appears to embody a postcolonial ethos. Postcolonial restorative justice conflates the two meanings of representation indicated by Marx. Representing community in restorative justice, for instance, seems to entail both a portrayal of community as a material entity and an attempt at making the community speak. This is a problematic operation since community is not a thing or place but an imagined and context-specific category without a literal referent (Kaasila-Pakanen, 2021). Analogously, victim and offender are represented as ontologically different entities, expressing completely different needs and erasing the multiple forms that harming and being harmed can take, including the nuanced overlap between them.

Restorative justice appears to be built on the cultural, social and economic foundations of the West, which inform the English-speaking academic world in particular. Additionally, the representation of colonised perspectives often comes from Western subjects – academics or policy entrepreneurs – who speak on behalf of non-Western constituencies. This is the paradigm of the postcolonial formation of the theoretical, empirical and normative foundations of restorative justice (Tauri, 2013). Restorative justice works as a novel criminological approach aiming to indigenise criminal justice. However, this operation is only superficially context-sensitive since it is aligned with the worldviews and interests of Western cultural institutions, policymakers and, ultimately, the neo-colonial state. The idea of Indigenous-informed restorative practices, the connection with state policymaking, the hegemony of Anglophone voices in shaping the restorative justice agenda and the professionalisation of practices are all claims with colonising effects. Similarly, restorative justice masterwords, which embrace a universalistic notion of human nature, can turn restorative practices into interventions exerting epistemic-normative control over non-Western individuals who are not aligned with these supposedly universal ideas (Tauri, 2013).

This critique highlights how certain restorative justice models, such as family group conferences (FGCs) in Australia and Aotearoa New Zealand, may not be as culturally sensitive as they are portrayed. FGCs are usually described as an example of context-specific restorative justice or, even more often, as the offspring of traditional justice practices. However, researchers have persuasively argued that, rather than a model of culturally appropriate justice practice, FGCs are perceived by some Māori participants as imposing Western, formulaic and standardised processes, rejecting the notion that they are truly culture-sensitive (Moyle and Tauri, 2016).

Similarly, by foregrounding notions of guilt and responsibility, restorative justice disavows the role of systemic, colonial factors leading to criminalisation. This is encapsulated by the offender's acknowledgement of responsibility as a condition to enter restorative justice programs. Yet guilt and responsibility are distinctively Western concepts with specific historical roots which do not reflect any preliminary cultural engagement with non-Western understandings of conflict and harm (Winterdyk, 2021). Likewise, the stereotypical idea that Indigenous worldviews primarily rely on healing and interconnectedness, as opposed to state-centric ideas of fairness, rights and equality, is a hyper-simplifying binary opposition which orientalises Indigenous struggles within postcolonial states, undermining their effectiveness (Smith, 2022).

The categorisation of restorative justice as an Indigenous form of justice, or a justice rooted in local justice traditions, can be read ultimately as a postcolonial state's attempt to justify Western crime-control models. This endeavour is expressed by the claim that those practices are intended to assist Indigenous offenders, ultimately resulting in legitimising state interventions (Smith, 2022). The Indigenous participant, in this way, is turned into a commodified 'native informant' (Spivak, 1999: ix), an infantilised and passive subject who is written out of any significant ethical existence by those postcolonial justice narratives.

In short, postcolonial restorative justice seems to obliterate what Spivak calls the process of 'worlding' integral to any form of justice (1985: 247). This concept designates the intricate process of understanding the diverse, interconnected worlds inhabited by individuals and communities. Social categories such as Indigenous roots, guilt and responsibility are part of historically, culturally and geographically specific worlds. Using such concepts to market novel justice practices with a significant Western imprint (cf. Spivak, 2004) would cause epistemic distortions with detrimental ethical and political effects on those who are supposed to benefit from them – Indigenous people. The risk here is to make a political use of history to sell a state-friendly notion of restorative justice to policymakers around the world (Levers, 2023), irrespective of its effects on already marginalised constituencies (cf. Spivak, 2013: 57).

The political representations of the world embodied in these exercises of apparently benevolent postcolonial justice should be critically appraised. The worlding implicit in postcolonial restorative justice lacks awareness of how colonial histories have influenced the construction and perception of justice. The main concern here is how certain groups are represented in the process of postcolonial worlding, how their perspectives are disavowed and how their voices are spoken by others. This is a typical example of hegemonic political representation which 'flat-packs' the diverse ways in which people experience their worlds, standardising the complexities of various cultural contexts under overarching labels to make those practices more appealing (Blagg, 2017: 71).

Overall, postcolonial restorative justice seems unaware of the intersectional dimensions of people's experiences. It does not consider the possibility that individuals may inhabit multiple, intersecting social positions, such as gender, race, class, place and more, which shape their experience of the world.

Subaltern Restorative Justice

Ultimately, deconstruction poses ethical and political questions related to restorative justice's epistemic structure and material effects. Subalternity, used as a normative framework, can help address those questions turning restorative justice into an intersectional praxis aiming to redress unbalanced power dynamics. This reflection requires the awareness that any justice practice is epistemically and materially determined and that innocent and pure voices cannot be retrieved. Yet it is possible to engage in dialogues which try to incorporate different concepts of the world – and their power differentials – and which critically attend to different experiences of oppression (Spivak, 1990: 19).

Decolonising Restorative Justice

Subalternity, as argued earlier, designates interlocking dimensions of cultural, economic and gendered subordination. This condition is exacerbated when (benevolent) postcolonial scholars, activists or practitioners attempt to make subalterns 'speak'. The entanglement of subordinated voices and subordinating violence renders subaltern voices inevitably contaminated, and this impurity needs to be reckoned with. The challenge is, therefore, to acknowledge the power relationships imbricated with any form of encounter as a precondition to generating spaces for inclusive and expansive cross-cultural communication and then material emancipation.

Postcolonial restorative justice disempowers non-Western forms of justice by categorising them as mythical 'roots' lost in time, thus diminishing their actual significance (cf. Sylvester, 2003; Levers, 2023). A subaltern-sensitive restorative justice needs to acknowledge and understand its potential to compel people to adopt a Western-centric logic of justice – binary, abstracting, generalising, functionalist, conservative. The process of de-Westernisation requires postcolonial restorative justice to 'unlearn its privileges' (Danius, Jonsson and Spivak, 1993: 24). The masterwords characterising restorative justice, to which participants must adapt in order to be suitable to restorative justice, should be critically addressed and not passively accepted by or actively forced upon participants. Imposing this logic and its masterwords is another way of legitimising the hegemonic power of the West, where the West is the standard which often marks *the other* as backward and irrational, making Western justice fulfil a civilising mission. The issue is to think of a non-logocentric justice which deliberately challenges the epistemic violence and power imbalances enshrined in Western forms of justice.

A subaltern-sensitive restorative justice aims at establishing counter-hegemonic spaces that facilitate new interpretations of the world, paving the way for social and material transformations (Darder, 2018). These spaces are characterised by both diversity and resistance to a universally fixed language. This language, anchored in Western epistemologies of patriarchal dominance, class divisions and racialising reproduction, marginalises voices suspected of purportedly outmoded and uncivilised claims. There is a need to advance an approach that negotiates abstract and general notions of responsibility, guilt, victim, offender, state and community by incorporating other, creative, risk-taking, material, concrete and specific epistemological sensibilities (Darder, 2018).

The design of these spaces cannot be predetermined; they should entail collaboration with subaltern constituencies, the establishment of power-sharing partnerships between service agencies and subaltern individuals and groups, in contrast to the prevailing top-down, managerialist approach that prioritises administrative and measurable outcomes, such as victim satisfaction and reoffending (Moyle and Tauri, 2016). Restorative justice actors should be actively involved in the entire process – from identifying needs to designing and directly delivering the programs, including program evaluation. Decentralisation in the design and facilitation of these encounters requires a comprehensive understanding of the social context surrounding subaltern issues. The challenge lies in transitioning from a focus on efficiently delivering services and on Eurocentric notions of evidence-based policy to an emphasis on initiatives allowing for diversity, which avoid defining subalterns according to Western standards and treating their cultural beliefs and practices as mere add-ons (Moyle and Tauri, 2016).

As said earlier, this is not merely an epistemological effort but an epistemic-normative endeavour to reinvent a decolonising stance aimed at social transformation. Decolonisation, here, seeks to demystify the artificial limits imposed by racialised and gendered formations and economic hierarchies, recognising all cultures and linguistic systems as significant. This approach requires practitioners who are willing to think of themselves as active participants (not passive or neutral facilitators) and acknowledge their knowledge as inherently partial, unfinished and deeply influenced by specific gendered, historical, economic and cultural configurations (Darder, 2018).

More broadly, restorative justice must fulfil its potential as a politically transformative force; it must become an integral part of the struggle for effective decolonisation, challenging the norms of Western knowledge and questioning the assumptions underlying concepts of justice (Cunneen, 2002). From this angle, subaltern restorative justice embodies a non-harm principle, by minimising its possible detrimental effects on contexts, and an anti-oppressive aim, by challenging the power relations embedded in criminal justice systems. It then seeks to create a platform for individuals to articulate their unique experiences of hierarchy and disenfranchisement (Asadullah, 2021).

Restorative Justice and Political Pedagogy

Spivak provides pedagogical-political tactics which can be taken up to generate a subaltern-sensitive restorative justice. 'Strategic essentialism' designates the use of stereotypes by a group as a means of subverting the forces that oppress them (Danius, Jonsson and Spivak, 1993: 34). These stereotypes are adopted yet not completely adhered to by these individuals, who keep themselves at a critical distance from these labels. For example, the label 'Indian', as a designation of national identity, certainly oversimplified the diversity of people living in India, yet it helped create a sense of unity strategic to the struggle against British colonial rule. Strategic essentialism remains, therefore, an anti-essentialist tactic, justified by the political opportunity of reappropriating negative categories for emancipatory aims, though it requires that groups deliberately downplay their internal differences to create a sense of unity as a condition for political struggle.

Strategic essentialism (similarly to Butler's 'resignification' and Rancière's 'fatherless language'; see the previous chapters) can be adopted to counter marginalising discourses by using them against their intended outcomes. In the case of restorative justice, its postcolonial effects due to the use of Western-centric masterwords can be countered by appropriating critically some of those abstract labels. Concepts like victim, community and restoration, as well as offender, state and punishment, can confine groups within overly simplistic, restrictive epistemic spaces, limiting their self-understanding and self-representation. Yet, individuals and groups so defined can reappropriate those labels as a temporary tactic to enter restorative encounters and then to articulate their need to have their contexts and social histories recognised, pushing encounters away from imposing one-size-fits-all identities (Eide, 2016).

A related tactic is that of 'affirmative sabotage' (Spivak, 2013: 4). This consists of an overt challenge to epistemic-political principles in order to subvert instead of merely discarding them. Rather than seeking uncontaminated native knowledge or destroying everything as colonial, affirmative sabotage promotes a critical analysis of the complicity of certain restorative justice categories in limiting the transformative potential of restorative encounters. Restorative justice becomes problematic when it fails to comprehend its inevitable political and ethical situatedness. The core of this tactic involves the '*uncoercive* rearrangement of desires' (Spivak, 2004: 526), the process of reshaping subjectivity in both colonial and postcolonial restorative justice. This entails not only entering but also fully engaging with the discourse or system that is being criticised, undermining it from within. It is a form of subversion that acknowledges the need for insider engagement to bring about effective change.

Practitioners may play a crucial role here, though they need to embrace their function both politically and pedagogically (Spivak, 2013). We need practitioners fully engaged with a form of cultural literacy which culminates in unlearning their own privileges and then acting upon this new self-awareness. The aim would be to become a critical reader of culturally diverse contexts, develop a sensible readerly imagination and move beyond the identitarian confines dictated by masterwords. There is a need for imaginative training to assist practitioners to detect their own internalised cultural stereotypes, which work as taken-for-granted truths. Practitioners, for instance, are often deeply entrenched in technical and operational discourses, losing sight of how such discourses disguise the specific cultural roots of their training or practice.

The goal should be to unveil the constructed nature of the restorative masterwords and their hierarchical binary relations, identifying the concealed mechanisms behind the representation of peoples' needs. We need to imagine training as a space to reflect on how master narratives related to nationality, gender and class often produce stereotypes that obscure the subjectivity of others. Training, here, is about demythologising universal figures, critically questioning assumptions about the conditions of knowledge, disrupting assumed certainties and encouraging a critical engagement with concepts such as restoration or harm (cf. Castro Varela, 2020; Purcell, 2020).

Practitioners should be trained to acknowledge their situatedness by examining their role within restorative justice and the position of restorative justice within Western culture. Instead of passively letting participants 'speak', they should immerse themselves in the culture of participants in restorative encounters. In this way, practitioners can relate to participants, imaginatively entering their world, reading it as a text, whilst recognising their own liminality with respect to participants' lives.

Privilege – in the form of reliance on essentialist taxonomies and cultural reductionism – can create a form of isolation that disconnects those who possess it from certain forms of alternative knowledge. It is essential to acknowledge these limitations and address them, not merely as an inclusive gesture but to expand one's understanding. This involves critically scrutinising and challenging personal beliefs, biases and assumptions to grasp their origins and normalisation.

Adopting this approach amounts to undergoing an epistemic-political transformation that may help practitioners experience themselves *relationally*. This means rethinking participants not as mere objects of knowledge or as perfectly autonomous actors, but as subjects who navigate and construct their identities – not only in response to their personal stories and social histories but also in response to how practitioners relate to them.

Encountering Ethical Singularities

These tactics may constitute a viable political strategy only if they are combined with a broader ethical-political strategy. Restorative justice's postcolonial ethics is rooted in preconceived notions of what the other is and should be that inevitably infringe upon the distinctiveness of specific others. Representing the other erases differences, assumes stable identification and simplifies unique human experiences and narratives. Subaltern restorative encounters should instead be shaped by a call to address the ethical singularity of others and its political implications.

Spivak's engagement with ethics is closely linked to political responsibility. She encourages scholars and practitioners to be aware of their positions of privilege and to use their knowledge and agency to challenge oppressive structures. This can be seen as an ethical imperative to actively engage in transformative and socially just practices.

This awareness would lead to presenting new possibilities and ways of being, creating opportunities for encountering others dialogically. This process is not informed by any expert knowledge but by *justice* understood as the ethical interruption of the self by the demands of others (Spivak, 1990: 110).

Practitioners, scholars, advocates and policymakers have a crucial institutional responsibility and complicity when they claim to be neutral and let the people speak for themselves. They are complicit in the subtle suppression of the voice of the oppressed, especially of those culturally and materially affected by colonial capitalism.

The restorative justice movement finds itself entangled in the webs of Western universal categories and practices. In encounters with difference, we are compelled to consider our complicity and responsibility, both within knowledge/power relations and in the unequal material conditions that those categories and practices may perpetuate (Kaasila-Pakanen, 2021).

The challenge is then to imagine ethical encounters able to mitigate the inevitable othering effects which take place when facing differences. The acknowledgement of the limits of Western knowledge, of participants' situatedness, and the unlearning of privilege are first steps to creating such encounters. These steps, whilst attesting to epistemic, normative and material complicity with the capitalist system, would provide a space for a different ethical engagement with others. The *other* is no longer a transcendental, Westernised subject but a situated category to be 'broken down' as *others*, as 'unknowable' subjects (Spivak, 1993/2009: 185). This encounter calls for developing an intersubjective relation with someone we will never be able to know entirely, therefore configuring an impossibility which is generative of a new openness towards those we encounter. To some extent, this encounter marks the end of autonomous, identitarian, rational subjects and the birth of unknowable *inter-subjects*, who, as such, call for engagement and the negotiation of new foundations within specific contexts (Griffiths, 2017).

What animates these encounters is a notion of 'ethical singularity' (Spivak, 1995: xxv), understood as the process, unstable and never ending, of engaging with what cannot be disclosed, reached or represented when encountering others (Davis,

2002). This posture would help mitigate the risk of appropriating and then exploiting differences. Accepting this concealment, this shared incapacity to fully know, is what enables justice as a never entirely accessible condition, never completely expressed in any law, an experience of the impossible which drives the ethical encounter with one who is other than 'I'.

These are bodily encounters, where the body is the phenomenological stratification of one's experiences, unfolding in and enmeshed with the world (Kaasila-Pakanen, 2021). Here, responsibility means enabling an ethical response which is aware of the impossibility of total knowledge of those encountered. Ethical singularity, rooted in bodies, is founded upon and generates an ethics of the self-aware and self-limiting exchange, which can be transformative rather than merely restorative.

Beyond Spivak

Critical discussions around restorative justice must address the positionality of those involved in advocating for, studying or practising it as much as of those who engage with those practices, bringing their broken relations into restorative encounters in the hope of achieving restoration.

The gender- and class-sensitive deconstruction proposed in the previous pages is strategic in showing both the colonial nature of criminal justice and the (benevolent yet problematic) postcolonial premises and effects of restorative justice. Restorative justice, in fact, often represents the other as an essentialised constituency, which ends up silencing differences.

Engaging with subalternity demands imagining forms of justice which encounter differences without appropriating and exploiting the other. Subalternity captures intersectional forms of epistemic-normative and material oppression produced by colonial and postcolonial actions. A justice that aims to acknowledge instead of disavowing the contexts within which embodied others encounter each other must reckon with the materiality of the struggles of those disenfranchised and suffering. It must also tie these challenges to cultural production so that links between justice and cultural politics are unearthed.

Unlearning epistemic-material privileges, creating spaces for subaltern experiences to be addressed and criticising restorative justice's widely acclaimed Indigenous past generate opportunities for the development of active forces towards the establishment of a justice which is more than Western justice.

Specific epistemic-political strategies can contribute to unsettle those privileges and create those spaces, or at least reduce the impact of erasing or objectifying cultural and material differences. Strategic essentialism, the use of stereotypes by a group as a means of subverting the forces that oppress them, helps reappropriate marginalising categories for emancipatory aims. Then, the affirmative sabotage of epistemic-political principles promotes a critical analysis of the complicity of certain restorative justice categories in limiting the transformative potential of restorative encounters.

Spivak also aids us to understand what an ethical-political restorative justice may look like. This endeavour requires designing forms of training for practitioners that empower them to recognise their situatedness and acknowledge the impossibility of developing a full knowledge of the other, as well as their responsibility and complicity with the postcolonial state when refusing to address their own ethical and political position. Thinking of justice outside political struggles, material exploitation and cultural silencing means serving these forms of oppression, enabling their operation in disguise, within restorative encounters.

A way forward is to rethink the other as *others* and difference as *differences*. This is a precondition for encountering human beings as ethical singularities – that is, as illegible subjects who are situated at the intersection of cultural, material and gendered power relationships. Ultimately, encountering subalternity pushes those interested in appraising critically and reformulating politically restorative justice to develop an acute sensitivity to the inevitable epistemic-political contamination of justice. There is no struggle for justice devoid of cultural, material and gendered premises, implications and effects.

References

Asadullah, M. (2021) 'Decolonization and Restorative Justice: A Proposed Theoretical Framework'. *Decolonization of Criminology and Justice*, 3(1): 27–62.

Blagg, H. (2017) 'Doing Restorative Justice "Otherwise"'. In: Aertsen, I. and Pali, B. (eds.) *Critical Restorative Justice*, 61–78. Oxford: Hart.

Castro Varela, M. do M. (2020) 'Fundamental Education and Decolonization of the Mind'. *On_Education: Journal for Research and Debate*, 3(7), https://www.oneducation.net/no-07_april-2020/fundamental-education-and-decolonization-of-the-mind/.

Cunneen, C. (2002) 'Restorative Justice and the Politics of Decolonization'. In Weitekamp, E. G. M. and Kerner, H.-J. (eds.) *Restorative Justice: Theoretical Foundations*, 32–43. Portland: Willan.

Danius, S., Jonsson, S. and Spivak, G. C. (1993) 'An Interview with Gayatri Chakravorty Spivak'. *Boundary*, 2, 20(2): 24–50.

Darder, A. (2018) 'Decolonizing Interpretive Research: Subaltern Sensibilities and the Politics of Voice'. *Qualitative Research Journal*, 18(2): 94–104.

Davis, D. R. (2002) '(Love Is) the Ability of Not Knowing: Feminist Experience of the Impossible in Ethical Singularity'. *Hypatia*, 17(2): 145–61.

Derrida, J. (1967/1976) *Of Grammatology*, trans. Spivak, G. C., ix–lxxxviii. Baltimore, MD: Johns Hopkins University Press.

Eide, E. (2016) 'Strategic Essentialism'. In Naples, N. A. (ed.) *The Wiley Blackwell Encyclopedia of Gender and Sexuality Studies*. Hoboken: Wiley Blackwell.

Griffiths, M. (2017) 'For Speaking against Silence: Spivak's Subaltern Ethics in the Field'. *Transactions of the Institute of British Geographers*, 43(2): 299–311.

Hodgson, J. (2022) 'Offending Girls and Restorative Justice: A Critical Analysis'. *Youth Justice*, 22(2): 166–88.

Jülich, S. and Thorburn, N. (2017) 'Sexual Violence and Substantive Equality: Can Restorative Justice Deliver?' *Journal of Human Rights Social Work*, 2(1–2): 34–44.

Kaasila-Pakanen, A. L. (2021) 'Close Encounters: Creating Embodied Spaces of Resistance to Marginalisation and Disempowering Representation of Difference in Organisation'. *Gender, Work & Organization*, 28(5): 1805–22.

Koen, R. A. (2005) *Restorative Justice: A Marxist Analysis*. PhD Thesis, University of Cape Town, https://open.uct.ac.za/items/ead76917-f2a6-4025-9b14-ab5491d825be.

Levers, L. A. (2023) *Decolonising Restorative Justice: A Case of Policy Reform*. London: Routledge.

Maglione, G. (2017a) 'Communities at Large: An Archaeological Analysis of the "Community" within Restorative Justice Policy and Laws'. *Critical Criminology*, 25(3): 453–69.
Maglione, G. (2017b) 'Embodied Victims: An Archaeology of the "Ideal Victim" of Restorative Justice'. *Criminology & Criminal Justice*, 17(4): 401–17.
Morton, S. (2008) *Gayatri Spivak: Ethics, Subalternity and the Critique of Postcolonial Reason*. Cambridge, UK: Polity.
Moyle, P. and Tauri, J. M. (2016) 'Māori, Family Group Conferencing and the Mystifications of Restorative Justice'. *Victims & Offenders*, 11(1): 87–106.
Purcell, M. E. (2020) 'Cosmopolitanism as Transnational Literacy: Putting Spivak to Work'. *Asia Pacific Journal of Education*, 40(1): 61–73.
Rosenblatt, F. F. and Mazzucato, C. (eds.) (2023) 'Special Issue'. *The International Journal of Restorative Justice*, 6(3).
Sherman, L. (2003) 'Reason for Emotion: Reinventing Justice with Theories, Innovations, and Research – The American Society of Criminology 2002 Presidential Address'. *Criminology*, 41(1): 1–37.
Smith, J. (2022) 'Decolonizing Restorative Justice'. In Asadullah, M. (ed.) *Decolonization and Justice: An Introductory Overview*, 96–104. Regina, Canada: University of Regina Open Education and Publishing, https://opentextbooks.uregina.ca/decolonizingjustice/chapter/decolonizing-restorative-justice/.
Spivak, G. C. (1974) *Myself Must I Remake: The Life and Poetry of W. B. Yeats*. New York: Thomas Y. Crowell and Company.
Spivak, G. C. (1976) 'Translator's Preface'. In Derrida, J. (ed.) *Of Grammatology*, trans. Spivak, G. C., ix–lxxxviii. Baltimore, MD: Johns Hopkins University Press.
Spivak, G. C. (1981) 'French Feminism in an International Frame'. *Yale French Studies*, 62: 154–84.
Spivak, G. C. (1983) 'Displacement and the Discourse of Woman'. In Krupnik, M. (ed.) *Displacement: Derrida and After*, 169–95. Bloomington: Indiana University Press.
Spivak, G. C. (1985) 'The Rani of Sirmur: An Essay in Reading the Archives'. *History and Theory*, 24(3): 247–72.
Spivak, G. C. (trans.) (1995) *Imaginary Maps: Three Stories by Mahasweta Devi*. London: Routledge.
Spivak, G. C. (1996) *The Spivak Reader*, ed. Landry, D. and Maclean, G. London: Routledge.
Spivak, G. C. (1990) *The Post-Colonial Critic. Interviews, Strategies, Dialogues*. London: Routledge.
Spivak, G. C. (1999) *A Critique of Postcolonial Reason*. Cambridge, MA: Harvard University Press.
Spivak, G. C. (2004) 'Righting Wrongs'. *The South Atlantic Quarterly*, 103(2/3): 523–81.
Spivak, G. C. (1987/2006) *In Other Worlds: Essays in Cultural Politics*. London: Routledge.
Spivak, G. C. (1993/2009) *Outside in the Teaching Machine*. London: Routledge.
Spivak, G. C. (2013) *An Aesthetic Education in the Era of Globalization*. Cambridge, MA: Harvard University Press.
Spivak, G. C. (1985/2020) *Can the Subaltern Speak?* London: Afternall Books.
Sylvester, D. J. (2003) 'Myth in Restorative Justice History.' *Utah Law Review*, 1: 1445–96.
Tauri, J. M. (2013) 'Indigenous Critique of Authoritarian Criminology'. In Ball, M., Tauri, J. M., O'Brien, E. and Carrington, K. (eds.) *Crime, Justice and Social Democracy: International Perspectives*, 217–23. London: Palgrave Macmillan.
Van Ness, D. and Strong, H. (2022) *Restoring Justice*, 6th ed. Cincinnati, OH: Anderson.
Willis, R. (2020) '"Let's Talk about It": Why Social Class Matters to Restorative Justice'. *Criminology & Criminal Justice*, 20(2): 187–206.
Winterdyk, J. A. (2021) 'Comparing Aboriginal and Post-Colonial Restorative Justice: The Case of Canada'. In Gavrielides, T. (ed.) *Comparative Restorative Justice*, 107–29. Berlin: Springer.
Zehr, H. (2005) *Changing Lenses: A New Focus for Crime and Justice*, 3rd ed. Scottsdale, PA: Herald Press.

8 Conclusions, New Beginnings and Futures

Encountering difference, sovereignty, community, identity, equality and subalternity prompted a profound reconsideration of the foundations of restorative justice. It enabled a meditation, from different angles, on the political conditions, meanings, significance and effects of restorative justice. Ultimately, this intellectual endeavour challenged familiar notions in restorative justice theory and practice, through the lenses of the theories encountered. Mainstream conceptual, historical and practical issues morphed into something unexpectedly strange and demanded formulating original ways of thinking and innovative paths for action.

From an analytical standpoint, rethinking the history of restorative justice using the concept of assemblage; reframing the relationship between restorative justice and criminal justice through a political-ontological approach; exposing the problematic conceptualisation of community as a fusional entity in restorative justice; rethinking the role of identity in restorative encounters; analysing restorative dynamics as aesthetico-political processes; and unearthing the postcolonial legacies of restorative justice, contributed to generating new understandings of what restorative justice is. This book's analytical dimension is then inextricably bound to a normative perspective; thus, these explorations also involved outlining how restorative justice ought to be, its possible role in addressing relational, social, cultural and political oppression. Hence, the possibility of a nomadic restorative justice, a restorative justice to come, a restorative justice singular plural, a restorative justice otherwise, a democratic restorative justice and a subaltern restorative justice emerged.

Gilles Deleuze's contribution consisted in disassembling and then reassembling restorative justice, revealing it as a dynamic combination of multiple lines of different matter – semiotic and material, molar and molecular. Restorative justice is animated by a tangle of justice-desiring flows, while the institutionalisation of restorative justice is a manifestation of the coding and territorialisation of these flows into state apparatuses and their stratification into legal systems. Yet the assemblage served not only as an interpretive tool but also as a normative framework. It suggested avoiding any nostalgic yearning for returning restorative justice to an 'organic' form of justice. The justice-desiring flows, in fact, persist as an ever-present virtual stream within the institutionalised version of restorative justice, so that the issue becomes how to nurture them, harnessing their

DOI: 10.4324/9781003298359-8

life-generating potential. Ultimately, this encounter with Deleuze taught us that the focus of the restorative justice movement should be on fostering its capacity for radical transformation, becoming aware of its detrimental self-institutionalising tendencies, whilst generating new forms of solidarity across social, cultural and political spheres.

Through Giorgio Agamben's political ontology, it became possible to conceptualise the origin of restorative justice as the rediscovery of 'human presence', which is neutralised and concealed by criminal justice. However, this approach also helped us identify a fundamental similarity between restorative justice and (liberal) criminal justice. Both possess a ban-structure, that is, they both include by exclusion their very archē, the 'mere fact of life', which is relegated to outside the realm of justice. The mere fact of life is not simply erased, but it is positioned as a negative foundation, inside and yet outside (like a threshold) of both criminal and restorative justice. This chapter, then, proposed a similarly nuanced appreciation of the subjectivation processes which take place during restorative encounters.

The institutionalisation of restorative justice was critically reconsidered as a paradigmatic form of the sovereign appropriation of an informal justice model. The resulting commodification, bureaucratisation and technicisation of restorative justice leads to a loss of experience and the neutralisation of its potential to liberate life from oppressive apparatuses. Agamben's political ontology also provided a framework for reflecting on the future of restorative justice. By unveiling the inconsistencies of the presuppositional ban-structure of restorative justice and profaning the artificial removal of life at its core, it is possible to activate restorative encounters' political potential to support anti-authoritarian forms of life, whilst dismantling the legal violence inherent in institutionalised forms of justice.

Placed within Jean-Luc Nancy's conceptual framework, restorative justice emerged as a web of myths set against the backdrop of liberal criminal justice. This chapter showed how these myths evolve into institutional mythologies when particular historical conditions facilitate the diffusion and solidification of certain narratives at the expense of others. Along these lines, it became possible to understand institutional restorative justice as built upon the same self-generating and self-perpetuating subject that underlies both atomistic individualism and communitarian philosophy. This institutional development diminishes the ethical-political potential of human relationality, transforming it into organised uniformity.

This chapter proposed the development of a singular-plural restorative justice to interrupt mythologies that reduce justice to a unified normative theory, opening up new possibilities for shaping the world and reactivating our responsibility to restore multiplicity. This justice unfolds as an anarchic spacing, a dynamic encounter which involves an ethical-political challenge to the institutionalisation of justice. Nancy urged us to envision restorative justice not merely as a means to overcome the relational disruptions represented by a crime. Restorative justice should become an endeavour to create a more welcoming spacing, wherein the harm, as loss of coexistence, is encountered and addressed as an expression of human groundlessness. Ultimately, within this context, justice is nothing but an ongoing effort to resist the political and ethical totalisation of human existence inherent in the (capitalist) institutionalisation of human praxis.

Judith Butler's chapter provided a powerful transdisciplinary lens for critiquing restorative justice's basic tenets. Butler reminded us that the symbolic dynamics which take place when trying to restore just relationships shape people's identities, a process that can be inherently violent and thus warrants critical attention. This chapter also raised the issue that human interconnectedness, often used as an anthropological justification of restorative justice, is rooted in the idea of a social pact between atomic individuals akin to that which underpins liberal criminal justice. If our aim is to develop a critical restorative justice capable of embracing social complexities without imposing fixed identities, then we must rethink the foundation of restorative justice as social interdependence (instead of interconnectedness). Social interdependence is an ontological condition which precedes individuality and is therefore prior to those same individuals who purportedly entered into a social pact.

This chapter then argued for a non-violent restorative justice that embraces the ethical-political operation of disidentifying individuals and groups while generating competing frameworks to intensify resistance by fostering equality. The way to achieve this transformation is twofold. On the one hand, the roots of those symbolic forms of violence characteristic of institutionalised restorative justice (such as distinctive idealisations of victims and offenders, or the psychological notion of vulnerability that individualises harm and responsibility) must be detected and denounced; on the other hand, social precarity must be acknowledged and addressed, whilst recognising social precariousness. This dual movement, symbolic and embodied, cultural and material, was adopted to unearth the fundamental challenges and opportunities for connecting restorative justice with radically progressive politics.

Jacques Rancière's political theory aided us in reconstructing the historical-theoretical trajectory of restorative justice. It delineated the ethical components characterising both the early development of restorative justice and the more recent institutional growth propelled by the restorative justice movement's attempt to emulate criminal justice. This trajectory culminates in a rigidification of restorative justice characterised by the imposition of structures that constrain participants' narratives, thereby curtailing their ability to express their needs and interests beyond pre-established labels.

This approach led to advocating for a radical democratic reinterpretation of restorative justice, disrupting both the fixed scripting of restorative encounters and the process of communitarian de-institutionalisation. Rancière's agonistic, self-critical approach challenged not only the criminal justice identities of victims and offenders but also the nostalgic longings for an 'organic' restorative justice. It suggested broadening the scope of restorative encounters and redefining harms as political disputes and injustices. It encouraged the creation of spaces for expressing one's capacities by eliminating obstacles to equality and asking facilitators to evolve into political activists committed to helping parties realise their equality.

This chapter ultimately showed the intrinsic link between politics and justice, asserting that depoliticised justice inevitably succumbs to police orders. In contrast, democratic restorative justice constitutes an ongoing challenge to the tempting illusions of context-blind justice, emphasising the importance of sustaining a self-critical, disruptive and politically engaged approach to justice.

The chapter on Gayatri Chakravorty Spivak proposed a gender- and class-sensitive deconstructive perspective, highlighting the colonial nature of liberal criminal justice and the postcolonial premises and effects of restorative justice. Both treat the other as a homogeneous constituency, resulting in the suppression of differences into identities. To address this predicament, this chapter argued for engaging with subalternity to envision forms of justice that encounter differences without appropriating or exploiting the other. Subalternity exposes intersectional forms of epistemic-normative and material oppression stemming from colonial and postcolonial arrangements. A justice that seeks to acknowledge the contexts in which embodied others interact must grapple with the material struggles of marginalised people, connecting their challenges to cultural exploitation so as to unveil the ties between (in)justice and cultural politics.

This approach problematised restorative justice's celebrated Indigenous past, charged with a tendency to oversimplify cultural differences, turning them into Western identities. It also underscored specific epistemic-political strategies that can undermine Western cultural-material privileges in shaping restorative justice. Similarly, this chapter argued for enriching the training for restorative justice practitioners to empower them to recognise their situatedness, acknowledge the impossibility of fully understanding the other and recognise their complicity with the postcolonial state when failing to address their own position. Ultimately, a subaltern-sensitive restorative justice rethinks the other as others and recognises difference as differences, laying the groundwork for encountering human beings as ethical singularities.

While these approaches and their applications appeared as fundamentally distinct from each other, they also exhibited significant commonalities that now warrant attention. The recognition of this common ground provides a critical starting point for the development of a politically engaged restorative justice.

The authors encountered in this book share a conviction that the epistemic and normative, cultural and material, ethical and political dimensions that animate justice are intimately entangled. They blur the boundaries between these spheres, whilst simultaneously nurturing the tensions that traverse them. The different analyses of the foundations, development and institutionalisation of restorative justice, engage with fundamental domains of justice at multiple levels and reconstruct restorative justice as a layered and dynamic 'tension field'. Knowledge and power are intertwined, and their separation is at best a heuristic operation. The cultural and material dimensions are entangled as well, implying that there is no material reality which is not always already cultural, no body, action or object that is not already signified.

This analytical perspective is not normatively neutral. Instead, it is informed by the desire to challenge reifying authorities, interrupting the flow of command that tradition and the state place over us by generating fixed identities that constrain human potential. This desire, once again, is animated by a fluid entanglement between the ethical and political spheres. The reckoning of how individuals should behave is linked to how societies should act. Politics does not merely scale up the findings from ethics, and ethics does not merely individualise politics. There is neither a conflation nor a mere developmental link between these levels of human action. Instead, our authors showed the generative, mutual dependency between these two domains. In this context, justice is both ethical and political, and rethinking justice means rethinking it as an ethical-political endeavour to address human relations. This means that the micro and macro dimensions of human action – relational stories and social histories, personal harms and collective injuries – are inextricably linked and, therefore, must be treated together.

Politics is not merely a series of processes concerning the power to govern, to administer the economy and to design bureaucratic apparatuses for the management of social issues. It is about rising and addressing the very question of being and becoming human among other humans and then imagining, shaping and conducting the polity. Similarly, ethics is not merely the decision of how to live an individual life but of how to imagine and conduct one's life among other lives. The relationship between politics and ethics is therefore internal and agonistic, and yet of mutual implication: ethical principles presuppose and challenge politics, and political processes entail and affect ethical principles.

The ontological dimension of restorative justice, the connection between the quest for a justice that encounters other human beings and the question of being and becoming human among other humans, is therefore a crucial, common theme. From radically different perspectives, the six encounters addressed this reciprocally constitutive link between the normative and the ontological domains, unearthing both ontology's political implications and politics' ontological significance, once again highlighting the entanglement between apparently separate domains. In fact, it is exactly this artificial separation which limits the quest for justice to a purely regulatory means for the distribution of rights, duties and resources, neglecting the decisive role that the ontological question may play in envisioning forms of coexistence and addressing the sometimes-tragic manifestations of living together. Ontology, here, is not the search for some essential or natural substance, ahistorical and decontextualised. Instead, it is the active, relentless questioning of the conditions of being and becoming (or unbecoming) human within historical arrangements.

Here, humans are ethical-political creatures in a constant state of becoming, necessarily exposed to each other. The human condition, in fact, emerges as marked by fundamental sharedness, difference and groundlessness. Yet this condition manifests itself in various ways, depending on contingent social, cultural, economic and political factors. This entanglement between the ontological and normative spheres warrants crucial attention to the specific historical contexts wherein human coexistence takes place. This awareness demands envisioning justice as a dynamic, ethical and political form of life, which unfolds over time in specific environments. These contexts are often marked by struggles between those who have power and those who do not, demanding that justice be ontological yet context-specific.

This position then requires a self-critical acknowledgement of the contextuality of our own understandings of justice and their roots in distinctive sets of contingencies. By embracing a historical perspective, it is possible to access the dynamism which pertains to the human condition and, therefore, to the quest for justice. This reflexive historical posture, once again, is normatively charged. Embracing history, in fact, means refusing to accept the rigidification of the present, the perception that the present is our epochal horizon and, as such, can hardly be modified. History teaches us that change is possible. What there is and what we have are not our destiny, even when they seem immutable.

A further common theme is that there is a need to develop the embodied and creative nature of justice. A body, here, is not a biological object but the stratification of one's experiences plugged into the wider social, political, economic, cultural and physical environment. This body is not a static entity but a process, a becoming; body is the embodiment of being. Justice restores the body as a whole of affective experiential levels when interruptions of the process of embodiment take place. These diminutions of bodily agency are invariably intertwined with cultural constructs and are always contextual and contingent upon social arrangements. Justice, reactivating the flow of embodiment, enables intersubjectivity, for the concrete experience of others is rooted in the very fact of the body. This does not mean that restorative justice is a justice only for bodily individuals; instead, it considers human embodiment as integral to the non-human and other-than-human worlds. Altering non-human and other-than-human realms always affects human embodiments, and vice versa, since this process is inextricably enmeshed with the world, as much as the world is integral to human embodiment.

Justice's creative element refers to the body's actual capacity to create, artistically. Art is not simply a tool for justice. Art *is* justice when it generates tangible spaces which alter the common understanding and sensory perception of the world. Art is this embodied, affective, expressive disruption of both the 'I' and of technocratic and capitalist destruction, modelled not on the act of production but rather on humans' creative potential to generate new, non-violent, mutually enhancing social relationships.

From this angle, the pressing issue of the institutionalisation of restorative justice appears as historically related to techno-capitalist devastation. Institutionalisation is a process of collapsing difference into identity by technicising justice and neutralising those entanglements and the dynamic tensions that animate them. Technicisation, by undoing social interdependence, denying human experience and imposing unchangeable models of the world, turns justice into a means integral to capitalism. This becoming-technical of justice, in fact, involves a distinctive way of understanding the world as a passive resource to be instrumentally and limitlessly exploited (cf. Heidegger, 1954/2013). This process supports capitalism, understood as a religion without redemption (cf. Benjamin, 1921/2021), wherein production is an absolute priority, the self-engendering and self-perpetuating exploitation of humans and nature. Capitalism reifies difference by annulling it into fixed identities, covers over the human lack of foundations with taken-as-inevitable artefacts and impedes any genuine, non-utilitarian contact between human beings.

This damning diagnosis should not suggest a mere, naive call for de-institutionalisation, for the retrieval of a supposedly pure restorative justice. De-institutionalisation poses ethical and political questions as well, since the return to some imagined uncontaminated form of communitarian justice often results in a return to nostalgic identities, fixed hierarchies and conservatism. This would likely be another manifestation of capitalist injustice.

To counter this predicament, justice emerged across these chapters as an ever-coming, self-critical interruption of violence. This is a fragmented justice whose archē is the acknowledgement of human groundlessness, the necessarily mutual exposure of human beings and the fundamental difference which marks human existence. Justice needs to reckon with this ontological condition and address contextual injustices underpinned by the denial of groundlessness, the suspension of human interdependence and the disavowal of difference. This justice is not a free-floating entity but an earthly, embodied process, historical and social, relating both to people's ethical constitution and to the political organisation of communities. This results in a search for ways to forge new models of ethical self-constitution and innovative forms of solidarity, as well as radical and politically engaged tactics to counter injustices.

Along these lines, restorative justice emerges as an ontologically grounded political praxis implemented through critical encounters. Its overarching aim is to address human coexistence and its sometimes-tragic manifestations whilst countering its social preconditions, relational effects and rigidification in fixed identities. Critique means taking a stand about why certain interactions are deemed to be harms, their roots and effects, why certain individuals, organisations and human and non-human entities are deemed to be stakeholders and others not. Encountering entails addressing humans' mutual exposure, and its challenges, engaging in ways that honour the multidimensional entanglements which *are* human relations, recognising that some suffer more than others, that justice cannot be context blind and that imagining and practising justice is an ethical-political journey. But a justice of critical encounters is also a self-critical justice, a restless endeavour to uncover its own limitations, an attempt at addressing its own archē. This means questioning its foundations, establishing new relations, allowing new voices to emerge and resisting the temptation to affirm itself as the only justice and, in this way, neutralise its own potential to nurture life.

This is the restorative justice *I* stand for – a radical political movement (not a policy option, a practice or even less a penal mechanism) which challenges capitalist violence, advocating for democratic decision-making, non-violence and social interdependence. This challenge spans the epistemic, ontological and normative realms, concerning how we develop knowledge around social harms and conflicts, what we consider harms and conflicts to be and what aims we pursue in addressing them.

Epistemologically, *this* restorative justice necessitates a critical engagement not only with the structures and practices of traditional justice systems but also with the very frameworks through which *knowledge* about crime and justice is constructed and understood socially. To counter broader systems of oppression and inequality contributing to conflicts and harms, there is a need to encourage individuals and communities to critically examine the social, political and economic structures that enable the denial of human interdependence. This involves challenging dominant narratives about crime and justice, as well as advocating for opportunities that empower individuals and communities to better understand and face systems of power and oppression. Knowledge is viewed, here, as inherently decentralised, emerging from the lived experiences of individuals and communities and diverging from top-down, expert-driven models of knowledge production and decision-making.

Ontologically, this restorative justice prioritises *difference* over sameness, adapting to the evolving social and historical contexts wherein harms and conflicts take place. Hence, it emerges as a fragmentary justice rather than a coherent, totalising program. Embracing the inherent complexity and uncertainty of human interactions and social dynamics, this restorative justice prioritises dialogue, exploration and collective problem-solving in navigating these complexities. It is *prefigurative*, meaning that its non-violent end (restoring human potential) always demands non-violent means. It integrates both material and cultural dimensions, as culture manifests itself in bodies and their arrangements, and bodies are inherently imbued with cultural significance. Ultimately, this restorative justice actualises an ontological-political conception of justice, perpetually engaged in addressing the question of what it means to be human among other humans, within specific contexts.

Normatively, this restorative justice is not merely a practice but a *praxis* – an agonistic process which questions political organisation – working not simply against institutionalisation but towards the ongoing endeavour to de-institutionalise itself. It is a process of removing obstacles to human potential, unfolding within a tension field where one pole is 'archic' and the other 'anarchic', one institutional and the other non-institutional. This praxis navigates between these two points, critically, striving to maintain a balance by resisting the tendency to self-institutionalise that social movements often embrace, while simultaneously providing sufficient support to generate new answers for those affected by harm and conflict. Thus, this justice is inherently democratic, as this agonistic tendency seeks to render visible and audible bodies and voices that were previously unseen and unheard. This is a form of social-political justice which is relational, as relations exist only within the intricate fabric of social history into which they are interwoven. It is both historical and forward-looking, as people's understanding of history and their connection to it shape their aspirations for the future.

This understanding calls for the transformation of restorative practitioners into political activists committed to nurture social interdependence. It demands reframing harm and trauma in restorative justice as social and not only psychological phenomena which require critical scrutiny. It advocates for the expansion of the restorative ethos to inform systems, institutions and practices in a bid to make them more horizontal and non-violent. It urges the inclusion of non-human and other-than-human actors, such as the environment and animals, within the scope of restorative justice efforts. It challenges the preconceptions that dictate rigid differences between 'victims' and 'offenders', considering and managing power relationships beyond pre-set legal labels. It compels to rethink widely accepted notions of guilt, remorse and responsibility, acknowledging their problematic moral, political and cultural roots, towards the recognition of humans' shared mutual exposure. It calls for a critical examination of the criminal justice system and active efforts to overcome it, rather than supporting it. It emphasises the importance of investing in bottom-up initiatives which connect relational harms with social conflicts, personal stories and collective histories, and not only in policy entrepreneurship. It suggests culturally sensitive, un-scripted, training for practitioners. It encourages experimentation with flexible, contextual and inclusive languages, incorporating non-conventional forms of expression such as the arts to rewrite past injustices. In short, it urges the restorative justice movement to become aware (and in charge) of its own political conditions, functions and effects.

Ultimately, the critical encounters which constituted this book did not aim to form a comprehensive theory but to provide a set of instruments for the relentless quest for a justice that restores human potential. These encounters are like 'ladders' to be thrown away after the reader has climbed to the next level (Wittgenstein, 1922: 189).

References

Benjamin, W. (1921/2021) 'Capitalism as Religion'. In Fenves, P. and Ng, J. (eds.) *Toward the Critique of Violence*, 90–2. Stanford: Stanford University Press.
Heidegger, M. (1954/2013) *The Question Concerning Technology and Other Essays*. New York: Harper.
Wittgenstein, L. (1922) *Tractatus Logico-Philosophicus*. London: Keegan.

Index

FSC
www.fsc.org
MIX
Papier | Fördert
gute Waldnutzung
FSC® C083411

Kolibri 360 GmbH
Ferdinand-Jühlke-Straße 7
99095 Erfurt, Deutschland
produktsicherheit@kolibri360.de